W9-BKF-247

PROSE

LITERARY TERMS AND CONCEPTS

PROSE
LITERARY TERMS AND CONCEPTS

EDITED BY KATHLEEN KUIPER, MANAGER, ARTS AND CULTURE

Britannica
Educational Publishing

IN ASSOCIATION WITH

ROSEN
EDUCATIONAL SERVICES

Published in 2012 by Britannica Educational Publishing
(a trademark of Encyclopædia Britannica, Inc.)
in association with Rosen Educational Services, LLC
29 East 21st Street, New York, NY 10010.

Distributed exclusively by Rosen Educational Services.
For a listing of additional Britannica Educational Publishing titles, call toll free (800) 237-9932.

First Edition

Britannica Educational Publishing
Michael I. Levy: Executive Editor
J.E. Luebering: Senior Manager
Marilyn L. Barton: Senior Coordinator, Production Control
Steven Bosco: Director, Editorial Technologies
Lisa S. Braucher: Senior Producer and Data Editor
Yvette Charboneau: Senior Copy Editor
Kathy Nakamura: Manager, Media Acquisition
Kathleen Kuiper: Manager, Arts and Culture

Rosen Educational Services
Heather M. Moore Niver: Editor
Nelson Sá: Art Director
Cindy Reiman: Photography Manager
Nicole Russo: Designer
Matthew Cauli: Cover Design
Introduction by Kathleen Kuiper

Library of Congress Cataloging-in-Publication Data

Prose: literary terms and concepts / edited by Kathleen Kuiper. — 1st ed.
    p. cm. — (The Britannica guide to literary elements)
Includes bibliographical references and index.
ISBN 978-1-61530-494-3 (library binding)
1. Prose literature—History and criticism. I. Kuiper, Kathleen.
PN3335.P76 2012
808—dc22

                                                                    2010047949

Manufactured in the United States of America

Cover; pages 1, 44, 69, 98, 120, 134, 164, 180, 210 Shutterstock.com

CONTENTS

87

92

102

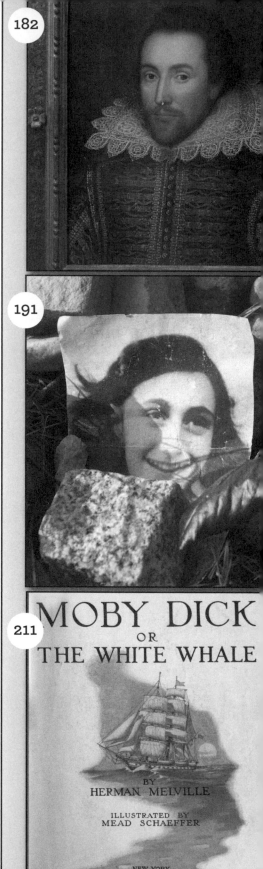

218

231

INTRODUCTION

Our lives, if you think about it, can be considered one long narrative, with characters, incidents, and trajectory. Each one is interwoven with several other narratives—those of parents, siblings, teachers, friends, and relatives. And yet, even though each is lived parallel with others at some points, each is unique—even those of identical twins. Only in extreme cases of isolation are they relatively uncomplicated. After all, even Robinson Crusoe salvaged, explored, built structures, and generally constructed his island life even before he met Friday.

Add to each story personal dreams, both the conscious visions we embrace for our futures and those we fashion late at night, when we weave stories in other worlds in which we can fly. Our brains build unconscious dreams in the spaces between synapses firing, setting off unconnected memories of scents, sights, and feelings. Thus do our personal narratives multiply.

And those stories take no account of the connection between us and the painters of human hands on cave walls or the lines of carbon in ancient rocks. We could also multiply those multigenerational and historical stories, expanding outward from our families to our neighbourhoods, our states, our country, our globe, the Milky Way, and the universe.

This book is about stories and storytelling of many varieties, from fables to short stories and novels. It further looks at specialized types of writing, such as science fiction, biography, romance, and literary criticism, with sidebars and brief examples. It focuses especially on prose, examining in particular the novel; the genre of science fiction; the ancient forms of fable, parable, and allegory; the romance genre; the saga; the short story; the style of writing called satire; the varieties of biography; and the origins and methodology of literary criticism.

Perhaps the most pervasive genre of literature in the 21st century is the novel. In its characteristic form, it is composed of several elements. It has a plot, meaning that something happens. For example, in Mark Twain's *The Adventures of Huckleberry Finn*, the captive Huck, needing to escape from his drunken father, fakes his own death and sets off down the Mississippi River on a raft.

Novels also require characters—agents to either bring about or react to the events. In the first of Ursula K. Le Guin's Earthsea novels (which, incidentally, preceded the Harry Potter books by a few decades), the boy Sparrowhawk determines that he possesses magic powers and is sent to a special school for wizards. Sparrowhawk's discovery sets the events of the series in motion.

Further, novels happen somewhere. This can be a real place, such as Sweden in the crime novels of Stieg Larsson, or a real place in an imagined future, such

Well-chosen words have the ability to evoke a wide range of responses in readers or listeners.
Shutterstock.com

as the post-apocalyptic Los Angeles of Philip K. Dick's *Do Androids Dream of Electric Sheep?* (source of the movie *Blade Runner*). The setting also, of course, can be fashioned by the author's imagination—J.R.R. Tolkien's Middle Earth, for example, or Lewis Carroll's Wonderland.

Novels and short stories also express a particular point of view. Charlotte Brontë's *Jane Eyre* is told from the perspective of the title character. Some stories have an omniscient narrator—one who knows what's happening to all the characters all the time and who speaks of them in the third person. More complicated are the stories told from the perspective of an unreliable narrator, such as the section of William Faulkner's *The Sound and the Fury* that is related by a mentally disabled adult. In fact, Faulkner's book is unusual in employing four distinct narrative voices.

Novels have many additional features, usually differing from short stories in word length as well as scope of chronology, though since the beginning of the 20th century this latter point is less common than it once was. Whereas Murasaki Shikibu's *The Tale of Genji* and Leo Tolstoy's *War and Peace* once represented the paradigm, and novels often covered decades or even generations, the 20th century brought us such works as James Joyce's *Ulysses*, which at great length describes a single day in the life of Leopold Bloom. Even chronological progression was challenged in the

20th century. The Argentine author Julio Cortázar, in his book *Hopscotch*, goes so far as to suggest an alternative order to the novel's chapters.

In addition to an arc of development, prose is also characterized by the use of symbols and motifs. The one immutable element of the novel is that it has a point, a greater significance, even when the author is positing the meaninglessness of life.

Of the fictional worlds available to us in the 21st century, that of science fiction is one of the youngest. Born of technological advances in society, it has become one of the more exciting genres, offering not only alternate histories and parallel universes, but also reflections on such topics as sex and gender, anthropology, utopias and dystopias, and many other subjects of contemporary interest.

Much more ancient are the related forms of fable, parable, and allegory. Each expects us to search below the surface of the text to find a hidden meaning. In his fables, Aesop sometimes presented animals behaving as humans would. The story of the fox and his unsuccessful attempt to reach some grapes on a vine, for example, reveals the human tendency to disdain what we cannot achieve.

Like the fable, the parable tends to be brief, though its agents are often humans rather than animals. It can be exemplified by the biblical story of the prodigal son, who unlike his dutiful brother spends his entire inheritance in riotous living. When he has lost everything and is hungry and hopeless, he determines to return to his father's house, as a servant if necessary, and throw himself on his father's mercy. Beyond his wildest expectations, his father rejoices at his return and welcomes his lost son back with a great feast. This parable of redemption is a sign of hope for those who know themselves to be less than perfect.

The allegory is the underlying form for both fable and parable. Its story conveys a meaning not explicitly set forth in the narrative. Allegory may have meaning on two or more levels that we can understand only through an interpretive process. Literary allegories typically describe situations and events or express abstract ideas in terms of material objects, persons, and actions.

Probably the most influential allegory of the Middle Ages, when the genre was at its peak, is the 13th-century French didactic poem *Romance of the Rose*. This poem illustrates the allegorical technique of personification, in which a fictional character—in this case, The Lover—transparently represents a concept or type. As in most allegories, the action of the narrative "stands for" something not explicitly stated. The Lover's eventual plucking of the crimson rose represents his conquest of his lady.

The medieval romance originated in ancient Greece. First signifying the use of vernacular language instead of the Latin known only to the scholarly elite, the term romance has come to have a variety of meanings—from a medieval narrative composition to a love affair, or, in modern publishing, a formulaic story about a love affair. Romance and its assortment of meanings are further explored in chapter four.

Another early genre, the saga, represents a rich tradition of northern Europe. In English the word *saga* is typically used to refer to the biographies of a hero (or group of heroes) written in Iceland between the 12th and 15th centuries. These heroes were most often kings of Norway, early founders of Iceland, or legendary Germanic figures of the 4th to the 8th century.

The oldest saga is the fragmentary *Ólafs saga helga* ("Saga of St. Olaf"), written about 1180. In form it is a hagiographic narrative, laying emphasis on miracles worked through the agency of the saint. It was probably written in the monastery of Þingeyrar, which played an important part in cultural life in the late 12th and early 13th centuries.

These sagas provide the most detailed descriptions available of the lifestyle of early Germanic peoples and constitute the most complete account of their literature and literary traditions. Although the sagas and poems were first written down by Christian scribes, they present a picture of a pre-Christian European culture that reached its heights of expression in Icelandic settlements.

Another genre with deep roots is the short story. Its early ancestors were ancient Greek fables and brief romances, the tales of the *Arabian Nights*, and the earthily realistic tales of Geoffrey Chaucer and Giovanni Boccaccio inserted within longer narratives. Short stories did not really emerge as a distinct literary genre until the early 19th century, however. Their development seems to have been prompted both by literary Romanticism and literary realism. Romanticism stimulated interest in the strange and fantastic, in abnormal sensation and heightened experience that could be explored within the compass of a brief prose narrative but did not have the duration appropriate to the scale of the novel.

The first true collections of short stories began to appear almost simultaneously in Germany, the United States, Russia, and France in the second and third decades of the 19th century. In Germany the tales of Heinrich von Kleist and E.T.A. Hoffmann made use of the fabulous as a means of exploring psychological and metaphysical problems. Washington Irving's *The Sketch Book* (1819–20) marked the beginning of the American short story. In the 1830s he was followed by Edgar Allan Poe and Nathaniel Hawthorne, the best American storywriters in the first half of the 19th century. Poe wrote many classic tales of horror and virtually invented the detective story. In his *Twice-Told Tales* (1837) Hawthorne displayed a Puritan-derived fascination with the ordeals of individual experience, particularly the experience of evil. Aleksandr Pushkin and Nikolay Gogol in Russia and authors in France also turned to the short story, but many preferred to examine the details of

ordinary life, rather than the fantastic and legendary.

Satire is a tool used chiefly by fiction and drama writers to censure the shortcomings of human society. It could take many forms, including ridicule, derision, burlesque, and irony. Satire is found embodied in an indefinite number of literary forms. In English literature alone, the form is manifested in the superb wit of Chaucer's *Canterbury Tales*, the comedies of Ben Jonson, the verses of John Dryden and of Alexander Pope, and Jonathan Swift's excoriation of civilized society in *Gulliver's Travels*. Satire is a major element in the plays of Molière, George Bernard Shaw, and Bertolt Brecht, among other dramatists, while François Rabelais and Gogol were among its best-known practitioners in fiction. Satire is also an important element in the fictional utopias of Thomas More, Aldous Huxley, and George Orwell.

One of the chief forms of nonfictional literature is biography, a recounting of the life of an individual. It can be seen as a branch of history, because it depends on a selective ordering and interpretation of materials, written and oral, established through research and personal recollection. It can also be seen as a branch of imaginative literature in that it seeks to convey a sense of the individuality and significance of the subject through creative sympathetic insight.

In its final chapter, this book takes a look at literary criticism, a discipline concerned with a range of enquiries about literature that have tended to fall into three broad categories: philosophical, descriptive, and evaluative. Criticism asks several questions: What is literature? What does literature do? What is literature worth?

And that's what each of us has to assess for ourselves as we read and relate to each other the events of the day. Why is it that a bad dream can haunt us for days as we puzzle over it? How did that writer manage to so involve us that we were crying as we finished a book? Why do we feel so hopeful at the conclusion of a good speaker's talk?

Words can give us hope or lead us to despair. The more aware we are of how words affect our lives, the better we know ourselves and understand the motivations of others. And that, after all, is what gives each of us power over our own lives.

Across the street a man sitting in a harness is washing windows on a four-story building. He has lived a life you know nothing about. But since you've seen him, he's a part—however small—of your memory banks. Maybe you'll remember seeing him two years from now, maybe you won't. Maybe, with fellow feeling, you can sense the wetness of his sleeve as the water drips down his right arm. What else do you see when you think about this? A Peeping Tom? A symbol of clear vision? How would *you* write this story?

CHAPTER 1

Novel

An invented prose narrative of considerable length and a certain complexity that deals imaginatively with human experience, usually through a connected sequence of events involving a group of persons in a specific setting, is called a novel. Within its broad framework, the genre of the novel has encompassed an extensive range of types and styles: picaresque, epistolary, Gothic, romantic, realist, historical—to name only some of the more important ones.

The novel is a genre of fiction, and fiction may be defined as the art or craft of contriving, through the written word, representations of human life that instruct or divert or both. The various forms that fiction may take are best seen less as a number of separate categories than as a continuum or, more accurately, a cline, with some such brief form as the anecdote at one end of the scale and the longest conceivable novel at the other. When any piece of fiction is long enough to constitute a whole book, as opposed to a mere part of a book, then it may be said to have achieved novelhood. But this state admits of its own quantitative categories, so that a relatively brief novel may be termed a novella (or, if the insubstantiality of the content matches its brevity, a novelette), and a particularly long novel may overflow the banks of a single volume and become a *roman-fleuve*, or river novel. Length is very much one of the dimensions of the genre.

The term *novel* is a truncation of the Italian word *novella* (from the plural of Latin *novellus*, a late variant of *novus*,

The shelves of libraries around the world support printed books on a vast assortment of subjects, written in a great variety of styles. Comstock/Thinkstock

meaning "new"), so that what is now, in most languages, a diminutive denotes historically the parent form. The *novella* was a kind of enlarged anecdote like those to be found in the 14th-century Italian classic Boccaccio's *Decameron*, each of which exemplifies the etymology well enough. The stories are little new things, novelties, freshly minted diversions, toys. They are not reworkings of known fables or myths, and they lack weight and moral earnestness. It is to be noted that, despite the high example of novelists of the most profound seriousness, such as Leo Tolstoy, Henry James, and Virginia Woolf, the term *novel* still, in some quarters, carries overtones of lightness and frivolity. And it is possible to descry a tendency to triviality in the form itself. The ode or symphony seems to possess an inner mechanism that protects it from aesthetic or moral corruption, but the novel can descend to shameful commercial depths of sentimentality or pornography. This section endeavours to consider the novel not solely in terms of great art but also as an all-purpose medium catering to all the strata of literacy.

Such early ancient Roman fiction as Petronius's *Satyricon* of the 1st century CE and Lucius Apuleius's *The Golden Ass* of the 2nd century contain many of the popular elements that distinguish the novel from the epic poem. In the fictional works, the medium is prose, the events described are unheroic, and the settings are streets and taverns, not battlefields and palaces. There is more low fornication than princely combat. Gods do not move the action. The dialogue is homely rather than aristocratic. It was, in fact, out of the need to find—in the period of Roman decline—a literary form that was anti-epic in both substance and language that the first prose fiction of Europe seems to have been conceived. When the most memorable character in Petronius is a *nouveau riche* vulgarian and the hero of Lucius Apuleius is turned into a donkey, nothing farther from epic can easily be imagined.

The medieval chivalric romance (from a popular Latin word, probably *Romanice*, meaning written in the vernacular, not in traditional Latin) restored a kind of epic view of humans—though now as heroic Christians, not heroic pagans. At the same time, it bequeathed its name to the later genre of continental literature, the novel, which is known in French as *roman*, in Italian as *romanzo*, etc. (The English term *romance*, however, carries a pejorative connotation.) But that later genre achieved its first great flowering in Spain at the beginning of the 17th century in an antichivalric comic masterpiece—the *Don Quixote* of Cervantes, which, on a larger scale than the *Satyricon* or *The Golden Ass*, contains many of the elements that have been expected from prose fiction ever since. Novels have heroes, but not in any classical or medieval sense. As for the novelist, he must, in the words of the contemporary British-American poet W.H. Auden,

*Become the whole of boredom,
subject to
Vulgar complaints like love,
among the Just
Be just, among the Filthy filthy
too,
And in his own weak person, if
he can,
Must suffer dully all the wrongs
of Man.*

The novel attempts to assume those burdens of life that have no place in the epic poem and to see individuals as unheroic, unredeemed, imperfect, even absurd. This is why there is room among its practitioners for writers of hard-boiled detective thrillers such as the 20th-century American writer Mickey Spillane or of sentimental melodramas such as the prolific 19th-century English novelist Mrs. Henry Wood, but not for someone of the unremitting elevation of outlook of a John Milton.

ELEMENTS

One of the principal ways to analyze a novel is by examining the myriad devices of which it is built. At the very least, these consist of plot, character, scene (or setting), narrative method and point of view, scope (or dimension), and myth, symbol, and significance.

PLOT

The novel is propelled through its hundred or thousand pages by a device known as the story or plot. This is frequently conceived by the novelist in very simple terms, a mere nucleus, a jotting on an old envelope: for example, Charles Dickens's *A Christmas Carol* (1843) might have been conceived as "a misanthrope is reformed through certain magical visitations on Christmas Eve," or Jane Austen's *Pride and Prejudice* (1813) as "a young couple destined to be married have first to overcome the barriers of pride and prejudice," or Fyodor Dostoyevsky's *Crime and Punishment* (1866) as "a young man commits a crime and is slowly pursued in the direction of his punishment." The detailed working out of the nuclear idea requires much ingenuity, because the plot of one novel is expected to be somewhat different from that of another, and there are very few basic human situations for the novelist to draw upon. The dramatist may take his plot ready-made from fiction or biography—a form of theft sanctioned by William Shakespeare—but the novelist has to produce what look like novelties.

The example of Shakespeare is a reminder that the ability to create an interesting plot, or even any plot at all, is not a prerequisite of the imaginative writer's craft. At the lowest level of fiction, plot need be no more than a string of stock devices for arousing stock responses of concern and excitement in the reader. The reader's interest may be captured at the outset by the promise of conflicts or mysteries or frustrations that will eventually be resolved, and he will gladly—so strong is his desire to be moved or entertained—suspend criticism of even the most trite modes of resolution. In the least sophisticated fiction, the knots to be untied are stringently physical, and the denouement often comes in a sort of triumphant violence. Serious fiction prefers its plots to be based on psychological situations,

Dust jacket designed by Vanessa Bell (the author's sister) for the first edition of Virginia Woolf's To the Lighthouse, *published by the Hogarth Press in 1927.* Between the Covers Rare Books, Merchantville, NJ

and its climaxes come in new states of awareness—chiefly self-knowledge—on the parts of the major characters.

Melodramatic plots, plots dependent on coincidence or improbability, are sometimes found in even the most elevated fiction. E.M. Forster's *Howards End* (1910) is an example of a classic British novel with such a plot. But the novelist is always faced with the problem of whether it is more important to represent the formlessness of real life (in which there are no beginnings, no ends, and very few simple motives for action) or to construct an artifact as well balanced and economical as a table or chair. Because he is an artist, the claims of art, or artifice, frequently prevail.

There are, however, ways of constructing novels in which plot may play a desultory part or no part at all. The traditional picaresque novel—a novel typically with a rogue as its central character—like Alain Lesage's *Gil Blas* (1715) or Henry Fielding's *Tom Jones* (1749), depends for movement on a succession of chance incidents. In the works of Virginia Woolf, the consciousness of the characters, bounded by some poetic or symbolic device, sometimes provides all the fictional material. Marcel Proust's great *roman-fleuve*, *À la recherche du temps perdu* (1913–27; *Remembrance of Things Past*, or *In Search of Lost Time*), has a metaphysical framework derived from the time theories of the philosopher Henri Bergson, and it moves toward a moment of truth that is intended to be literally a revelation of the nature of reality. Strictly, any scheme will do to hold a novel together—raw action, the hidden syllogism of the mystery story, prolonged solipsist contemplation—so long as the actualities or potentialities of human life are credibly expressed, with a consequent sense of illumination, or some lesser mode of artistic satisfaction, on the part of the reader.

CHARACTER

The inferior novelist tends to be preoccupied with plot. To the superior novelist the convolutions of the human personality, under the stress of artfully selected experience, are the chief fascination. Without character it was once accepted that there could be no fiction. In the period since World War II, the creators of what has come to be called the French *nouveau roman* (i.e., New Novel) have deliberately demoted the human element, claiming the right of objects and processes to the writer's and reader's prior attention. Thus, in books termed *chosiste* (literally "thing-ist"), they make the furniture of a room more important than its human incumbents. This may be seen as a transitory protest against the long predominance of character in the novel, but, even on the popular level, there have been indications that readers can be held by things as much as by characters. Henry James could be vague in *The Ambassadors* (1903) about the provenance of his chief character's wealth, but if he wrote today he would have to give his readers a tour around the factory or estate. The popularity of much undistinguished but popular fiction has nothing to do with its wooden characters. Machines, procedures, and organizations draw the reader. The success of Ian Fleming's British spy stories in the 1960s had much to do with James Bond's car, gun, and preferred way of mixing a martini.

But the true novelists remain creators of characters—prehuman, such as those in William Golding's *Inheritors* (1955); animal, as in Henry Williamson's *Tarka the Otter* (1927) or Jack London's *Call of the Wild* (1903); caricatures, as in much of Dickens; or complex and unpredictable entities, as in Tolstoy, Dostoyevsky, or Henry James. The reader may be prepared to tolerate the most wanton-seeming stylistic tricks and formal difficulties because of the intense interest of the central characters in novels as diverse as James Joyce's *Ulysses* (1922) and *Finnegans Wake* (1939) and Laurence Sterne's *Tristram Shandy* (1759–67).

It is the task of literary critics to create a value hierarchy of fictional character, placing the complexity of the Shakespearean view of humanity—as found in the novels of Tolstoy and Joseph Conrad—above creations that may be no more than simple personifications of some single characteristic, like some of those by Dickens. It frequently happens, however, that the common reader prefers surface simplicity—easily memorable cartoon figures like Dickens's never-despairing Mr. Micawber and devious Uriah Heep—to that wider view of personality, in which character seems to

engulf the reader, subscribed to by the great novelists of France and Russia. The whole nature of human identity remains in doubt, and writers who voice that doubt—like the French exponents of the *nouveau roman* Alain Robbe-Grillet and Nathalie Sarraute, as well as many others—are in effect rejecting a purely romantic view of character. This view imposed the author's image of himself—the only human image he properly possessed—on the rest of the human world. For the unsophisticated reader of fiction, any created personage with a firm position in time–space and the most superficial parcel of behavioral (or even sartorial) attributes will be taken for a character. Though the critics may regard it as heretical, this tendency to accept a character is in conformity with the usages of real life. The average person has at least a suspicion of his own complexity and inconsistency of makeup, but he sees the rest of the world as composed of much simpler entities. The result is that novels whose characters are created out of the author's own introspection are frequently rejected as not "true to life." But both the higher and the lower orders of novel readers might agree in condemning a lack of memorability in the personages of a work of fiction, a failure on the part of the author to seem to add to the reader's stock of remembered friends and acquaintances. Characters that seem, on recollection, to have a life outside the bounds of the books that contain them are usually the ones that earn their creators the most regard. Depth of psychological penetration, the ability to make a character real as oneself, seems to be no primary criterion of fictional talent.

SCENE, OR SETTING

The makeup and behaviour of fictional characters depend on their environment quite as much as on the personal dynamic with which their author endows them: indeed, in Émile Zola, environment is of overriding importance, because he believed it determined character. The entire action of a novel is frequently determined by the locale in which it is set. Thus, Gustave Flaubert's *Madame Bovary* (1857) could hardly have been placed in Paris, because the tragic life and death of the heroine have a great deal to do with the circumscriptions of her provincial milieu. But it sometimes happens that the main locale of a novel assumes an importance in the reader's imagination comparable to that of the characters and yet somehow separable from them. Wessex is a giant brooding presence in Thomas Hardy's novels, whose human characters would probably not behave much differently if they were set in some other rural locality of England. The popularity of Sir Walter Scott's "Waverley" novels is in part because of their evocation of a romantic Scotland. Swedish novelist Henning Mankell's Wallander crime novels have a sense of place so strong that the place itself almost becomes a character. Setting may be the prime consideration of some readers, who can be drawn to Conrad because he depicts life at sea or in the East Indies. They may be less interested in the complexity of human relationships that he presents.

The regional novel is a recognized species. The sequence of four novels that Hugh Walpole began with *Rogue Herries* (1930) was the result of his desire to do homage to the part of Cumberland, in England, where he had elected to live. The great Yoknapatawpha cycle of William Faulkner, a classic of 20th-century American literature set in an imaginary county in Mississippi, belongs to the category as much as the once-popular confections about Sussex that were written about the same time by the English novelist Sheila Kaye-Smith. Many novelists, however, gain a creative impetus from avoiding the same setting in book after book and deliberately seeking new locales. The English novelist Graham Greene apparently needed to visit a fresh scene in order to write a fresh novel. His ability to encapsulate the essence of an exotic setting in a single book is exemplified in *The Heart of the Matter* (1948). His contemporary Evelyn Waugh stated that the West Africa of that book replaced the true remembered West Africa of his own experience. Such power is common: the Yorkshire moors have been romanticized because Emily Brontë wrote of them in *Wuthering Heights* (1847), and literary tourists have visited Stoke-on-Trent, in northern England, because it comprises the "Five Towns" of Arnold Bennett's novels of the early 20th century. Others go to the Monterey, California, of John Steinbeck's novels in the expectation of experiencing a *frisson* added to the locality by an act of creative imagination. James Joyce, who remained inexhaustibly stimulated by Dublin, exalted that city in a manner that even 21st-century guidebooks recognize.

The setting of a novel is not always drawn from a real-life locale. The literary artist sometimes prides himself on his ability to create the totality of his fiction—the setting as well as the characters and their actions. In the Russian expatriate Vladimir Nabokov's *Ada* (1969) there is an entirely new space–time continuum, and the English scholar J.R.R. Tolkien in his *Lord of the Rings* (1954–55) created an "alternative world" that appeals greatly to many who are dissatisfied with the existing one. The world of interplanetary travel was imaginatively created long before the first moon landing. The properties of the future envisaged by H.G. Wells's novels or by Aldous Huxley in *Brave New World* (1932) are still recognized in an age that those authors did not live to see. The composition of place can be a magical fictional gift.

Whatever the locale of his work, every true novelist is concerned with making a credible environment for his characters, and this really means a close attention to sense data—the immediacies of food and drink and colour—far more than abstractions like "nature" and "city." The London of Charles Dickens is as much incarnated in the smell of wood in lawyers' chambers as in the skyline and vistas of streets.

ÉMILE ZOLA

(b. April 2, 1840, Paris, France—d. Sept. 28, 1902, Paris)

French novelist, critic, and political activist Émile Zola was the most prominent French novelist of the late 19th century. Raised in straitened circumstances, Zola worked at a Paris publishing house for several years during the 1860s while establishing himself as a writer. In the gruesome novel Thérèse Raquin (1867), he put his "scientific" theories of the determination of character by heredity and environment into practice for the first time. These ideas established him as the founder of naturalism in literature. In 1870 he began the ambitious project for which he is best known, the Rougon-Macquart Cycle (1871–93), a sequence of 20 novels documenting French life through the lives of the violent Rougon family and the passive Macquarts. It includes L'Assommoir (1877), a study of alcoholism that is among his most successful and popular novels; Nana (1880); Germinal (1885), his masterpiece; and La Bête humaine (1890). Among his other works are two shorter novel cycles and treatises explaining his theories on art, including The Experimental Novel (1880). He is also notable for his involvement in the Alfred Dreyfus affair, especially for his open letter, "J'accuse" (1898), denouncing the French army general staff for concealing the truth in the wrongful conviction of the Jewish army officer for treason. Zola died under suspicious circumstances, overcome by carbon-monoxide fumes in his sleep.

NARRATIVE METHOD AND POINT OF VIEW

Where there is a story, there is a story-teller. Traditionally, the narrator of the epic and mock-epic alike acted as an intermediary between the characters and the reader. The method of Fielding is not so different from the method of Homer. Sometimes the narrator boldly imposed his own attitudes. Always he assumed an omniscience that tended to reduce the characters to puppets and the action to a predetermined course with an end implicit in the beginning. Many novelists have been unhappy about a narrative method that seems to limit the free will of the characters, and innova-tions in fictional technique have mostly sought the objectivity of the drama, in which the characters appear to work out their own destinies without prompting from the author.

The epistolary method, most notably used by Samuel Richardson in *Pamela* (1740) and by Jean-Jacques Rousseau in *La nouvelle Héloïse* (1761), has the advan-tage of allowing the characters to tell the story in their own words, but it is hard to resist the uneasy feeling that a kind of divine editor is sorting and ordering the letters into his own pattern. The device of making the narrator also a character in the story has the disadvantage of limiting the material available for the narration, because the narrator-character can know only those events in which he partici-pates. There can, of course, be a number of secondary narratives enclosed in the main narrative, and this device—though it sometimes looks artificial—has been used triumphantly by Conrad and, on a lesser scale, by W. Somerset Maugham. A, the main narrator, tells what he knows directly of the story and introduces what B and C and D have told him about the parts that he does not know.

Seeking the most objective narrative method of all, Ford Madox Ford used, in *The Good Soldier* (1915), the device of the storyteller who does not under-stand the story he is telling. This is the technique of the "unreliable observer." The reader, understanding better than the narrator, has the illusion of receiv-ing the story directly. Joyce, in both his major novels, uses different narra-tors for the various chapters. Most are unreliable, and some approach the imper-sonality of a sort of disembodied parody. In *Ulysses*, for example, an episode set in a maternity hospital is told through the medium of a parodic history of English prose style. But, more often than not, the sheer ingenuity of Joyce's techniques draws attention to the manipulator in the shadows. The reader is aware of the author's cleverness where he should be aware only of the characters and their actions. The author is least noticeable when he is employing the stream of con-sciousness device, by which the inchoate thoughts and feelings of a character are presented in interior monologue— apparently unedited and sometimes deliberately near-unintelligible. It is because this technique seems to draw fic-tion into the psychoanalyst's consulting room (presenting the raw material of either art or science, but certainly not art itself), however, that Joyce felt impelled to impose the shaping devices referred to earlier. Joyce, more than any novelist, sought total objectivity of narration technique but ended as the most subjective and idiosyncratic of stylists.

The problem of a satisfactory narrative point of view is, in fact, nearly insoluble. The careful exclusion of comment, the limitation of vocabulary to a sort of reader's lowest common denominator, the paring of style to the absolute minimum—these puritanical devices work well for an Ernest Hemingway (who, like Joyce, remains, nevertheless, a highly idiosyncratic stylist) but not for a novelist who believes that, like poetry, his art should be able to draw on the richness of word play, allusion, and symbol. For even the most experienced novelist, each new work represents a struggle with the unconquerable task of reconciling all-inclusion with self-exclusion. It is noteworthy that Cervantes, in *Don Quixote*, and Nabokov, in *Lolita* (1955), join hands across four centuries in finding most satisfactory the device of the fictitious editor who presents a manuscript story for which he disclaims responsibility. But this highly useful method presupposes in the true author a scholarly, or pedantic, faculty not usually associated with novelists.

SCOPE, OR DIMENSION

No novel can theoretically be too long, but if it is too short it ceases to be a novel.

It may or may not be accidental that the novels most highly regarded by the world are of considerable length—Cervantes's *Don Quixote*, Dostoyevsky's *Brothers Karamazov*, Tolstoy's *War and Peace*, Dickens's *David Copperfield*, Proust's *À la recherche du temps perdu*, and so on. On the other hand, since World War II, brevity has been regarded as a virtue in works like the later novels of the Irish absurdist author Samuel Beckett and the *ficciones* of the Argentine Jorge Luis Borges, and it is only an aesthetic based on bulk that would diminish the achievement of Ronald Firbank's short novels of the post-World War I era or the Evelyn Waugh who wrote *The Loved One* (1948). It would seem that there are two ways of presenting human character—one, the brief way, through a significant episode in the life of a personage or group of personages; the other, which admits of limitless length, through the presentation of a large section of a life or lives, sometimes beginning with birth and ending in old age. The plays of Shakespeare show that a full delineation of character can be effected in a very brief compass, so that, for this aspect of the novel, length confers no special advantage. Length, however, is essential when the novelist attempts to present something bigger than character—when, in fact, he aims at the representation of a whole society or period of history.

No other cognate art form—neither the epic poem nor the drama nor the film—can match the resources of the novel when the artistic task is to bring to immediate, sensuous, passionate life the somewhat impersonal materials of the historian. *War and Peace* is the great triumphant example of the panoramic study of a whole society—that of early 19th-century Russia—which enlightens as the historian enlightens and yet also conveys directly the sensations and emotions of living through a period of cataclysmic change. In the 20th century, another Russian, Boris Pasternak, in his *Doctor Zhivago* (1957), expressed—though on a less than Tolstoyan scale—the personal immediacies of life during the Russian Revolution. Though of much less literary distinction than either of these two books, Margaret Mitchell's *Gone with the Wind* (1936) showed how the American Civil War could assume the distanced pathos, horror, and grandeur of any of the classic struggles of the Old World.

Needless to say, length and weighty subject matter are no guarantee in themselves of fictional greatness. Among American writers, for example, James Jones's celebration of the U.S. Army on the eve of World War II in *From Here to Eternity* (1951), though a very ambitious project, repels through indifferent writing and sentimental characterization; Norman Mailer's *Naked and the Dead* (1948), an equally ambitious military novel, succeeds much more because of a tautness, a concern with compression, and an astringent objectivity that Jones was unable to match. Diffuseness is the great danger in the long novel, and diffuseness can mean slack writing, emotional self-indulgence, and sentimentality.

Even the long picaresque novel—which, in the hands of a Fielding or his contemporary Tobias Smollett, can rarely be accused of sentimentality—easily betrays itself into such acts of self-indulgence as the multiplication of incident for its own sake, the coy digression, the easygoing jogtrot pace that subdues the sense of urgency that should lie in all fiction. If Tolstoy's *War and Peace* is a greater novel than Fielding's *Tom Jones* or Dickens's *David Copperfield*, it is not because its theme is nobler, or more pathetic, or more significant historically; it is because Tolstoy brings to his panoramic drama the compression and urgency usually regarded as the monopolies of briefer fiction.

Sometimes the scope of a fictional concept demands a technical approach analogous to that of the symphony in music—the creation of a work in separate books, like symphonic movements, each of which is intelligible alone but whose greater intelligibility depends on the theme and characters that unify them. The French author Romain Rolland's *Jean-Christophe* (1904–12) sequence is, very appropriately since the hero is a musical composer, a work in four movements. Among works of English literature, Lawrence Durrell's *Alexandria Quartet* (1957–60) insists in its very title that it is a tetralogy rather than a single large entity divided into four volumes; the concept is "relativist" and attempts to look at the same events and characters from four different viewpoints. Anthony Powell's *A Dance to the Music of Time*, a multivolume series of novels that began in 1951 (collected 1962), may be seen as a study of a segment of British society in which the chronological approach is eschewed, and events are brought together in one volume or another because of a kind of parachronic homogeneity. C.P. Snow's *Strangers and Brothers*, a comparable series that began in 1940 and continued to appear throughout the '50s and into the '60s, shows how a fictional concept can be realized only in the act of writing, since the publication of the earlier volumes antedates the historical events portrayed in later ones. In other words, the author could not know what the subject matter of the sequence would be until he was in sight of its end. Behind all these works lies the giant example of Proust's *roman-fleuve*, whose length and scope were properly coterminous with the author's own life and emergent understanding of its pattern.

Myth, Symbolism, Significance

The novelist's conscious day-to-day preoccupation is the setting down of incident, the delineation of personality, the regulation of exposition, climax, and denouement. The aesthetic value of the work is frequently determined by subliminal forces that seem to operate independently of the writer, investing the properties of the surface story with a deeper significance. A novel will then come close to myth, its characters turning into symbols of permanent human states or impulses, particular incarnations of general truths perhaps only realized for the first time in the act of reading. The ability to perform a quixotic act anteceded *Don Quixote*, just as *bovarysme* existed before Flaubert found a name for it.

But the desire to give a work of fiction a significance beyond that of the mere story is frequently conscious and deliberate, indeed sometimes the primary aim. When a novel—like Joyce's *Ulysses*, Ursula K. Le Guin's *Lavinia* (2008), or Anthony Burgess's *Vision of Battlements* (1965)—is based on an existing classical myth, there is an intention of either ennobling a lowly subject matter, satirizing a debased set of values by referring them to a heroic age, or merely providing a basic structure to hold down a complex and, as it were, centrifugal picture of real life. Of *Ulysses* Joyce said that his Homeric parallel (which is worked out in great and subtle detail) was a bridge across which to march his 18 episodes. After the march the bridge could be "blown skyhigh." But there is no doubt that, through the classical parallel, the account of an ordinary summer day in Dublin is given a richness, irony, and universality unattainable by any other means.

The mythic or symbolic intention of a novel may manifest itself less in structure than in details, which, though they appear naturalistic, are really something more. The shattering of the eponymous golden bowl in Henry James's 1904 novel makes palpable, and hence truly symbolic, the collapse of a relationship. Even the choice of a character's name may be symbolic. Sammy Mountjoy, in William Golding's *Free Fall* (1959), has fallen from the grace of heaven, the mount of joy, by an act of volition that the title makes clear. The eponym of *Doctor Zhivago* is so called because his name, meaning "The Living," carries powerful religious overtones. In the Russian version of the Gospel According to St. Luke, the angels ask the women who come to Christ's tomb: "*Chto vy ischyote zhivago mezhdu myortvykh?*"—"Why do you seek the living among the dead?" And his first name, Yuri, the Russian equivalent of George, has dragon-slaying connotations.

The symbol, the special significance at a subnarrative level, works best when it can fit without obtrusion into a context of naturalism. The optician's trade sign of a huge pair of spectacles in F. Scott Fitzgerald's *Great Gatsby* (1925) is acceptable as a piece of scenic detail, but an extra dimension is added to the tragedy of Gatsby, which is the tragedy of a whole epoch in American life, when it is taken also as a symbol of divine myopia. Similarly, a cinema poster in Malcolm Lowry's *Under the Volcano* (1947), advertising a horror film, can be read as naturalistic background, but evidently the author expects the illustrated fiend—a concert pianist whose grafted hands are those of a murderer—to be seen also as a symbol of Nazi infamy. The novel is set at the beginning of World War II, and the last desperate day of the hero, Geoffrey Firmin, stands also for the collapse of Western civilization.

There are symbolic novels whose infranarrative meaning cannot easily be stated, because it appears to subsist on an unconscious level. Herman Melville's *Moby Dick* (1851) is such a work, as is D.H. Lawrence's novella *St. Mawr* (1925), in which the significance of the horse is powerful and mysterious.

USES

Just as people read novels for different reasons—to escape from the daily grind, to experience the perspective of a much-loved writer, to gain insight into the human condition—so too novelists present their work in many ways and for many reasons. Whatever else may be said about a novel of any sort, it must reveal how the author thinks about the world.

INTERPRETATION OF LIFE

Novels are not expected to be didactic, like tracts or morality plays. Nevertheless, in varying degrees of implicitness, even the "purest" works of fictional art convey a philosophy of life. The novels of Jane Austen, designed primarily as superior entertainment, imply a desirable ordered existence, in which the comfortable decorum of an English rural family is disturbed only by a not-too-serious shortage of money, love affairs that go temporarily wrong, and the intrusion of self-centred stupidity. The good, if unrewarded for their goodness, suffer from no permanent injustice. Life is seen, not only in Jane Austen's novels but in the whole current of bourgeois Anglo-American fiction, as fundamentally reasonable and decent. When wrong is committed, it is usually punished, thus fulfilling Miss Prism's summation in Oscar Wilde's play *The Importance of Being Earnest* (1895), to the effect that in a novel the good characters end up happily and the bad characters unhappily: "that is why it is called fiction."

That kind of fiction called realistic, which has its origins in 19th-century France, chose the other side of the coin, showing that there was no justice in life and that the evil and the stupid must prevail. In the novels of Thomas Hardy there is a pessimism that may be taken as a corrective of bourgeois Panglossianism—the philosophy that everything happens for the best, satirized in Voltaire's *Candide* (1759)—because the universe is presented as almost impossibly malevolent. This tradition is regarded as morbid, and it has been deliberately ignored by most popular novelists. The "Catholic" novelists—such as François Mauriac in France, Graham Greene in England, and others—see life as mysterious, full of wrong and evil and injustice inexplicable by human canons but necessarily acceptable in terms of the plans of an inscrutable God. Between the period of realistic pessimism, which had much to do with the agnosticism and determinism of 19th-century science, and the introduction of theological evil into the novel, writers such as H.G. Wells attempted to create a fiction based on optimistic liberalism. As a reaction, there was the depiction of "natural man" in the novels of D.H. Lawrence and Ernest Hemingway.

For the most part, the view of life common to American and European fiction in the second half of the 20th century posited the existence of evil—whether theological or of that brand discovered by the French Existentialists, particularly Jean-Paul Sartre—and assumed that people are imperfect and life possibly absurd. The fiction of the former communist Europe was based on a far different assumption, one that seems naïve and old-fashioned in its collective optimism to readers in the disillusioned democracies. It is to be noted that in the erstwhile Soviet Union, aesthetic evaluation of fiction was replaced by ideological judgment. From this perspective, the works of the popular British writer A.J. Cronin—because they seem to depict personal tragedy as an emanation of capitalistic infamy—were ranked above those of Conrad, James, and their peers.

ENTERTAINMENT OR ESCAPE

In a period that takes for granted that the written word should be "committed"—to the exposure of social wrong or the propagation of progressive ideologies—novelists who seek merely to take the reader out of his dull or oppressive daily life are not highly regarded, except by that reading public that has never expected a book to be anything more than a diversion. Nevertheless, the provision of laughter and dreams has been for many centuries a legitimate literary occupation. It can be condemned by serious devotees of literature only if it falsifies life through oversimplification and tends to corrupt its readers into belief that reality is as the author presents it. The novelettes once beloved of mill girls and domestic servants, in which the beggar maid was elevated to queendom by a king of high finance, were a mere narcotic, a sort of enervating opium of the oppressed. The encouragement of such subliterature might well be one of the devices of social oppression. Adventure stories and spy novels may have a healthy enough astringency, and the very preposterousness of some adventures can be a safeguard against any impressionable young reader's neglecting the claims of real life to dream of becoming a secret agent. The subject matter of some humorous novels—such as the effete British aristocracy created by P.G. Wodehouse, which is no longer in existence if it ever was—can never be identified with a real human society. The dream is accepted as a dream. The same may be said of Evelyn Waugh's early novels—such as *Decline and Fall* (1928) and *Vile Bodies* (1930)—but these are raised above mere entertainment by touching, almost incidentally, on real human issues (the relation of the innocent to a circumambient malevolence is a persistent theme in all Waugh's writing).

Any reader of fiction has a right to an occasional escape from the dullness or misery of his existence, but he has the critical duty of finding the best modes of escape—in the most efficiently

engineered detective or adventure stories, in humour that is more than sentimental buffoonery, in dreams of love that are not mere pornography. The fiction of entertainment and escape frequently sets itself higher literary standards than novels with a profound social or philosophical purpose. Books such as John Buchan's *Thirty-nine Steps* (1915), Graham Greene's *Travels with My Aunt* (1969), Dashiell Hammett's *Maltese Falcon* (1930), Raymond Chandler's *Big Sleep* (1939), and Walter Mosley's *Gone Fishin'* (1997) are distinguished pieces of writing that, while diverting and enthralling, keep a hold on the realities of human character. Ultimately, all good fiction is entertainment, and, if it instructs or enlightens, it does so best through enchanting the reader.

PROPAGANDA

The desire to make the reader initiate certain acts—social, religious, or political—is the essence of all propaganda, and, though it does not always accord well with art, the propagandist purpose has often found its way into novels whose prime value is an aesthetic one. The *Nicholas Nickleby* (1839) of Charles Dickens attacked the abuses of schools to some purpose, as his *Oliver Twist* (1838) drew attention to the horrors of poorhouses and his *Bleak House* (1853) to the abuses of the law of chancery. The weakness of propaganda in fiction is that it loses its value when the wrongs it exposes are righted, so that the more successful a propagandist novel is, the briefer the life it can be expected to enjoy. The genius of Dickens lay in his ability to transcend merely topical issues through the vitality with which he presented them, so that his contemporary disclosures take on a timeless human validity—chiefly through the power of their drama, character, and rhetoric.

The pure propagandist novel—which Dickens was incapable of writing—quickly becomes dated. The "social" novels of H.G. Wells, which propounded a rational mode of life and even blueprinted utopias, were quite quickly exploded by the conviction of man's irredeemable irrationality that World War I initiated and World War II corroborated, a conviction Wells came to share toward the end of his life. But the early scientific romances of Wells remain vital and are seen to have been prophetic. Most of the fiction of the former Soviet Union, which either glorified the regime or refrained from criticizing it, was dull and unreal, and the same can be said of communist fiction elsewhere. Propaganda too frequently ignores humanity as a totality, concentrating on it aspectively—in terms of politics or sectarian religion. When a didactic attack on a system, as in Harriet Beecher Stowe's attack on slavery in the United States in *Uncle Tom's Cabin* (1852), seems to go beyond mere propaganda, it is because the writer makes the reader aware of wrongs and injustices that are woven into the permanent human fabric. The reader's response may be a modification of his own sensibility, not an immediate desire for action, and this is one of the legitimate effects of serious fiction. The propagandist Dickens calls for the immediate righting of wrongs, but the novelist Dickens says, mainly through implication, that all people—not just schoolmasters and state hirelings—should become more humane. If it is possible to speak of art as possessing a teaching purpose, this is perhaps its only lesson.

HARRIET BEECHER STOWE

(b. June 14, 1811, Litchfield, Conn., U.S.—d. July 1, 1896, Hartford, Conn.)

The American writer and philanthropist Harriet Beecher Stowe (née Harriet Elizabeth Beecher) was the daughter of the famous revivalist Presbyterian minister Lyman Beecher. She taught school in Hartford and in Cincinnati, where she came into contact with fugitive slaves and learned about life in the South, and later settled in Maine with her husband, a professor of theology and an eminent biblical scholar. Her antislavery novel Uncle Tom's Cabin *(1852) had so great an effect that it was often cited (by Abraham Lincoln, among others) among the causes of the American Civil War. The book was an immediate sensation and was taken up eagerly by abolitionists while, along with its author, it was vehemently denounced in the South, where reading or possessing the book became an extremely dangerous enterprise. It had the effect of helping to solidify both pro- and antislavery sentiment. Her other works include the novels* Dred *(1856), also against slavery, and* The Minister's Wooing *(1859).*

REPORTAGE

The division in the novelist's mind is between his view of his art as a contrivance, like a Fabergé watch, and his view of it as a record of real life. The versatile English writer Daniel Defoe, on the evidence of such novels as his *Journal of the Plague Year* (1722), a recreation of the London plague of 1665, believed that art or contrivance had the lesser claim and proceeded to present his account of events of which he had had no direct experience in the form of plain journalistic reportage. This book, like his *Robinson Crusoe* (1719) and *Moll Flanders* (1722), is more contrived and cunning than it appears, and the hurried, unshaped narrative is the product of careful preparation and selective ordering. His example, which could have been rather fruitful, was not much followed until the 20th century, when the events of the real world became more terrifying and marvelous than anything the novelist could invent and seemed to ask for that full imaginative treatment that only the novelist's craft can give.

In contemporary American literature, John Hersey's *Hiroshima* (1946), though it recorded the actual results of the nuclear attack on the Japanese city in 1945, did so in terms of human immediacies, not scientific or demographic abstractions, and this approach is essentially novelistic. Truman Capote's *In Cold Blood* (1966) took the facts of a multiple murder in the Midwest of the United States and presented them with the force, reality, tone, and (occasionally) overintense

writing that distinguish his genuine fiction. Norman Mailer, in *The Armies of the Night* (1968), recorded, in great personal detail but in a third-person narration, his part in a citizens' protest march on Washington, D.C. Mailer seemed to have a talent for merging the art of fiction and the craft of reportage, and his *Of a Fire on the Moon* (1970), which deals with the American lunar project, reads like an episode in an emergent *roman-fleuve* of which Mailer is the central character.

The presentation of factual material as art is the purpose of such thinly disguised biographies as Somerset Maugham's *The Moon and Sixpence* (1919), undisguised biographies fleshed out with supposition and imagination like Helen Waddell's *Peter Abelard* (1933), and many autobiographies served up—out of fear of libel or of dullness—as novels. Conversely, invented material may take on the lineaments of journalistic actuality through the employment of a Defoe technique of flat understatement. This is the way of such science fiction as Michael Crichton's *Andromeda Strain* (1969), which uses sketch maps, computer projections, and simulated typewritten reports.

AGENT OF CHANGE IN LANGUAGE AND THOUGHT

Novelists, being neither poets nor philosophers, rarely originate modes of thinking and expression. Poets such as Chaucer and Shakespeare have had much to do with the making of the English language, and Byron was responsible for the articulation of the new romantic sensibility in it in the early 19th century. Books such as the Bible, Karl Marx's *Das Kapital*, and Adolf Hitler's *Mein Kampf* may underlie permanent or transient cultures, but it is hard to find, except in the early Romantic period, a novelist capable of arousing new attitudes to life (as opposed to aspects of the social order) and forging the vocabulary of such attitudes.

With the 18th-century precursors of Romanticism—notably Richardson, Sterne, and Rousseau—the notion of sentiment entered the European consciousness. Rousseau's *Nouvelle Héloïse* fired a new attitude toward love—more highly emotional than ever before—as his *Émile* (1762) changed educated views on how to bring up children. The romantic wave in Germany, with Johann Wolfgang von Goethe's *Sorrows of Young Werther* (1774) and the works of Jean-Paul Richter a generation later, similarly aroused modes of feeling that rejected the rational constraints of the 18th century. Nor can the influence of Sir Walter Scott's novels be neglected, both on Europe and the American South (where Mark Twain thought it had had a deplorable effect). With Scott came new forms of regional sentiment, based on a romantic reading of history.

A novelist rarely makes a profound mark on a national language, as opposed to a regional dialect (to which, by using it for a literary end, he may impart a fresh dignity). It is conceivable that Alessandro Manzoni's *I promessi sposi* (1825–27; *The Betrothed*), often called the greatest modern Italian novel, gave 19th-century Italian intellectuals some notion of a viable modern prose style in an Italian that might be termed "national," but even this is a large claim. Günter Grass, in post-Hitler Germany, sought to revivify a language that had been corrupted by the Nazis. He threw whole dictionaries at his readers in the hope that new freedom, fantasy, and exactness in the use of words might influence the publicists, politicians, and teachers in the direction of a new liberalism of thought and expression.

It is difficult to say whether the French Existentialists, such as Sartre and Albert Camus, influenced their age primarily through their fiction or their philosophical writings. Certainly, Sartre's early novel *Nausea* (1938) established unforgettable images of the key terms of his philosophy, which haunted a whole generation, as Camus's novel *The Stranger* (1942) created for all time the lineaments of "Existential man." In the same way, the English writer George Orwell's *Nineteen Eighty-four* (1949) incarnated brilliantly the nature of the political choices that were open to 20th-century humanity, and, with terms like "Big Brother" (i.e., the leader of an authoritarian state) and "doublethink" (belief in contradictory ideas simultaneously), modified the political vocabulary. But a novelist's influence has yet to surpass that of the poet, who can give a language a soul and define, as Shakespeare and Dante did, the scope of a culture.

EXPRESSION OF THE SPIRIT OF ITS AGE

The novelist, like the poet, can make the inchoate thoughts and feelings of a society come to articulation through the exact and imaginative use of language and symbol. In this sense, his work seems to precede the diffusion of new ideas and attitudes and to be the agent of change. But it is hard to draw a line between this function and that of expressing an existing climate of sensibility. Usually, the nature of a historical period—that spirit known in German as the *Zeitgeist*—can be understood only in long retrospect, and it is then that the novelist can provide its best summation. The sickness of the Germany that produced Hitler had to wait some time for fictional diagnosis in such works as Thomas Mann's *Doctor Faustus* (1947) and, later, Günter Grass's *Tin Drum* (1959). Evelyn Waugh waited several years before beginning, in the trilogy *Sword of Honour*, to depict that moral decline of English society that started to manifest itself in World War II, the conduct of which was both a cause and a symptom of the decay of traditional notions of honour and justice.

The novel can certainly be used as a tool for the better understanding of a departed age. The period following World War I had been caught forever in Hemingway's *Sun Also Rises* (1926; called *Fiesta* in England), F. Scott Fitzgerald's novels and short stories about the so-called Jazz Age, the *Antic Hay* (1923) and *Point Counter Point* (1928) of Aldous Huxley, and D.H. Lawrence's *Aaron's Rod* (1922) and *Kangaroo* (1923). The spirit of the English 18th century, during which social, political, and religious ideas associated with rising middle classes conflicted with the old Anglican Tory rigidities, is better understood through reading Smollett and Fielding than by taking the cerebral elegance of Pope and his followers as the typical expression of the period.

Similarly, the unrest and bewilderment of the young in the decades after World War II still speak in novels such as J.D. Salinger's *Catcher in the Rye* (1951) and Kingsley Amis's *Lucky Jim* (1954). Douglas Coupland's *Generation X* (1991), while not as accomplished a work of art as Salinger's or Amis's, was almost single-handedly responsible for naming a generation of Americans born during the 1960s and 1970s. It is notable that with novels like these—as well as the Beat-generation books of Jack Kerouac; the American-Jewish novels of Saul Bellow, Bernard Malamud, Anzia Yezierska, and Philip Roth; the novels of African American experience by Ralph Ellison and James Baldwin; and the works of Native American writers Louise Erdrich and Sherman Alexie—it is a segmented spirit that is expressed, the spirit of an age group, social group, or racial group, and not the spirit of an entire society in a particular phase of history. But probably a *Zeitgeist* has always been the emanation of a minority, the majority being generally silent. Only in the 20th century did minorities begin to find a voice.

CREATOR OF LIFESTYLE AND ARBITER OF TASTE

Novels have been known to influence, though perhaps not very greatly, modes of social behaviour and even, among the particularly impressionable, conceptions of personal identity. But more young men have seen themselves as Hamlet or Childe Harold than as Julien Sorel, the protagonist of Stendhal's novel *The Red and the Black* (1830), or the sorrowing Werther. Richardson's eponymous novel may popularize Pamela, or Galsworthy's *Forsyte Saga* (1906–22) Jon, as a baptismal name, but it rarely makes a deeper impression on the mode of life of literate families. Conversely, the capacity of Oscar Wilde's *Picture of Dorian Gray* (1891) to influence young men in the direction of sybaritic amorality, or of D.H. Lawrence's *Lady Chatterley's Lover* (1928) to engender a freer attitude to sex, deserves further assessment. With the lower middle class reading public, the effect of devouring *The Forsyte Saga* was to engender genteelisms—cucumber sandwiches for tea, supper renamed dinner—rather than to learn that book's sombre lesson about the decline of the old class structure. Similarly, the ladies who read Scott in the early 19th century were led to barbarous ornaments and tastefully arranged folk songs.

Fiction has to be translated into one of the dramatic media—stage, film, or television—before it can begin to exert a large influence. *Tom Jones* as a film in 1963 modified table manners and coiffures and gave American visitors to Great Britain a new (and probably false) set of expectations. The stoic heroes of Hemingway, given to drink, fights, boats, and monosyllables, became influential only when they were transferred to the screen. They engendered other, lesser heroes—incorruptible private detectives, partisans brave under interrogation—who in their turn have influenced the impressionable young when seeking an identity. Ian Fleming's James Bond led to a small revolution in martini ordering. But all these influences are a matter of minor poses, and such poses are most readily available in fiction easily adapted to the mass media—which means lesser fiction. Proust, though he recorded French patrician society with painful fidelity, had little influence on it, and it is hard to think of Henry James disturbing the universe even fractionally. Films, television programs, and the Internet dictate taste and behaviour more than the novel ever could.

STYLE

The grammatical and lexical choices novelists make are a yardstick of their achievement. These will reveal not only the special artistry and techniques they have mastered, but also the spirit of the age in which they live and their approach to life.

ROMANTICISM

The Romantic movement in European literature is usually associated with those social and philosophical trends that prepared the way for the French Revolution, which began in 1789. The somewhat subjective, anti-rational, emotional currents of romanticism transformed intellectual life in the revolutionary and Napoleonic periods and remained potent for a great part of the 19th century. In the novel, the romantic approach to life was prepared in the "sentimental" works of Richardson and Sterne and attained its first major fulfillment in the novels of Rousseau. Sir Walter Scott, in his historical novels, turned the past into a great stage for the enactment of events motivated by idealism, chivalry, and strong emotional impulse, using an artificially archaic language full of remote and magical charm. The exceptional soul—poet, patriot, idealist, madman—took the place of dully reasonable fictional heroes, such as Tom Jones, and sumptuous and mysterious settings ousted the plain town and countryside of 18th-century novels.

The romantic novel must be seen primarily as a historical phenomenon, but the romantic style and spirit, once they had been brought into being, remained powerful and attractive enough to sustain a whole subspecies of fiction. The cheapest love story can be traced back to the example of Charlotte Brontë's *Jane Eyre* (1847), or even Rousseau's earlier *Nouvelle Héloïse*. Similarly, best-selling historical novels, even those devoid of literary merit, can find their progenitor in Scott, and science fiction in Mary Shelley's *Frankenstein* (1818), a romantic novel subtitled *The Modern Prometheus*,

as well as in Jules Verne and H.G. Wells. The aim of romantic fiction is less to present a true picture of life than to arouse the emotions through a depiction of strong passions or fire the imagination with exotic, terrifying, or wonderful scenes and events. When it is condemned by critics, it is because it seems to falsify both life and language. The pseudopoetical enters the dialogue and *récit* alike, and humanity is seen in only one of its aspects—that of feeling untempered with reason.

If such early romantic works as those of Scott and of the Goethe of *The Sorrows of Werther* have long lost their original effect, the romantic spirit still registers power and truth in the works of the Brontës—particularly in Emily Brontë's *Wuthering Heights*, in which the poetry is genuine and the strange instinctual world totally convincing. Twentieth-century romantic fiction records few masterpieces. Writers such as Daphne du Maurier, the author of *Jamaica Inn* (1936), *Rebecca* (1938), and many others, are dismissed as mere purveyors of easy dreams. It is no more possible in the 21st century to revive the original romantic élan in literature than it is to compose music in the style of Beethoven. Despite the attempts of Lawrence Durrell to achieve a kind of decadent romantic spirit in his *Alexandria Quartet*, the strong erotic feeling, the exotic setting, the atmosphere of poetic hallucination, the pain, perversion, and elemental force seem to be contrivances, however well they fulfill the original romantic prescription.

MARY WOLLSTONECRAFT SHELLEY

(b. Aug. 30, 1797, London, Eng.—d. Feb. 1, 1851, London)

The English Romantic novelist Mary Wollstonecraft Shelley is noted for her part Gothic, part philosophical novel Frankenstein; or, The Modern Prometheus *(1818, revised 1831), which resonated with readers into the 21st century. The only daughter of the English social philosopher William Godwin and the English writer and feminist Mary Wollstonecraft, she met and eloped with the poet Percy Bysshe Shelley in 1814. (They married in 1816 after his first wife committed suicide.) Mary Shelley's* Frankenstein *narrates the dreadful consequences that arise after a scientist artificially creates a human being. After her husband's death in 1822, she devoted herself to publicizing his writings and educating their son. Of her several other novels, the best,* The Last Man *(1826), is an account of the future destruction of the human race by a plague.*

REALISM

Certain major novelists of the 19th century, particularly in France, reacted against romanticism by eliminating from their work those "softer" qualities—tenderness, idealism, chivalric passion, and the like—which seemed to them to hide the stark realities of life in a dreamlike haze. In Gustave Flaubert's works there are such romantic properties—his novel *Salammbô* (1862), for instance, is a sumptuous representation of a remote pagan past—but they are there only to be punctured with realistic irony. On one level, his *Madame Bovary* may be taken as a kind of parable of the punishment that fate metes out to the romantic dreamer, and it is the more telling because Flaubert recognized a strong romantic vein in himself: "Madame Bovary, c'est moi" ("I am Madame Bovary"). Stendhal and Balzac, on another level, admit no dreams and present life in a grim nakedness without poetic drapery.

Balzac's mammoth fictional work—the 20-year succession of novels and stories he published under the collective title *La Comédie humaine* (*The Human Comedy*)—and Stendhal's novels of the same period, *The Red and the Black* (1830) and *The Charterhouse of Parma* (1839), spare the reader nothing of those baser human instincts that militate against, and eventually conquer, many human aspirations. Rejecting romanticism so energetically, however, they swing to an extreme that makes "realism" a synonym for unrelenting pessimism. Little comes right for the just or the weak, and base human nature is unqualified by even a modicum of good. But there is a kind of affirmative richness and energy about both writers that seems to belie their pessimistic thesis.

In England, George Eliot in her novel *Middlemarch* (1871–72) viewed human life grimly, with close attention to the squalor and penury of rural life. If "nature" in works by romantic poets like Wordsworth connoted a kind of divine benevolence, only the "red in tooth and claw" aspect was permitted to be seen in the novels of the realists. George Eliot does not accept any notion of Divine Providence, whether Christian or pantheistic, but her work is instinct with a powerful moral concern: her characters never sink into a deterministic morass of hopelessness, because they have free will, or the illusion of it. With Thomas Hardy, who may be termed the last of the great 19th-century novelists, the determinism is all-pervasive, and his final novel, *Jude the Obscure* (1896), represents the limit of pessimism. Behind him one is aware of the new science, initiated by the biologists Charles Darwin and T.H. Huxley, which displaces humans as free beings, capable of choice, by a view of them as the product of blind mechanistic forces over which they have little control.

Realism in this sense has been a continuing impulse in the 21st-century novel, but few writers would go so far as Hardy in positing humanity's near-total impotence in a hostile universe. Realism in the Existentialist fiction of 20th-century France, for instance, made humans not merely wretched but absurd, yet it did not diminish the power of self-realization through choice and action. Realism has frequently been put in the service of a reforming design, which implies a qualified optimism. War novels, novels about the sufferings of the oppressed (in prison, ghetto, totalitarian state), studies of human degradation that are bitter cries against man-made systems—in all of these the realistic approach is unavoidable, and realistic detail goes much further than anything in the first realists. But there is a difference in the quality of the anger the reader feels when reading the end of Hardy's *Tess of the D'Urbervilles* (1891) and that generated by Upton Sinclair's *Jungle* (1906) or Erich Maria Remarque's *All Quiet on the Western Front* (1929). In Hardy's novel, pessimistic determinism, reducing human character to pain, frustration, and impotent anger, was—paradoxically—appropriate to an age that knew no major cataclysms or oppressions. The novels of Sinclair and Remarque reflect the 20th century, which saw the origin of all wrong in the human will, and set on a program of diagnosis and reform.

NATURALISM

The naturalistic novel is an offshoot of realism, and it is, again, in France that its first practitioners are to be found, with Émile Zola leading. It is difficult to separate the two categories, but naturalism seems characterized not only by a pessimistic determinism but also by a more thoroughgoing attention to the physical and biological aspects of human existence. Individuals are less souls aspiring upward to their divine source than products of natural forces, as well as genetic and social influences, and the novelist's task is to present the physical essence of humans and their environment. The taste of Balzac's and Stendhal's audiences was difficult to accommodate to utter frankness about the basic processes of life, and the naturalists had to struggle against prejudice, and often censorship, before their literary candour could prevail. Writers in the 20th century took the naturalistic approach for granted, but they were more concerned with a technique of presentation than with the somewhat mechanistic philosophy of Zola and his followers.

Naturalism received an impetus after World War I, when novelists felt they had a duty to depict the filth, suffering, and degradation of the soldier's life, without euphemism or circumlocution. Joyce's *Ulysses*, when it appeared in 1922, was the first novel to seek to justify total physical candour in terms of its artistic, as opposed to moral, aim—which was to depict with almost scientific objectivity every aspect of an ordinary urban day. Though Joyce had read Zola, he seems to invoke the spirit of a far earlier naturalistic writer—the ribald French author of the 16th century, François Rabelais—and this is in keeping with the Catholic tradition that Joyce represents. Zola, of course, was an atheist.

The technique of the interior monologue, which presented the unedited flow of a character's unspoken thought and emotion, called for the utmost frankness in dealing with natural functions and urges. Joyce, it is now recognized, had no prurient or scatological intent. His concern was with showing life as it is (without any of the didactic purpose of Zola), and this entailed the presentation of lust, perversion, and blasphemy as much as any of the traditionally acceptable human functions.

The naturalistic novelists have had their social and legal problems—obscenity indictments, confiscation, emasculation by timid publishers—but the cause was ultimately won, at least in Great Britain and the United States, where there are few limits placed on the contemporary novelist's proclaimed right to be true to nature. In comparison with much contemporary fiction the pioneer work of Zola seems positively reticent.

IMPRESSIONISM

The desire to present life with frank objectivity led certain early 20th-century novelists to question the validity of long-accepted narrative conventions. If truth was the novelist's aim, the tradition of the omniscient narrator would have to go, to be replaced by one in which a fallible, partially ignorant character—one involved in the story and hence himself subject to the objective or naturalistic approach—recounted what he saw and heard. But the Impressionist painters of late 19th-century France had proclaimed a revision of the whole seeing process: they distinguished between what the observer assumed he was observing and what he actually observed. That cerebral editing which turned visual data into objects of geometric solidity had no place in Impressionist painting. The visible world became less definite, more fluid, resolving into light and colour.

The German novelists Thomas Mann and Hermann Hesse, moving from the realist tradition, which concentrated on closely notated detail in the exterior world, sought the lightness and clarity of a more elliptical style, and were proclaimed Impressionists. But in England Ford Madox Ford went much further in breaking down the imagined rigidities of the space–time continuum, liquidating step-by-step temporal progression and making the visual world shimmer, dissolve, reconstitute itself. In Ford's tetralogy *Parade's End* (1924–28), the reader moves freely within the time continuum, as if it were spatial, and the total picture is perceived through an accumulation of fragmentary impressions. Ford's masterpiece, *The Good Soldier*, pushes the technique to its limit: the narrator tells his story with no special dispensation to see or understand more than a fallible being can, and, in his reminiscences, he fragments whole sequences of events as he ranges freely through time (such freedom had traditionally been regarded as a weakness, a symptom of the disease of inattention).

In the approach to dialogue manifested in a book that Ford wrote jointly with Conrad—*The Inheritors* (1901)—a particular aspect of literary impressionism may be seen whose suggestiveness has been ignored by other modern novelists. As the brain imposes its own logical patterns on the phenomena of the visual world, so it is given to editing into clarity and conciseness the halting utterances of real-life speech. The characters of most novels are impossibly articulate. Ford and Conrad attempted to present speech as it is actually spoken, with many of the meaningful solidities implied rather than stated. The result is sometimes exasperating, but only as real-life conversation frequently is.

The interior monologue, which similarly resists editing, may be regarded as a development of this technique. To show pre-articulatory thought, feeling, and sensuous perception unordered into a rational or "literary" sequence is an impressionistic device that, beginning in Édouard Dujardin's minor novel *Les Lauriers sont coupés* (1888; *We'll to the Woods No More*), served fiction of high importance, from Dorothy Richardson, Joyce, and Virginia Woolf to William Faulkner and Samuel Beckett.

Novelists such as Ronald Firbank and Evelyn Waugh (who studied painting and was a competent draftsman) learned, in a more general sense, how to follow the examples of the Impressionist and Post-Impressionist painters in their fiction. A spare brilliance of observation, like those paintings in which a whole scene is suggested through carefully selected points of colour, replaced that careful delineation of a whole face, or inventorying of a whole room, that had been the way of Balzac and other realists. In four or five brief lines of dialogue Waugh can convey as much as the 19th-century novelists did in as many pages.

EXPRESSIONISM

Expressionism was a German movement that found its most congenial media in painting and drama. The artist's aim was to express, or convey the essence of, a particular theme, to the exclusion of such secondary considerations as fidelity to real life. The typical Expressionist play, by Bertolt Brecht, for example, concerns itself with a social or political idea that is hurled at the audience through every possible stage device—symbols, music, cinematic insertions, choral speech, dance. Human character is less important than the idea of humanity, and probability of action in the old realist sense is the least of the dramatist's concerns. The emotional atmosphere is high-pitched, even ecstatic, and the tone is more appropriate to propaganda than to art. Expressionistic technique, as the plays of Brecht prove, was an admirable means of conveying a communist program, and it was in the service of such a program that John Dos Passos, in the trilogy of novels *U.S.A.* (1937), used literary devices analogous to the dramatic ones of Brecht—headlines, tabloid biographies, popular songs, lyric soliloquies, and the like.

But the Austro-Czech Franz Kafka, the greatest of the Expressionist novelists, sought to convey what may crudely be termed man's alienation from his world in terms that admit of no political interpretation. When Joseph K., the hero of Kafka's novel *The Trial* (1925), is accused of a nameless crime, he seeks to arm himself with the apparatus of a defense. And he is finally executed—stabbed with the utmost courtesy by two men in a lonely place. The hallucinatory atmosphere of that novel, as also of his novel *The Castle* (1926), is appropriate to nightmare, and indeed Kafka's work has been taken by many as an imaginative forecast of the nightmare through which Europe was compelled to live during the Hitler regime. But its significance is more subtle and universal. One element is original sin and another is filial guilt. In the story *The Metamorphosis* (1915), a young man changes into an enormous insect, and the nightmare of alienation can go no further.

Kafka's influence has been considerable. Perhaps his most distinguished follower is the English writer Rex Warner, whose *Wild Goose Chase* (1937) and *Aerodrome* (1941) use fantasy, symbol, and improbable action for an end that is both Marxist and Freudian. The filial guilt, however, seems to be taken directly from Kafka, with an innocent hero caught in a monstrously oppressive web that is both the totalitarian state and paternal tyranny. More recently, the American writer William Burroughs has developed his own Expressionistic techniques in *The Naked Lunch* (1959), which is concerned with the alienation from society of the drug addict. His later novels *Nova Express* (1964) and *The Ticket That Exploded* (1962) use obscene fantasy to present a kind of metaphysical struggle between free spirit and enslaved flesh, evidently an extrapolation of the earlier drug theme. Burroughs is a didactic novelist, and didacticism functions best in a fictional ambience that rejects the complexities of character and real-life action.

AVANT-GARDISM

Many innovations in fiction can be classified under headings already considered. Even so revolutionary a work as Joyce's *Finnegans Wake* represents an attempt to show the true nature of a dream. This can be regarded as a kind of Impressionism pushed so far that it looks like Surrealism. The brief novels of Samuel Beckett (which, as they aim to demonstrate the inadequacy of language to express the human condition, become progressively more brief) seem to have a kind of Expressionist derivation, because everything in them is subordinated to a central image of man as a totally deprived creature, resentful of a God he does not believe in. The French New Novel (or antinovel), dethroning the individual as a primary concern of fiction, may represent one of the few true breaks with traditional technique since the beginning of the 20th century.

Dissatisfaction not only with the content of the traditional novel but with the manner in which readers have been schooled to approach it has led the contemporary French novelist Michel Butor, in *Mobile* (1962), to present his material in the form of a small encyclopaedia, so that the reader finds his directions obliquely, through an alphabetic taxonomy and not through the logic of sequential events. Nabokov, in *Pale Fire* (1962), gives the reader a poem of 999 lines and critical apparatus assembled by a madman. Again the old sense of direction (beginning at the beginning and going on to the end) has been liquidated, yet *Pale Fire* is a true and highly intelligible novel. In England, B.S. Johnson published similar "false-directional" novels, though the influence of Sterne makes them seem accessible, even cozily traditional. One of Johnson's books is marketed as a bundle of disjunct chapters—which may thus be dealt aleatorially and read in any order.

Available avant-garde techniques are innumerable, though not all of them are salable. There is the device of counterpointing a main narrative with a story in footnotes, which eventually rises like water and floods the other. At least one novel has been written in which the words are set (rather like the mouse's tail or tale in *Alice in Wonderland*) to represent graphically the physical objects in the narrative. Burroughs experimented with a tricolumnar technique, in which three parallel narratives demand the reader's attention. But the writers like Borges and Nabokov go beyond mere technical innovation: they ask for a reconsideration of the very essence of fiction. In one of his *ficciones*, Borges strips from the reader even the final illusion that he is reading a story, for the story is made to dissolve, the artist evidently losing faith in his own artifact. Novels, as Borges, Nabokov, and many others have shown, can turn into poems or philosophical essays, but they cannot, while remaining literature, turn into compositions disclaiming all interest in the world of feeling, thought, and sense. Novelists can do anything they please with their art so long as they interpret, or even just present, a world that the reader recognizes as existing, or capable of existing, or capable of being dreamed of as existing.

JORGE LUIS BORGES

(b. Aug. 24, 1899, Buenos Aires, Arg.—d. June 14, 1986, Geneva, Switz.)

The Argentine poet, essayist, and short-story writer Jorge Luis Borges wrote extraordinary fiction in a classic, unobtrusive style. Educated in Switzerland, Borges recognized early that he would have a literary career. From the 1920s on he was afflicted by a growing hereditary blindness. In 1938 a severe head wound seemed to free his deepest creative forces. His blindness was total by the mid 1950s and forced him to abandon the writing of long texts and begin dictating his works. From 1955 he held the honorary post of director of Argentina's national library. Much of his work is rich in fantasy and metaphorical allegory, including the story collections Ficciones *(1944), which won him an international following, and* The Aleph *(1949).* Dreamtigers *(1960) and* The Book of Imaginary Beings *(1967) almost erase the distinctions between prose and poetry. Though he later repudiated it, he is credited with establishing in South America the modernist Ultraist movement, a rebellion against the decadence of the established writers of the Generation of '98.*

NOVEL: TERMS AND CONCEPTS

Some of the categories into which novels are placed overlap. The first two terms, for example, are variations of each other and may be used more or less interchangably. This grouping also includes a sampling of types of novels.

APPRENTICESHIP NOVEL

A biographical novel that deals with the period of a young person's social and moral initiation into adulthood is called an apprenticeship. The class derives from Goethe's *Wilhelm Meisters Lehrjahre* (1795–96; *Wilhelm Meister's Apprenticeship*). In German literature, where it is called *Bildungsroman*, it became a traditional novel form. An English example is Dickens's *David Copperfield* (1850). Thomas Wolfe's *Look Homeward, Angel* (1929) represents a 20th-century American example. French writer Colette discussed the period of her life in which she first married, moved to Paris, and wrote the Claudine novels as *Mes Apprentissages* (1936; *My Apprenticeships*).

BILDUNGSROMAN

A class of novel that deals with the maturation process, with how and why the protagonist develops, both morally and psychologically. The German word *Bildungsroman* means "novel of education" or "novel of formation."

The folklore tale of the dunce who goes out into the world seeking adventure and learns wisdom the hard way was raised to literary heights in Wolfram von Eschenbach's medieval epic *Parzival* and in Hans Grimmelshausen's picaresque tale *Simplicissimus* (1669). The first novelistic development of this theme was Christoph Martin Wieland's *Geschichte des Agathon* (1766–67; *History of Agathon*). It was followed by Goethe's *Wilhelm Meisters Lehrjahre* (1795–96; *Wilhelm Meister's Apprenticeship*), which remains the classic example of the genre. Other examples are Adalbert Stifter's *Nachsommer* (1857; *Indian Summer*) and Gottfried Keller's *Der grüne Heinrich* (1854–55; *Green Henry*).

The bildungsroman traditionally ends on a positive note, though its action may be tempered by resignation and nostalgia. If the grandiose dreams of the hero's youth are over, so are many foolish mistakes and painful disappointments, and, especially in 19th-century novels, a life of usefulness lies ahead. In the 20th century and beyond, however, the bildungsroman more often ended in resignation or death. Classic examples include *Great Expectations* (1861) by Charles Dickens, *Anne of Green Gables* (1908) by Lucy Maud Montgomery, *Sons and Lovers* (1913) by D.H. Lawrence, *Member of the Wedding* (1946) by Carson McCullers, *Catcher in the Rye* (1951) by J.D. Salinger, *To Kill a Mockingbird* (1960) by Harper Lee, *Oranges Are Not the Only Fruit* (1985) by Jeanette Winterson, and *Black Swan Green* (2006) by David Mitchell.

Jeanette Winterson. David Levenson/Getty Images

A common variation of the bildungsoman is the *Künstlerroman*, a novel dealing with the formative years of an artist. Such other variations as the *Erziehungsroman* ("novel of upbringing") and the *Entwicklungsroman* ("novel of [character] development") differ only slightly from the bildungsroman, and these terms are sometimes used interchangeably.

DIME NOVEL

Dime novels were a type of inexpensive, usually paperback, melodramatic novel of adventure popular in the United States roughly between 1860 and 1915. They often featured a western theme. One of the best-known authors of such works was E.Z.C. Judson, whose stories, some based on his own adventures, were written under the pseudonym Ned Buntline. The dime novels were eventually replaced by pulp magazines, a term that refers to the cheap paper on which they were printed. "Penny dreadfuls" and "shilling shockers" are genres similar to the dime novel in their lurid and often tawdry stories.

EPISTOLARY NOVEL

When a novel is told through the medium of letters written by one or more of the characters, it is termed an epistolary novel. Originating with Samuel Richardson's *Pamela; or, Virtue Rewarded* (1740), the story of a servant girl's victorious struggle against her master's attempts to seduce her, it was one of the earliest forms of novel to be developed and remained one of the most popular up to the 19th century. The epistolary novel's reliance on subjective points of view makes it the forerunner of the modern psychological novel.

The advantages of the novel in letter form are that it presents an intimate view of the character's thoughts and feelings without interference from the author and that it conveys the shape of events to come with dramatic immediacy. Also, the presentation of events from several points of view lends the story dimension and verisimilitude. Though the method was most often a vehicle for sentimental novels, it was not limited to them. Of the outstanding examples of the form, Richardson's *Clarissa* (1748) has tragic intensity, Tobias Smollett's *Humphry Clinker* (1771) is a picaresque comedy and social commentary, and Fanny Burney's *Evelina* (1778) is a novel of manners. Jean-Jacques Rousseau used the form as a vehicle for his ideas on marriage and education in *La Nouvelle Héloïse* (1761; "The New Eloise"), and Goethe used it for his statement of Romantic despair, *Die Leiden des jungen Werthers* (1774; *The Sorrows of Young Werther*). The letter novel of Pierre Choderlos de Laclos, *Les Liaisons dangereuses* (1782; *Dangerous Acquaintances*), is a work of penetrating and realistic psychology.

Some disadvantages of the form were apparent from the outset. Dependent on the letter writer's need to "confess" to virtue, vice, or powerlessness, such confessions were susceptible to suspicion or ridicule. The servant girl Pamela's remarkable literary powers and her propensity for writing on all occasions were cruelly burlesqued in Henry Fielding's *Shamela* (1741), which pictures his heroine in bed scribbling, "I hear him coming in at the Door," as her seducer enters the room. From 1800 on, the popularity of the form declined, though novels combining letters with journals and narrative were still common, as in Bram Stoker's *Dracula* (1897). In the 20th century, letter fiction was often used to exploit the linguistic humour and unintentional character revelations of such semiliterates as the hero of Ring Lardner's *You Know Me Al* (1916).

GOTHIC NOVEL

The Gothic novel is a form of European Romantic, pseudomedieval fiction having a prevailing atmosphere of mystery and terror. Its heyday was the 1790s, but it underwent frequent revivals in subsequent centuries.

Called Gothic because its imaginative impulse was drawn from medieval buildings and ruins, such novels commonly used such settings as castles or monasteries equipped with subterranean passages, dark battlements, hidden panels, and trapdoors. The vogue was initiated in England by Horace Walpole's immensely successful *Castle of Otranto* (1765). His most respectable follower was Ann Radcliffe, whose *Mysteries of Udolpho* (1794) and *Italian* (1797) are among the best examples of the genre. A more sensational type of Gothic romance exploiting horror and violence flourished in Germany and was introduced to England by Matthew Gregory Lewis with *The Monk* (1796). Other landmarks of Gothic fiction are William Beckford's Oriental romance *Vathek* (1786) and Charles Robert Maturin's story of an Irish Faust, *Melmoth the Wanderer* (1820). The classic horror stories *Frankenstein* (1818), by Mary Wollstonecraft Shelley, and *Dracula* (1897), by Bram Stoker, are in the Gothic tradition but introduce the existential nature of humankind as its definitive mystery and terror.

Easy targets for satire, the early Gothic romances died of their own extravagances of plot, but Gothic atmospheric machinery continued to haunt the fiction of such major writers as the Brontë sisters, Edgar Allan Poe, Nathaniel Hawthorne, and even Dickens in *Bleak House* and *Great Expectations*. In the second half of the 20th century, the term was applied to paperback romances having the same kind of themes and trappings similar to the originals.

ANN RADCLIFFE

(b. July 9, 1764, London, Eng.—d. Feb. 7, 1823, London)

The most representative of English Gothic novelists was Ann Radcliffe (née Ann Ward). Brought up in a well-to-do family, in 1787 she married a journalist who encouraged her literary pursuits. Her first two novels were published anonymously. She achieved fame with her third novel, The Romance of the Forest *(1791), a tale of 17th-century France. With her fourth,* The Mysteries of Udolpho *(1794), she became the most popular novelist in England. It tells how the orphaned Emily St. Aubert is subjected to cruelties by guardians, threatened with the loss of her fortune, and imprisoned in castles but is finally freed and united with her lover. Strange and fearful events take place in the haunted atmosphere of the solitary castle of Udolpho, set high in the dark and majestic Apennines.* The Italian *(1797), which displays rare psychological insight, reveals her full powers. It shows not only improved dialogue and plot construction, but its villain—Schedoni, a monk of massive physique and sinister disposition—is treated with a psychological insight unusual in her work. In Radcliffe's tales, scenes of terror and suspense are infused with an aura of romantic sensibility.*

HISTORICAL NOVEL

Any novel that has as its setting a period of history and that attempts to convey the spirit, manners, and social conditions of a past age with realistic detail and fidelity (which is in some cases only apparent fidelity) to historical fact is considered to be a historical novel. The work may deal with actual historical personages, as does Robert Graves's *I, Claudius* (1934), or it may contain a mixture of fictional and historical characters. It may focus on a single historic event, as does Franz Werfel's *Forty Days of Musa Dagh* (1934), which dramatizes the defense of an Armenian stronghold. More often it attempts to portray a broader view of a past society in which great events are reflected by their effect on the private lives of fictional individuals. Since the appearance of the first historical novel, Sir Walter Scott's *Waverley* (1814), this type of fiction has remained popular. Some historical novels, such as Leo Tolstoy's *War and Peace* (1865–69), are of the highest artistic quality. One type of historical novel is the purely escapist costume romance, which, making no pretense to historicity, uses a setting in the past to lend credence to improbable characters and adventures.

I NOVEL

The form or genre of 20th-century Japanese literature that is characterized by self-revealing narration, with the author usually as the central character is known in English as the I novel (in Japanese, *watakushi shōsetsu*, or *shishōsetsu*).

The I novel grew out of the naturalist movement that dominated Japanese literature during the early decades of the 20th century. The term is used to describe two different types of novel, the confessional novel (characterized by prolonged, often self-abasing, revelation) and the "mental attitude" novel (in which the writer probes innermost thoughts or attitudes toward everyday events in life). Notable I novelists of the first type include Kasai Zenzō, Kamura Isota, and Uno Kōji; writers of the latter type, headed by Shiga Naoya, include Amino Kiku, Takii Kōsaku, and Ozaki Kazuo.

INDIANISTA NOVEL

The Brazilian literary genre of the 19th century that idealizes the simple life of the South American Indian and incorporates words of indigenous peoples to name flora, fauna, and customs is that of the Indianista novel. The tone of the Indianista novel is one of languid nostalgia and *saudade*, a brooding melancholy and reverence for nature. The Indian had appeared as a fictional character in Brazilian literature from the late 18th century. It was not until the following century, however, that José de Alencar initiated the vogue of the Brazilian Indianista novel by contributing what remain two of the most popular works to the genre, *O Guarani* (1857) and *Iracema* (1865), romantic tales of love between Indian and white and of the conflict between the Indians and their Portuguese conquerors.

NEW NOVEL

The New Novel (French *nouveau roman*), also called (more broadly) the *antinovel,* is an avant-garde novel of the mid-20th century that marked a radical departure from the conventions of the traditional novel in that it ignores such elements as plot, dialogue, linear narrative, and human interest. Starting from the premise that the potential of the traditional novel had been exhausted, the writers of New Novels sought new avenues of fictional exploration. In their efforts to overcome literary habits and to challenge the expectations of their readers, they deliberately frustrated conventional literary expectations, avoiding any expression of the author's personality, preferences, or values. They rejected the elements of entertainment, dramatic progress, and dialogue that serve to delineate character or develop plot.

The term *antinovel* (or, more precisely, *anti-roman*) as a descriptor was first used by Jean-Paul Sartre in an introduction to Nathalie Sarraute's *Portrait d'un inconnu* (1948; *Portrait of a Man Unknown*). This term has often been applied to the fiction of such writers as Sarraute, Claude Simon, Alain Robbe-Grillet, Marguerite Duras, and Michel Butor and is therefore usually associated with the French *nouveau roman* of

the 1950s and '60s. In place of reassuring conventions, these French authors offered the reader more demanding fiction, presenting compressed, repetitive, or only partially explained events whose meaning is rarely clear or definitive. In Robbe-Grillet's *La Jalousie* (1957; *Jealousy*), for example, the narrator's suspicions of his wife's infidelity are never confirmed or denied. The story is not laid out chronologically, but rather the reader is subject to the narrator's obsessive review of observed details and events.

Though the word *antinovel* is of relatively recent coinage, the nonlinear approach to novel writing is at least as old as the works of Laurence Sterne. Works contemporary with the *nouveau roman* but written in other languages—such as the German novelist Uwe Johnson's *Mutmassungen über Jakob* (1959; *Speculations About Jakob*) and the British author Rayner Heppenstall's *Connecting Door* (1962)—share many of the characteristics of the New Novel, such as vaguely identified characters, casual arrangement of events, and ambiguity of meaning.

NONFICTION NOVEL

The name *nonfiction novel* is applied to any story of actual people and actual events told with the dramatic techniques of a novel. The American writer Truman Capote claimed to have invented this genre with his book *In Cold Blood* (1965).

A true story of the brutal murder of a Kansas farm family, the book was based on six years of exacting research and interviews with neighbours and friends of the victims and the two captured murderers. The story is told from the points of view of different "characters," and the author attempts not to intrude his own comments or distort fact. Critics pointed out earlier precedents for this type of journalistic novel, such as John Hersey's *Hiroshima* (1946), an account of the World War II atomic bombing of the Japanese city told through the histories of six survivors. Norman Mailer's *The Executioner's Song* (1979) is another notable example of the genre.

NOVEL OF MANNERS

A work of fiction that re-creates a social world, conveying with finely detailed observation the customs, values, and mores of a highly developed and complex society is called a novel of manners. The conventions of the society dominate the story, and characters are differentiated by the degree to which they measure up to the uniform standard, or ideal, of behaviour or fall below it. The range of a novel of manners may be limited, as in the works of Jane Austen, which deal with the domestic affairs of English country gentry families of the 19th century and ignore elemental human passions and larger social and political determinations. It may also be sweeping, as in the novels of Balzac, which mirror the 19th century in all its complexity in stories dealing with Parisian life, provincial life, private life, public life, and military life. Notable writers of the novel of manners from the end of the 19th century into the 20th include Henry James, Evelyn Waugh, Edith Wharton, and John Marquand.

JANE AUSTEN

(b. Dec. 16, 1775, Steventon, Hampshire, Eng.—d. July 18, 1817, Winchester, Hampshire)

The English novelist Jane Austen gave the novel its distinctly modern character through her treatment of ordinary people in everyday life. The daughter of a rector, she lived in the circumscribed world of minor landed gentry and country clergy that she was to use in her writing; her closest companion was her sister, Cassandra. Her earliest known writings are mainly parodies, notably of sentimental fiction. In her six full-length novels—Sense and Sensibility (1811), Pride and Prejudice (1813), Mansfield Park (1814), Emma (1815), Persuasion (1817), and Northanger Abbey (published 1817 but written before the others)—she created the comedy of manners of middle-class English life in her time. Her writing is noted for its wit, realism, shrewd sympathy, and brilliant prose style. She published her novels anonymously; two appeared only after her death, which probably resulted from Addison disease.

NOVELLA

A short and well-structured narrative, often realistic and satiric in tone, the novella influenced the development of the short story and the novel throughout Europe. Originating in Italy during the Middle Ages, the novella was based on local events that were humorous, political, or amorous in nature. The individual tales often were gathered into collections along with anecdotes, legends, and romantic tales. Writers such as Giovanni Boccaccio, Franco Sacchetti, and Matteo Bandello later developed the novella into a psychologically subtle and highly structured short tale, often using a frame story to unify the tales around a common theme.

Geoffrey Chaucer introduced the novella to England with *The Canterbury Tales*. During the Elizabethan period, William Shakespeare and other playwrights extracted dramatic plots from the Italian novella. The realistic content and form of these tales influenced the development of the English novel in the 18th century and the short story in the 19th century.

The novella flourished in Germany, where it is known as the *Novelle*, in the 18th, 19th, and early 20th centuries in the works of writers such as Heinrich von Kleist, Gerhart Hauptmann, Goethe, Thomas Mann, and Franz Kafka. As in Boccaccio's *Decameron*, the prototype of the form, German *Novellen* are often encompassed within a frame story based on a catastrophic event (such as plague, war, or flood), either real or imaginary. The individual tales are related by various reporter-narrators to divert the audience from the misfortune they are experiencing. Characterized by brevity, self-contained plots that end on a note of irony, a literate and facile style, restraint of emotion, and objective rather than subjective presentation, these tales were a major stimulant to the development of the modern short story in Germany. The *Novelle* also survived as a unique form, although unity of mood and style often replaced the traditional unity of action. The importance of the frame was diminished, as was the necessity for maintaining absolute objectivity.

Examples of works usually considered to be novellas, rather than novels or short stories, are Leo Tolstoy's *Smert Ivana Ilicha* (*The Death of Ivan Ilich*), Fyodor Dostoyevsky's *Zapiski iz podpolya* (*Notes from the Underground*), Joseph Conrad's *Heart of Darkness,* and Henry James's *The Aspern Papers*.

PICARESQUE NOVEL

An early form, the picaresque novel is usually a first-person narrative, relating the adventures of a rogue or low-born adventurer (Spanish *pícaro*) as he drifts from place to place and from one social milieu to another in his effort to survive. In its episodic structure the picaresque novel resembles the long, rambling romances of medieval chivalry, to which it provided the first realistic counterpart. Unlike the idealistic knight-errant hero, however, the picaro is a cynical and amoral rascal who, if given half a chance, would rather live by his wits than by honourable work. The picaro wanders about and has adventures among people from all social classes and professions, often just barely escaping punishment for his own lying, cheating, and stealing. He is a casteless outsider who feels inwardly unrestrained by prevailing social codes and mores, and he conforms outwardly to them only when it serves his own ends. The picaro's narrative becomes in effect an ironic or satirical survey of the hypocrisies and corruptions of society, while also offering the reader a rich mine of observations concerning people in low or humble walks of life.

The picaresque novel originated in Spain with *Lazarillo de Tormes* (1554; doubtfully attributed to Diego Hurtado de Mendoza), in which the poor boy Lazaro describes his services under seven successive lay and clerical masters, each of whose dubious character is hidden under a mask of hypocrisy. The irreverent wit of *Lazarillo* helped make it one of the most widely read books of its time. The next picaresque novel to be published, Mateo Alemán's *Guzmán de Alfarache* (1599), became the true prototype of the genre and helped establish realism as the dominant trend in the Spanish novel. The supposed autobiography of the son of a ruined Genoese moneylender, this work is richer in invention, variety of episode, and presentation of character than *Lazarillo*, and it too enjoyed extraordinary popularity.

Among *Guzmán*'s numerous successors were several short novels by Miguel de Cervantes in the picaresque manner, notably *Rinconete y Cortadillo* (1613) and *El Coloquio de los perros* (1613; "Colloquy of the Dogs"). Francisco López de Úbeda's *La picara Justina* (1605; "Naughty Justina") tells the story of a woman picaro who deceives her lovers just as the picaro does his masters. Francisco Gómez de Quevedo's *Vida del Buscón* (1626; "The Life of a Scoundrel") is a masterpiece of the genre, in which the profound psychological depiction of a petty thief and swindler is underlain by a deep concern for moral values. After *Buscón* the picaresque novel in Spain declined gradually into the novel of adventure.

In the meantime, however, the picaro had made his way into other European literatures after *Lazarillo de Tormes* was translated into French, Dutch, and English in the later 16th century. The first picaresque novel in England was Thomas Nashe's *Unfortunate Traveller, or, the Life of Jacke Wilton* (1594). In Germany the type was represented by H.J. von Grimmelshausen's *Simplicissimus* (1669). In England the female picaro was revived in Daniel Defoe's *Moll Flanders* (1722), and many picaresque elements can be found in Henry Fielding's *Jonathan Wild* (1725), *Joseph Andrews* (1742), and *Tom Jones* (1749), and Tobias Smollett's *Roderick Random* (1748), *Peregrine Pickle*

(1751), and *Ferdinand, Count Fathom* (1753). The outstanding French example is Alain-René Lesage's *Gil Blas* (1715–35), which preserves a Spanish setting and borrows incidents from forgotten Spanish novels but portrays a gentler, more humanized picaro.

In the mid-18th century the growth of the realistic novel with its tighter, more elaborated plot and its greater development of character led to the final decline of the picaresque novel, which came to be considered somewhat inferior in artistry. But the opportunities for satire provided by the picaresque novel's mingling of characters from all walks of life, its vivid descriptions of industries and professions, its realistic language and detail, and above all its ironic and detached survey of manners and morals helped to enrich the realistic novel and contributed to that form's development in the 18th and 19th centuries. Elements of the picaresque novel proper reappeared in such mature realistic novels as Nikolay Gogol's *Dead Souls* (1842–52), Mark Twain's *Huckleberry Finn* (1884), and Thomas Mann's *Confessions of Felix Krull* (1954).

PSYCHOLOGICAL NOVEL

The psychological novel is a work of fiction in which the thoughts, feelings, and motivations of the characters are of equal or greater interest than is the external action of the narrative. In a psychological novel the emotional reactions and internal states of the characters are influenced by and in turn trigger external events in a meaningful symbiosis. This emphasis on the inner life of characters is a fundamental element of a vast body of fiction: William Shakespeare's *Hamlet* is perhaps the prime early example of it in dramatic form. Although an overtly psychological approach is found among the earliest English novels, such as Samuel Richardson's *Pamela* (1740), which is told from the heroine's point of view, and Laurence Sterne's introspective first-person narrative *Tristram Shandy* (1759–67), the psychological novel reached its full potential only in the 20th century. Its development coincided with the growth of psychology and the discoveries of Sigmund Freud, but it was not necessarily a result of this. The penetrating insight into psychological complexities and unconscious motivations characteristic of the works of Fyodor Dostoyevsky and Leo Tolstoy, the detailed recording of external events' impingement on individual consciousness as practiced by Henry James, the associative memories of Marcel Proust, the stream-of-consciousness technique practiced by James Joyce and William Faulkner, and the continuous flow of experience present in some of the works of Virginia Woolf were each arrived at independently.

In the psychological novel, plot is subordinate to and dependent upon the probing delineation of character. Events may not be presented in chronological order but rather as they occur in the character's thought associations, memories, fantasies, reveries, contemplations, and dreams. In the complex and ambiguous works of Franz Kafka, for example, the subjective world is externalized, and events that appear to be happening in reality are governed by the subjective logic of dreams.

ROMAN À CLEF

The roman à clef (a French phrase meaning "novel with a key") has the extraliterary interest of portraying well-known real people more or less thinly disguised as fictional characters.

The tradition goes back to 17th-century France, when fashionable members of the aristocratic literary coteries, such as Mlle de Scudéry, enlivened their historical romances by including in them fictional representations of well-known figures in the court of Louis XIV. In the 20th century, Somerset Maugham's *The Moon and Sixpence* (1919) was thought to be related to the life of the painter Paul Gauguin, and his *Cakes and Ale* (1930) was said to contain caricatures of the novelists Thomas Hardy and Hugh Walpole. More common romans à clef are Aldous Huxley's *Point Counter Point* (1928) and Simone de Beauvoir's *Mandarins* (1954), in which the disguised characters are immediately recognizable only to a small circle of insiders. Jack Kerouac fictionalized his own experiences in *On the Road* (1957). *Primary Colors* (1996) drew widespread

attention in the United States as much for its protagonist—based closely on U.S. Pres. Bill Clinton—as for its anonymous author, later revealed to be political journalist Joe Klein.

SENTIMENTAL NOVEL

Broadly, any novel that exploits the reader's capacity for tenderness, compassion, or sympathy to a disproportionate degree by presenting a beclouded or unrealistic view of its subject can be considered a sentimental novel. In a restricted sense the term refers to a widespread European novelistic development of the 18th century, which arose partly in reaction to the austerity and rationalism of the Neoclassical period. The sentimental novel exalted feeling above reason and raised the analysis of emotion to a fine art. An early example in France is Antoine-François Prévost's *Manon Lescaut* (1731), the story of a courtesan for whom a young seminary student of noble birth forsakes his career, family, and religion and ends as a card shark and confidence man. His downward progress, if not actually excused, is portrayed as a sacrifice to love.

The assumptions underlying the sentimental novel were Jean-Jacques Rousseau's doctrine of the natural goodness of man and his belief that moral development was fostered by experiencing powerful sympathies. In England, Samuel Richardson's sentimental novel *Pamela* (1740) was recommended by clergymen as a means of educating the heart. In the 1760s the sentimental novel developed into the "novel of sensibility," which presented characters possessing a pronounced susceptibility to delicate sensation. Such characters were not only deeply moved by their feelings toward others but also reacted emotionally to the beauty inherent in natural settings and works of art and music. The prototype was Laurence Sterne's *Tristram Shandy* (1759–67), which devotes several pages to describing Uncle Toby's horror of killing a fly. The literature of Romanticism adopted many elements of the novel of sensibility, including responsiveness to nature and belief in the wisdom of the heart and in the power of sympathy. It did not, however, assimilate the novel of sensibility's characteristic optimism.

SOCIAL PROBLEM NOVEL

A novel in which a prevailing social problem, such as gender, race, or class prejudice, is dramatized through its effect on the characters is sometimes categorized as a social problem novel (though it may be called a problem novel or a social novel). The type emerged in Great Britain and the United States in the mid-19th century. An early example is Elizabeth Gaskell's *Ruth* (1853), which portrays a humane alternative to the "fallen woman's" usual progress to social ostracism and prostitution during the period. If the work is strongly weighted to convert the reader to the author's stand on a social question, as is the case with Harriet Beecher Stowe's antislavery novel *Uncle Tom's Cabin* (1852), it is sometimes called a propaganda novel. Usually, a social problem novel limits itself to exposure of a problem. A personal solution may be arrived at by the novel's characters, but the author does not insist that it can be applied universally or that it is the only one. Most social problem novels derive their chief interest from their novelty or timeliness. For example, in 1947 Laura Z. Hobson's *Gentleman's Agreement*, revealing the unwritten code of anti-Semitism upheld in American middle-class circles, created a stir among a public freshly shocked by the Holocaust.

STREAM OF CONSCIOUSNESS

The narrative technique intended to render the flow of myriad impressions—visual, auditory, physical, associative, and subliminal—that impinge on the consciousness of an individual and form part of his awareness along with the trend of his rational thoughts is known as stream of consciousness. The term was first used by the psychologist William James in *The Principles of Psychology* (1890). As the psychological novel developed in the 20th century, some writers attempted to capture the total flow of their characters' consciousness, rather than limit themselves to rational thoughts. To represent the full richness, speed, and subtlety of the mind at work, the writer incorporates snatches of incoherent thought, ungrammatical constructions, and free association of ideas, images, and words at the pre-speech level.

The stream-of-consciousness novel commonly uses the narrative techniques of interior monologue. Probably the most famous example is James Joyce's *Ulysses* (1922), a complex evocation of the inner states of the characters Leopold and Molly Bloom and Stephen Dedalus. Other notable examples include *Leutnant Gustl* (1901) by Arthur Schnitzler, an early use of stream of consciousness to re-create the atmosphere of pre-World War I Vienna; William Faulkner's *The Sound and the Fury* (1929), which records the fragmentary and impressionistic responses in the minds of three members of the Compson family to events that are immediately being experienced or events that are being remembered; and Virginia Woolf's *The Waves* (1931), a complex novel in which six characters recount their lives from childhood to old age.

WESTERN

A genre of storytelling (novels, short stories, motion pictures, and television and radio shows) set in the American West, usually in the period from the 1850s to the end of the 19th century. Though basically an American creation, the western had its counterparts in the gaucho literature of Argentina and in tales of the settlement of the Australian outback. The genre reached its greatest popularity in the early and middle decades of

the 20th century and declined somewhat thereafter.

The western has as its setting the immense plains, rugged tablelands, and mountain ranges of the portion of the United States lying west of the Mississippi River, in particular the Great Plains and the Southwest. This area was not truly opened to white settlement until after the American Civil War (1861–65), at which time the Plains Indians were gradually subdued and deprived of most of their lands by white settlers and by the U.S. cavalry. The conflict between European pioneers and Indians forms one of the basic themes of the western. Another subset sprang out of the class of men known as cowboys, who were hired by ranchers to drive cattle across hundreds of miles of Western pasturelands to railheads where the animals could be shipped eastward to market. The cattle and mining industries spurred the growth of towns, and the gradual imposition of law and order that such settled communities needed was accomplished by another class of men who became staple figures in the western, the town sheriff and the U.S. marshal. Actual historical persons in the American West have figured prominently in latter-day re-creations of the era. Wild Bill Hickok, Wyatt Earp, and other lawmen have frequently been portrayed, as have such outlaws as Billy the Kid and Jesse James.

In literature, the western story had its beginnings in the first adventure narratives that accompanied the opening of the West to white settlement shortly before the Civil War. Accounts of the Western plainsmen, scouts, buffalo hunters, and trappers were highly popular in the East. Perhaps the earliest and finest work in this genre was James Fenimore Cooper's *The Prairie* (1827), though the high artistic level of this novel was perhaps atypical in regard to what followed. An early writer to capitalize on the popularity of western adventure narratives was E.Z.C. Judson, whose pseudonym was Ned Buntline. Also known as "the father of the dime novel," he wrote dozens of western stories and was responsible for transforming Buffalo Bill into an archetype. Owen Wister, who first saw the West while recuperating from an illness, wrote the first western that won critical praise, *The Virginian* (1902). Classics of the genre have been written by men who actually worked as cowboys. One of the best loved of these was *Bransford in Arcadia* (1914; reprinted 1917 as *Bransford of Rainbow Range*) by Eugene Manlove Rhodes, a former cowboy and government scout. Andy Adams incorporated many autobiographical incidents in his *Log of a Cowboy* (1903).

By far the best-known and one of the most prolific writers of westerns was Zane Grey, an Ohio dentist who became famous with the classic *Riders of the Purple Sage* (1912). In all, Grey wrote more than 80 books, many of which retained wide popularity. Another popular and prolific writer of westerns was Louis L'Amour.

JAMES FENIMORE COOPER

(b. Sept. 15, 1789, Burlington, N.J., U.S.—d. Sept. 14, 1851, Cooperstown, N.Y.)

The first major American novelist was James Fenimore Cooper. He grew up in a prosperous family in the settlement of Cooperstown, founded by his father. The Spy (1821), set during the American Revolution, brought him renown. His best-known novels, the series The Leatherstocking Tales, feature the frontier adventures of the wilderness scout Natty Bumppo and include The Pioneers (1823), The Last of the Mohicans (1826), The Prairie (1827), The Pathfinder (1840), and The Deerslayer (1841). He also wrote popular sea novels, notably The Pilot (1823), and a history of the U.S. Navy (1839). Though internationally celebrated, he was troubled by lawsuits and political conflicts in his later years, and his popularity and income declined.

Western short stories have also been among America's favourites. A.H. Lewis (c. 1858–1914), a former cowboy, produced a series of popular stories told by the "Old Cattleman." Stephen Crane created a comic classic of the genre with "The Bride Comes to Yellow Sky" (1898), and Conrad Richter (1890–1968) wrote a number of stories and novels of the Old Southwest. The Western Writers of America, formed in 1952, has cited many fine western writers, including Ernest Haycox (1899–1950); W.M. Raine (1871–1954), a former Arizona ranger who wrote more than 80 western novels; and B.M. Bower (1871–1940), a woman whose talent for realistic detail convinced thousands of readers that she was a real cowboy writing from personal experience. Other western classics are Walter van Tilburg Clark's *The Ox-Bow Incident* (1940), which used a Nevada lynching as a metaphor for the struggle for justice; A.B. Guthrie, Jr.'s *The Big Sky* (1947), about frontier life in the early 1840s, and *The Way West* (1949). Many western novels and short stories first appeared in pulp magazines, such as *Ace-High Western Stories* and *Double Action Western*, that were specifically devoted to publishing works in the genre. Larry McMurtry wrote a Pulitzer Prize-winning paean to the bygone cowboy, *Lonesome Dove* (1985). Also worthy of note in this regard are the collections of Wyoming stories (1999, 2004, 2008) by E. Annie Proulx.

CHAPTER 2

SCIENCE FICTION

The form of fiction that deals principally with the effect of actual or imagined science upon society or individuals is called science fiction, or in shortened form sci-fi or SF. The term *science fiction* was popularized, if not invented, in the 1920s by one of the genre's principal advocates, the American publisher Hugo Gernsback. The Hugo Awards, given annually since 1953 by the World Science Fiction Society, are named after him. These achievement awards are given to the top SF writers, editors, illustrators, films, and "fanzines."

THE WORLD OF SCIENCE FICTION

Science fiction is a modern genre. Though writers in antiquity sometimes dealt with themes common to modern science fiction, their stories made no attempt at scientific and technological plausibility, the feature that distinguishes science fiction from earlier speculative writings and other contemporary speculative genres such as fantasy and horror. The genre formally emerged in the West, where the social transformations wrought by the Industrial Revolution first led writers and intellectuals to extrapolate the future impact of technology. By the beginning of the 20th century, an array of standard science fiction "sets" had developed around certain themes, among them space travel, robots, alien beings, and time travel (see Major Science Fiction Themes section in the following text). The customary "theatrics" of science fiction include prophetic warnings, utopian aspirations, elaborate scenarios for entirely imaginary worlds, titanic disasters, strange voyages, and political agitation of many extremist flavours, presented in the form of sermons, meditations, satires, allegories, and parodies—exhibiting every conceivable attitude toward the process of techno-social change, from cynical despair to cosmic bliss.

Science fiction writers often seek out new scientific and technical developments to prognosticate freely the techno-social changes that will shock the readers' sense of cultural propriety and expand their consciousness. This approach was central to the work of H.G. Wells, a founder of the genre and likely its greatest writer. Wells was an ardent student of the 19th-century British scientist T.H. Huxley, whose vociferous championing of Charles Darwin's theory of evolution earned him the epithet "Darwin's Bulldog." Wells's literary career gives ample evidence of science fiction's latent radicalism, its affinity for aggressive satire and utopian political agendas, as well as its dire predictions of technological destruction.

This dark dystopian side can be seen especially in the work of T.H. Huxley's grandson, Aldous Huxley, who was a social satirist, an advocate of psychedelic drugs, and the author of a dystopian classic, *Brave New World* (1932). The sense of dread was also cultivated by H.P. Lovecraft, who invented the famous *Necronomicon*, an imaginary book of knowledge so ferocious that any scientist who dares to read it succumbs to madness. On a more personal level, the works of Philip K. Dick (often adapted for film) present metaphysical conundrums about identity, humanity, and the nature of reality. Perhaps bleakest of all, the English philosopher Olaf Stapledon's mind-stretching novels picture all of human history as a frail, passing bubble in the cold galactic stream of space and time.

Stapledon's views were rather specialized for the typical science fiction reader. When the genre began to gel in the early 20th century, it was generally disreputable, particularly in the United States, where it first catered to a juvenile audience. Following World War II, science fiction spread throughout the world from its epicentre in the United States, spurred on by ever more staggering scientific feats, from the development of nuclear energy and atomic bombs to the advent of space travel, human visits to the Moon, and the real possibility of cloning human life.

By the 21st century, science fiction had become much more than a literary genre. Its avid followers and practitioners constituted a thriving worldwide subculture. Fans relished the seemingly endless variety of SF-related products and pastimes, including books, movies, television shows, computer games, magazines, paintings, comics, and, increasingly, collectible figurines, Web sites, DVDs, and toy weaponry. They frequently held

J.K. Rowling's wildly popular Harry Potter and the Order of the Phoenix, *fifth in her series of seven books featuring the young wizard named in the title, has reached well beyond the printed page and fostered yearly conventions, games, apps, and films.* James Devaney/WireImage/Getty Images

well-attended, well-organized conventions, at which costumes were worn, handicrafts sold, and folk songs sung.

THE ANTECEDENTS OF SCIENCE FICTION

Antecedents of science fiction can be found in the remote past. Among the earliest examples is the 2nd-century CE Syrian-born Greek satirist Lucian, who in *Trips to the Moon* describes sailing to the Moon. Such flights of fancy, or fantastic tales, provided a popular format in which to satirize government, society, and religion while evading libel suits, censorship, and persecution. The clearest forerunner of the genre, however, was the 17th-century swashbuckler Cyrano de Bergerac, who wrote of a voyager to the Moon finding a utopian society of men free from war, disease, and hunger. The voyager eats fruit from the biblical tree of knowledge and joins lunar society as a philosopher—that is, until he is expelled from the Moon for blasphemy. Following a short return to Earth, he travels to the Sun, where a society of birds puts him on trial for humanity's crimes. In creating his diversion, Cyrano took it as his mission to make impossible things seem plausible. Although this and his other SF-like writings were published only posthumously and in various censored versions, Cyrano had a great influence on later satirists and social critics. Two works in particular—Jonathan Swift's *Gulliver's Travels* (1726) and Voltaire's *Micromégas* (1752)—show Cyrano's mark with their weird monsters, gross inversions of normalcy, and similar harsh satire.

Another precursor was Louis-Sébastien Mercier's *L'An deux mille quatre cent quarante* (c. 1771; "The Year 2440"; *Memoirs of the Year Two Thousand Five Hundred*), a work of French political speculation set in a 25th-century utopian society that worships science. While many writers had depicted some future utopian "Kingdom of God" or a utopian society in some mythical land, this was the first work to postulate a utopian society on Earth in the realizable future. The book was swiftly banned by the French ancien régime, which recognized that Mercier's fantasy about "the future" was a thin disguise for his subversive revolutionary sentiments. Despite this official sanction—or perhaps because of it—Mercier's book became an international best seller. Both Thomas Jefferson and George Washington owned copies.

PROTO-SCIENCE FICTION AND JULES VERNE

In 1818 Mary Wollstonecraft Shelley took the next major step in the evolution of science fiction when she published *Frankenstein: or, The Modern Prometheus*. Champions of Shelley as the "mother of science fiction" emphasize her innovative fictional scheme. Abandoning the occult folderol of the conventional Gothic novel, she made her protagonist a practicing "scientist"—though the term *scientist* was not actually coined until 1834—and gave him an interest in galvanic electricity and vivisection, two of the advanced technologies of the early 1800s. Even though reanimated corpses remain fantastic today, Shelley gave her story an air of scientific plausibility. This masterly manipulation of her readers established a powerful new approach to creating thrilling sensations of wonder and fear. *Frankenstein* has remained in print since its first publication, and it has been adapted for film repeatedly since the first silent version in 1910. Frankenstein's monster likewise remained a potent metaphor at the turn of the 21st century, when opponents of genetically engineered food coined the term *Frankenfood* to express their concern over the unknown effects of the human manipulation of foodstuffs.

Another significant 19th-century forerunner was Edgar Allan Poe, who wrote many works loosely classifiable as science fiction. *The Balloon Hoax* of 1844, originally published in the *New York Sun*, is but one example of Poe's ability to provide meticulous technical descriptions intended to mislead and impress the gullible.

More significant to the genre's formation than Poe was Jules Verne, who counted Poe among his influences and was arguably the inventor of science fiction. Verne's first novel, *Paris au XXième siècle (Paris in the Twentieth Century)*—written in 1863 but not published until 1994—is set in the distant 1960s and contains some of his most accurate prognostications: elevated trains, automobiles, facsimile machines, and computer-like banking machines. Nevertheless, the

book's depiction of a dark and bitter dystopian world without art was too radical for Jules Hetzel, Verne's publisher.

Hetzel, who published a popular-science magazine for young people, the *Magasin illustré d'éducation et de récréation*, was a shrewder judge of public taste than Verne. With Hetzel's editorial guidance, Verne abandoned his far-fetched futurism and set to work on the first of his *Voyages extraordinaires—Cinq semaines en ballon* (1863; *Five Weeks in a Balloon*). In this series of contemporary techno-thrillers, the reader learns of balloons, submarines, trains, mechanical elephants, and many other engineering marvels, all described with unmatchable technical accuracy and droll humour.

Verne's novels achieved remarkable international success, and he became a legend in his own time. His major works, which were adapted for film many times, remained popular into the 21st century, and the "scientific romance" became a permanent fixture of Western popular entertainment.

Another uncannily prescient figure was the French illustrator Albert Robida. His graphic cartoons and essays appeared in *Le Vingtième Siècle* (1882; *The 20th Century*), *La Vie électrique* (1883; "The Electric Life"), and the particularly ominous and impressive *La Guerre au vingtième siècle* (1887; "War in the 20th Century"). Although Robida's shrewd extrapolations were created for comic effect, they proved remarkably akin to the 20th century's reality. In fact, since Robida's time, science fiction has

Jules Verne's novels gained popularity for their wit as well as the unparalleled mechanical detail he provided while describing fantastic feats of engineering. Hulton Archive/Getty Images

often proved most prophetic not at its magisterial heights of moral sobriety but at its most louche and peculiar.

CLASSIC BRITISH SCIENCE FICTION

Great Britain as well as France experienced a flowering of creative imagination in the 1880s and '90s. Literary landmarks of the period included such innovative works as Robert Louis Stevenson's *Strange Case of Dr. Jekyll and Mr. Hyde* (1886) and H.G. Wells's phenomenal trio of *The Time Machine* (1895), *The Invisible Man* (1897), and *The War of the Worlds* (1898). Never before had fantastic events of seeming scientific plausibility erupted right in the midst of humdrum daily life. These works used the worldview presented by science to rip aggressively at the fabric of Victorian reality. As the 20th century dawned, many of science fiction's most common themes—space travel, time travel, utopias and dystopias, and encounters with alien beings—bore British postmarks.

The technophilic tenor of the times, as well as 19th-century laissez-faire capitalism, also inspired a reaction from those who longed for a return to a preindustrial life. William Morris's *News from Nowhere* (1890) envisioned a 21st-century pastoral utopia that combined the author's socialist theories with the lucid and placid values of the 14th century. While some critics dismissed Morris's work as a communist tract, C.S. Lewis praised its style and language. Indeed, Lewis,

Lord Dunsany, E.R. Eddison, J.R.R. Tolkien, and a growing host of imitators imbued pastoral settings with heroic and mythic elements, often borrowing from Christian ethos. Examples of this type of work existed even across the Atlantic, notably in two novels by William Dean Howells, the dean of late 19th-century American letters. In Howells's *A Traveler from Altruria* (1894) and *Through the Eye of the Needle* (1907), he described Altruria, a utopian world that combined the foundations of Christianity and the U.S. Constitution to produce an "ethical socialism" by which society was guided. Though heroic fantasy remained a minority taste in Britain and elsewhere for many decades, during the second half of the 20th century, it began to dominate bookstore shelves and book clubs.

MASS MARKETS AND JUVENILE SCIENCE FICTION

Publishing trends brought about an important shift in the development of the genre. The most crucial change in Britain was a decline in the publication of "three-decker" Victorian novels and an accompanying expansion of magazine publication. This adjustment proved highly advantageous to shorter works of science fiction. It brought about a new subgenre, as seen, for example, in George Chesney's short story *The Battle of Dorking* (1871). First published in *Blackwood's Magazine*, *The Battle of Dorking* darkly postulated a Prussian defeat of a poorly armed, weak, and unwary Britain and established the military techno-thriller. Chesney used his urgent narrative of the near future to warn against what he perceived as symptoms of Britain's decline.

Magazine publication was encouraged by an even more pronounced publishing trend that began in the early 1880s. With the development of a cheap process for converting wood pulp into paper and the increasing mechanization of the printing process, inexpensive "pulp" magazines began to deliver stories to a mass audience. During this period in the United States, "dime novels" (shoddily produced pamphlets that usually sold for a nickel) and boys' adventure magazines proliferated. The stories distributed in these books and magazines, such as Luis Senarens's *Frank Reade, Jr., and His Steam Wonder* (1884), often boasted SF elements that appealed to the young reader's sense of wonder and adventure. While Verne's influence is evident in them, dime novels lacked both Verne's knowledge of technology and his literary skill. Senarens's work, for example, epitomizes the worst aspects of the type: they are poorly written and filled with sadistic racism directed toward Native Americans, African Americans, Irish Americans, Mexicans, and Jews.

Edgar Rice Burroughs, with his serialized story *Under the Moons of Mars* (1912; novelized as *A Princess of Mars* and *Under the Moons of Mars*), transformed European-style "literary" science fiction into a distinctly American genre directed at a juvenile audience. Combining European elements of fantasy and horror with the naive expansionist style of early American westerns, Burroughs had his hero John Carter outwit various inferior green, yellow, and black Martians. He also marries a red Martian and has a child by her, despite the fact that she reproduces by laying eggs. Burroughs's hero remained an SF archetype, especially for "space operas," through the 1950s.

The success of juvenile SF stories inculcated a love of science fiction that culminated in the founding of adult-oriented SF pulp magazines in the 1920s, a circumstance that moved the centre of the genre decisively into American hands.

THE "GOLDEN AGE" OF SCIENCE FICTION

The previously mentioned Hugo Gernsback, an emigrant from Luxembourg based in New York City, made a living publishing technical magazines for radio and electrical enthusiasts. Noting the growing fondness of his youthful audience for fictional accounts of thrilling technical wonders, Gernsback began to republish the works of Verne and Poe and the early writings of H.G. Wells in great profusion.

Gernsback's magazine *Amazing Stories* (founded 1926) broke ground for many imitators and successors, including his own later periodicals *Science Wonder Stories*, *Air Wonder Stories*, and *Scientific Detective Monthly* (later known as *Amazing Detective Tales*), and a torrent of other pulp publications.

This practice soon yielded so much fruit that many people, especially Americans, falsely assumed that Americans had created science fiction.

By 1934 SF readership in the United States was large enough to support the establishment of the Science Fiction League, Gernsback's professionally sponsored fan organization (with local chapters in the United Kingdom and Australia). Like a kind of freemasonry, SF fandom spread across the United States. Eager young devotees soon had their own stories published, and, as time passed, they became the hardened, canny professionals of the SF pulp world. Literary groups such as New York's Futurians, Milwaukee's Fictioneers, and the Los Angeles Science Fiction League argued ideology in amateur presses. Conventions were held, feuds and friendships flourished, and science fiction began its long climb, never to respectability but rather toward mass acceptance.

Another influential figure was John W. Campbell, Jr., who from 1937 to 1971 edited *Astounding Science Fiction*. Campbell's insistence on accurate scientific research (he attended the Massachusetts Institute of Technology and received his B.S. in physics from Duke University) and some sense of literary style shaped the career of almost every major American science fiction writer from the period. As a writer, Campbell is noteworthy for his story *Who Goes There?* (1938) and its two film versions, *The Thing* (1951 and 1982), but he is best remembered as an editor. Many fans refer to Campbell's early years at *Astounding*, roughly 1938–46, with its frequent publication of stories by Robert Heinlein, Isaac Asimov, A.E. Van Vogt, and Theodore Sturgeon, as SF's golden age.

Certain literary critics countered wittily that the "golden age" of science fiction is the chronological age of 14—the reputed age at which many fans become hooked on science fiction and the all-too-typical literary level of a genre relished far more for its new scientific "ideas" than its literary merits. Nevertheless, even the sharpest critic would have to admit that for all its often juvenile nature—particularly as conceived in the United States—science fiction was a singular source of scientific wonder and discovery that inspired generations of scientists and engineers to pursue in reality what they had dreamed about in their youth.

SOVIET SCIENCE FICTION

Only the gargantuan world of Soviet state publishing could match the production of U.S. science fiction. The Soviet promotion of "scientific socialism" created a vital breathing space for science fiction within Soviet society. The genre's often allegorical nature gave Soviet writers of science fiction many creative opportunities for relatively free expression.

Soviet science fiction was broad and deep enough to spawn several subgenres, such as the techno-thriller Red Detective stories of Marxist world revolution and many Cosmonaut space operas. Among its masterpieces were the Constructivist silent film *Aelita* (1924), based on the 1923 novel of the same title by Aleksey Tolstoy. The film's imaginative set and costume designs had a strong artistic influence on Fritz Lang's film *Metropolis* (1927). Both *Aelita*'s design and its scenes of an Earthman leading a Martian proletarian revolt against an oppressive regime were echoed in the 1930s American film serial *Flash Gordon*. Another notable work of this period was Yevgeny Zamyatin's *My* (written in 1920, circulated in manuscript and not published in Russian until 1952; translated into English as *We* in 1924), which won a wide readership overseas, though the author's satiric daring led to his banishment under Joseph Stalin. The book's depiction of life under a totalitarian state influenced the other two great dystopian novels of the 20th century, Aldous Huxley's *Brave New World* (1932) and George Orwell's *Nineteen Eighty-four* (1949).

MAJOR SCIENCE FICTION THEMES

Since its first appearance as the dream-world of adolescent boys, science fiction has gained a modicum of respectability. Students of the genre often discuss these works according to the themes they examine. Several more or less clearly defined topics can be discerned.

UTOPIAS AND DYSTOPIAS

Sir Thomas More's learned satire *Utopia* (1516)—the title is based on a pun of the Greek words *eutopia* ("good place") and *outopia* ("no place")—shed an analytic light on 16th-century England along rational, humanistic lines. *Utopia* portrayed an ideal society in a hypothetical "no-place" so that More would be perceived as undertaking a thought experiment, giving no direct offense to established interests.

Since More's time, utopias have been attractive primarily to fringe political thinkers who have little practical redress within the power structures of the day. Under these conditions, a published thought experiment that airs hidden discontents can strike with revelatory force and find a broad popular response.

Utopias can be extravagant castles-in-the-air, nostalgic Shangri-Las, provocative satires, and rank political tracks thinly disguised as novels. Society's esteem for utopian thinking has fluctuated with the times. The failure of Soviet communism caused an immense archive of utopian work to shift catastrophically in value from sober social engineering to dusty irrelevancy. The line between reforming insight and political crankdom is often thin.

Utopias thrived amid the 19th century's infatuation with scientific progress. Many philosophers—Karl Marx included—thought that historical forces and the steady accumulation of rational knowledge would someday yield an "end state" for history. According to this way of thinking, the thoughtful futurist needed only to spot and nurture tomorrow's dominant progressive trends and kill off the feudal superstitions of false consciousness. Then social perfection would arrive as surely as the ticking of a clock.

Fictional successes along this line included Edward Bellamy's *Looking Backward* (1888), in which a Bostonian awakes from a mystical sleep in the year 2000 to find industry nationalized, equal distribution of wealth to all citizens, and class divisions eradicated—a process that Bellamy called Nationalism. Bellamy Nationalist clubs sprang up nationwide to discuss his ideals, and the Nationalists were represented at the 1891 Populist Party convention. Socialist leader Eugene V. Debs adopted many of the tenets of the Nationalist program. William Morris, who was appalled by Bellamy's depiction of a rational, bureaucratized industrial state, countered with *News from Nowhere*, a British vision of a pastoral utopia.

German politician Walther Rathenau wrote technological utopias, *Von Kommenden Dingen* (1917; *In Days to Come*) and *Der neue Staat* (1919; *The New Society*), in which he rejected nationalized industries in favour of greater worker participation in management. In the turbulence of Weimar society, he was assassinated by anti-Semitic nationalists.

H.G. Wells became a particularly ardent and tireless socialist campaigner. In works such as *A Modern Utopia* (1905), *Men Like Gods* (1923), *The Open Conspiracy: Blue Prints for a World Revolution* (1928), and *The Shape of Things to Come* (1933), he foresaw a rationalized, technocratic society. Yet Wells lived long enough to see the atomic bomb, and his last essay, "Mind at the End of Its Tether" (1945), darkly prophesied extinction for the human race, which, in his later opinion, lacked the creative flexibility to control its own affairs.

In B.F. Skinner's *Walden Two* (1948), rewards and punishments are employed to condition the members of a small communal society. In *Walden Two Revisited* (1976), Skinner was more explicit: "Russia after fifty years is not a model we wish to emulate. China may be closer to the solutions I have been talking about, but a communist revolution in America is hard to imagine."

Technocratic utopias like those envisioned by Wells and Skinner have a serious conceptual difficulty: where, how, and why is the process of "improvement" to stop? It is hard to champion "progress" by depicting a world in which further progress is impossible. This paradox does not apply to the pastoral utopia, which turns its back on technology to seek a timeless world of stability and peace. The pastoral utopia generally functions as an imaginary refuge from the technological forces that are so visibly warping the author's real-world landscape. Pastorals tend to be quiet, thoughtful village retreats devoid of smokestacks, newspapers, bank loans, and annoying traffic jams. Major works in this vein include Morris's *News from Nowhere*, Samuel Butler's satiric *Erewhon* (1872), James Hilton's *Lost Horizon* (1933), Aldous

Huxley's psychedelic *Island* (1962), and Ernest Callenbach's green postindustrial *Ecotopia* (1975).

Ursula K. Le Guin's *The Dispossessed* (1974) depicts an anarchist state striving to fulfill its own ideals, but like most modern SF utopias, it emphasizes ambiguity rather than claiming that history is on the author's side. Kim Stanley Robinson's Martian Trilogy—*Red Mars* (1992), *Green Mars* (1994), and *Blue Mars* (1996)—describes planetary settlers creating an idealist pioneer society under Martian physical conditions.

A central difficulty of utopian fiction is the lack of dramatic conflict. A state of perfection is inherently uneventful. The counter to utopia is dystopia, in which hopes for betterment are replaced by electrifying fears of the ugly consequences of present-day behaviour. Utopias tended to have a placid gloss of phony benevolence, while dystopias displayed a somewhat satanic thunder.

Utopias commonly featured "moderns" undergoing a conversion experience to the utopian mind-set—after which, all action stopped. In dystopias, a character representing moderns is excitingly chased down, persecuted, degraded, and commonly killed. In Huxley's *Brave New World*, an intellectual dissident is singled out and exiled by fatuous world rulers anxious to preserve their numbing status quo. George Orwell's hellish *Nineteen Eighty-four* stopped the march of history in its tracks with its famous image of the future as "a boot stamping on a human face—forever." Terry Gilliam's satiric film *Brazil* (1985) veers between pathos and absurdity with its bizarre blend of Orwell's dystopian vision of the future and Kafkaesque elements.

E.M. Forster's much-anthologized story *The Machine Stops* (1909) was written as a counterblast to Wellsian technical optimism. The story depicts a soulless push-button, heavily networked world. The sudden collapse of Forster's dystopia supplies motive force to the plot—a scheme so common in science fiction that it is known as the "house-of-cards" plot.

In Norman Spinrad's black comedy *The Iron Dream* (1972), a frustrated Adolf Hitler immigrates and becomes an American pulp SF novelist, to weirdly convincing effect. Whether pleasant or sinister, heavenly or apocalyptic, utopias and dystopias shared a sublime sense of ahistoricality. All solutions were necessarily final solutions, and the triumph, or calamity, would surely last at least a thousand years.

ALTERNATIVE SOCIETIES

If one abandons the odd notion that the passage of time must make things worse or better, the spectrum of possibility expands dramatically. Science fiction writers have spent much effort conceiving societies that are neither perfect nor horrific but excitingly different, alien to human experience. Robert Heinlein's greatest popular success, the novel *Stranger in a Strange Land* (1961), paints the fate of a prophet and social reformer who was raised by Martians. A Martian human has no earthly shibboleths, so the story's weird hero cuts briskly through almost every pious human custom relating to sex, death, religion, and money. For obvious reasons, Heinlein's work was a counter-cultural icon in the 1960s.

Many SF writers, like Heinlein, took particular pleasure in upsetting the most basic tenets of the human condition. John Varley's *The Ophiuchi Hotline* (1977) is an archive of methods to shatter old human verities: characters die and are reborn as clones, change sex with ease and alacrity, make backup tapes of their personalities, and undergo drastic acts of surgery—all in a space-dwelling society that accepts such things as normal.

William Gibson's *Neuromancer* was widely noted for its intense depiction of a postnational world order ruled by feudal global corporations. Artificial intelligences, owned by the wealthy few, are hugely powerful entities, yet they pass almost unheeded over a seething, fractured society of outlaw geneticists, information criminals, colourful street gangs, and orbiting Rastafarians.

In Neal Stephenson's *Snow Crash* (1992), a future globalized society has abandoned conventional land-based government and reformed itself along the lines of electronic cults and mobile interest groups. The Mafia delivers pizza, the CIA is a for-profit organization, Hong Kong is a global franchise of capitalist Chinatowns, and life online is often of more consequence than real life.

SEX AND GENDER

Because it is difficult to legislate relations between the sexes by conventional political reform, and because works of fiction can present a multiplicity of new arrangements, science fiction has had a particular affinity for feminism, and the attraction was mutual. In *Mizora* (1890), Mary Bradley Lane presented an early feminist utopia, and Charlotte Perkins Gilman in *Herland* (1915) imagined a society of women who reproduce by parthenogenesis.

The subject also interested some male authors. Theodore Sturgeon's *Venus Plus X* (1960) examined the limits of gender in a world where sexuality and reproduction are surgical add-ons. One of the more thoughtful explorations of the theme was Ursula K. Le Guin's *The Left Hand of Darkness* (1969), which posited a human society on a distant planet where humans have no sexual identity but become sexual beings for a brief period once a month. Each can become either male or female during this time. Le Guin works out the consequences of this sort of arrangement in meticulous anthropological detail and creates a revelatory tour de force.

Because science fiction was by nature receptive to technical solutions to all sorts of issues, including gender, readers embraced Shulamith Firestone's feminist tract *The Dialectic of Sex: The Case for a*

Feminist Revolution (1970). Although the book was not written with a science fiction audience in mind, it nevertheless declared that women could never be free of oppression until the physical acts of childbearing and child rearing were industrialized. The influence of Firestone's book could be seen in works such as Marge Piercy's *Woman on the Edge of Time* (1976) and Suzy McKee Charnas's *Motherlines* (1978).

URSULA K. LE GUIN

(b. Oct. 21, 1929, Berkeley, Calif., U.S.)

The American writer Ursula K. Le Guin is known for her tales of science fiction and fantasy imbued with concern for character development and language. The daughter of the distinguished anthropologist A.L. Kroeber and writer Theodora Kroeber, she attended Radcliffe College (B.A., 1951) and Columbia University (M.A., 1952). The methods of anthropology influenced her science-fiction stories, which often feature highly detailed descriptions of alien societies. Her first three novels, Rocannon's World *(1966),* Planet of Exile *(1966), and* City of Illusions *(1967), introduce beings from the planet Hain, who established human life on habitable planets, including Earth. Although her Earthsea series—*A Wizard of Earthsea *(1968),* The Tombs of Atuan *(1971),* The Farthest Shore *(1972),* Tehanu *(1990),* Tales from Earthsea *(2001), and* The Other Wind *(2001)—was written for children, Le Guin's skillful writing and acute perceptions attracted a large adult readership. She tapped the young adult market again with her* Annals of the Western Shore *series, which includes* Gifts *(2004),* Voices *(2006), and* Powers *(2007). Le Guin also wrote a series of books about cats with wings, which includes* Catwings Return *and* Jane on Her Own, *both published in 1999.*

Le Guin's most philosophically significant novels exhibit the same attention to detail that characterizes her science fiction and high fantasy works. The Left Hand of Darkness *(1969) is about a race of androgynous people who may become either male or female. In* The Dispossessed *(1974), she examined two neighbouring worlds that are home to antithetical societies, one capitalist, the other anarchic, both of which stifle freedom in particular ways. The destruction of indigenous peoples on a planet colonized by Earth is the focus of* The Word for World Is Forest *(1972).* Always Coming Home *(1985) concerns the Kesh, survivors of nuclear war in California. This book includes poetry, prose, legends, autobiography, and a tape recording of Kesh music. In 2008 Le Guin made literary news with* Lavinia, *a metatextual examination of a minor character from Virgil's* Aeneid *and her role in the historical development of early Rome.*

Le Guin also wrote many essays on fantasy fiction, feminist issues, writing, and other topics, some of them collected in The Language of the Night *(1979),* Dancing at the Edge of the World *(1989),* Steering the Craft *(1998), and* The Wave in the Mind *(2004). In 2000 she was awarded the Living Legend medal by the Library of Congress.*

Although feminist SF tended to hope for gender justice and to declare "if only" rather than to ask "what if," a powerful dystopian school of feminist science fiction suggested that relationships between men and women might slide from poor to downright catastrophic. Nazi cults of crazed masculinity haunt Katharine Burdekin's *Swastika Night* (1937). Joanna Russ's much-praised *The Female Man* (1975) suggests through its title that "femininity" is a weird condition forced on one by oppressors. Even Russ's feminist classic paled by comparison to Margaret Atwood's evocative dystopian misogyny in *The Handmaid's Tale* (1985). Drawn from dark contemporary trends, the bitter world of *The Handmaid's Tale* is ruled by a repressive American religious regime. This dystopia finally collapses from its own hostility to women—to be succeeded by yet another historical epoch. In this sense, *The Handmaid's Tale* makes an intellectual peace with historical process and transcends the customary limits of utopias and dystopias.

ALIEN ENCOUNTERS

Because human beings are the only known form of fully sentient life, any encounter with nonhuman intelligence is necessarily speculative. Writers in the 17th and 18th centuries produced many tales of travel to and from other inhabited worlds, but works such as Voltaire's *Micromégas* did not depict Saturnians as alien beings. They were men, though of Saturn-sized proportions.

A fuller knowledge of natural history enabled writers to imagine that life on other worlds might develop differently from life on Earth. In 1864 the astronomer and science popularizer Camille Flammarion published *Les Mondes imaginaires et les mondes réels* ("Imaginary Worlds and Real Worlds"), depicting otherworldly forms of life that could evolve within alien biological environments. This Gallic conceptual breakthrough was first exploited in fiction by J.H. Rosny Aîné, whose short story *Les Xipéhuz* (1887) describes an evolutionary war of extermination between prehistoric humans and a menacing crystal-based life-form.

Aliens were thus first conceived as Darwinian competitors with mankind, a scheme worked out in spooky Huxleyan detail by H.G. Wells, whose slimy, blood-sucking Martians possessed intellects "vast, and cool, and unsympathetic." Wells's *The War of the Worlds* (1898) was all the more successful for its implication that the highly advanced British Empire was finally experiencing from the other side the gunboat diplomacy that it had meted out to others. In 1938 Orson Welles's radio adaptation of *The War of the Worlds* was mistaken by the gullible for actual news reportage of marauding Martians sacking and looting New Jersey. The episode provoked a famous attack of mass panic, making it perhaps the most famous radio drama of all time.

Wells's *The First Men in the Moon* (1901) boosted antlike aliens into a sinister lunar analog for human society.

The spate of alien invasion stories that followed were often strident in tone and genocidal in their predictions of coming doom. The "bug-eyed monster" became a staple of science fiction. Stanley G. Weinbaum won immediate and lasting acclaim with his more sophisticated approach in *A Martian Odyssey* (1934), which presented aliens whose behaviour, though whimsical, harmless, and colourful, was profoundly inexplicable to human mentality. In Raymond Z. Gallun's *Old Faithful* (1934), the Martians tended to be quite decent sorts.

Authors of "serious" literature, such as Olaf Stapledon, also dealt with alien life forms. His *Star Maker* (1937) follows an Englishman whose disembodied mind travels across space and time, observing aliens as metaphysical actors in a fiery cosmic drama remote from all human concern, and encounters the creator of the universe (Star Maker). This critically acclaimed book is more a philosophical treatise on science, human nature, and God than a traditional novel. Stapledon's descriptions and social-philosophical discourses on galactic empires, symbiotic alien life-forms, genetic engineering, ecology, and overpopulation inspired a number of SF writers, including Arthur C. Clarke, during the 1940s and '50s.

As dramatic actors within a narrative, aliens pose unique difficulties. If too humanlike, they are of little use; if genuinely alien, they defy the fictional conventionalities of motive, conflict, and plot. In Stanisław Lem's *Solaris* (1961; filmed 1972, 2002), the sentience on an alien planet is so metaphysically distant from humanity that it causes its cosmonaut investigators to hallucinate and collapse. The Solaris alien is a permanent enigma, completely unframable by any human thought process. Hal Clement's *Mission of Gravity* (1954) was a tour de force in that its hero is a tiny, intelligent centipede-like creature who breathes poison gas in the crushing gravity of an alien world. This description alone makes it clear just how difficult imagining the alien can be. As a result, science fiction writers often centred their energies on a first contact with aliens, such as those found in Steven Spielberg's film *Close Encounters of the Third Kind* (1977). In the "first contact" narrative, one can enjoy the novel thrill of alienness without having to confront the implications of everyday interactions with aliens.

Alien-invasion motifs persist in science fiction, as in the film *Alien* (1979) with its ruthless, parasitic monsters. Yet a distinct and growing trend within science fiction depicted aliens as coworkers, science officers, technical specialists, sidekicks, and even love interests. Two of the most prominent examples of this come from the various television shows, films, and novels based on the worlds of *Star Trek* and *Alien Nation*. It is also increasingly common for human characters to have undergone such extensive warping and mutation—as in Paul Di Fillipo's *Ribofunk* (1996)—that they themselves are as exotic as aliens.

Aliens are supposed evolutionary products of life on different worlds, while intelligent robots are supposed mechanical, industrial creations. Robots and aliens therefore serve similar thematic purposes for science fiction. The first robots were introduced by Czech dramatist Karel Čapek as characters in his play *R.U.R.* (1921). In a rather standard alien-menace maneuver, Čapek's robots outcompete humanity within the new milieu of industrial mass production and attempt to exterminate the human race.

Robots remain primarily theatrical inventions, but they are central figures in science fiction thought experiments intended to provoke debate about humanity's place within a technological environment. Isaac Asimov, for example, devoted much effort to creating an ethical system for humans and robots. Asimov's famous Three Laws of Robotics are as follows:

> *(1) a robot may not injure a human being or, through inaction, allow a human being to come to harm; (2) a robot must obey the orders given it by human beings except where such orders would conflict with the First Law; (3) a robot must protect its own existence as long as such protection does not conflict with the First or Second Law.*

Asimov was able to derive an entertaining set of novels and stories from these three premises—even though his imaginary laws have never been used for the control of any real-world robot. Quite to the contrary, 21st-century robotics are probably best represented by semiautonomous military devices such as the cruise missile, specifically designed to blow itself up as it reaches its target and to do considerable damage.

The robot as a reflection of humanity received a classic outing in Lester del Rey's short story *Helen O'Loy* (1938). Helen was not the first female robot—her famous predecessor is the sinister celluloid robot Maria from the aforementioned film *Metropolis* (1927). Helen, by contrast, somehow establishes her womanhood by marrying her inventor and then sacrificing her own mechanical life upon her husband's death. Male robots, in the hands of authors such as Tanith Lee (*The Silver Metal Lover*, 1981) and Marge Piercy (*He, She, and It*, 1991), became distorted images of human men.

Humanoid robots, or androids, remain the photogenic darlings of SF cinema, appearing in a host of productions, including *Westworld* (1973), *The Stepford Wives* (1975, 2004), *Star Wars* (1977), *Bicentennial Man* (1999), *Artificial Intelligence: A.I.* (2001), and *I, Robot* (2004).

SPACE TRAVEL

Flight into outer space is the classic SF theme. Verne's pioneering *De la terre à la lune* (1865; *From the Earth to the Moon*) was the first fiction to treat space travel as a coherent engineering problem—to recognize explicitly that gravity would cease, that there could be no air, and so forth. Because Verne found no plausible way to land his cannon-fired passengers on the

Jedi master Yoda (with light sabre), as projected for the audience during a 2009 concert conducted by composer John Williams to celebrate Star Wars, a six-film cycle that constitutes one of the most recognizable space operas made for the wide screen. Jason Squires/WireImage/Getty Images

lunar surface, they merely whiz by the Moon at close range, cataloging craters in a geographic ecstasy. At the conceptual dawn of space travel, it was enough just to be up there, escaping earthly bonds to revel in sheer extraterrestrial possibility. Given that Georges Méliès filmed a fictional trip to the Moon with his pioneering camera in 1902, science fiction cinema is as old as cinema itself.

A certain disenchantment with this theme necessarily set in after the actual Moon landing in 1969, for human life in outer space proved less than heavenly. Far from swashbucklers, astronauts and cosmonauts were highly trained technicians whose primary motive was to preserve their hardware. They grappled with strict limits in fuel, power, water, oxygen, and privacy, along with cramped personal quarters—a life more akin to submarine service than to a romantic flight aboard a luxury starship.

The SF works that treat space travel with nuts-and-bolts realism are a minority taste. Science fiction far more commonly omits the unromantic aspects of space travel, especially through one of the genre's commonest stage devices, the "faster-than-light drive," or "warp drive." Although this imaginary technology is no more technically plausible than lifelike androids, it is a necessity for the alien-planet adventure story. Science fiction writers cheerfully sacrifice the realities of astrophysics in the service of imaginary worlds.

Much creative energy has been invested in "space opera," science fiction at its most romantic. The space opera is an action-adventure, commonly of galactic scale, of which the film cycle *Star Wars* (1977, 1980, 1983, 1999, 2002, 2005) is the best-known exemplar. It presents a unique type of "widescreen baroque," with all the riches of pulp fiction in a single package. *Star Wars*, for example, offered not only advanced scientific technology—presumably necessary to build the starships and orbiting battle stations—but also princesses, smugglers, robots, sword fights, mystical doctrines, levitating gurus, monsters, barroom brawls, heroes of dubious birth, elaborate chase scenes, and gothic death traps.

Like the black-clad figures who move the props in Japanese Noh theatre, the fantastic aspects of space opera are simply and gratefully accepted by its devotees. Writers of 20th-century space opera are among the most respected figures in science fiction. Their ranks include E.E. ("Doc") Smith, Edmond Hamilton, John W. Campbell, Jack Williamson, A.E. Van Vogt, Jack Vance, Anne McCaffrey, Lois McMaster Bujold, and C.J. Cherryh. Nor is space opera by any means moribund, for a particularly extravagant form of space opera is the signature of the New British Science Fiction, the first SF literary movement of the 21st century. Introverted postimperial insularity had long characterized British science fiction, but in the 21st century a cluster of writers—including Iain M. Banks, Stephen Baxter, Justina Robson, Peter F. Hamilton, Charles Stross, and Ken MacLeod—reengineered the universe in gaudy bursts of star-smashing neo-cosmology.

TIME TRAVEL

A complement to travel through space is travel through time. A prototype of the time travel story is Charles Dickens's *A Christmas Carol* (1843). The story features the Ghost of Christmas Yet to Come, who is magically able to immerse the hapless Scrooge in the dire consequences of his own ungenerous actions. But for all their familiarity, Scrooge's time travels were mere ghostly dreammongering. The SF version of time travel arrived when H.G. Wells suggested in *The Time Machine* (1895) that the process might be done mechanically.

For a genre whose central issues involve processes of historical change, time travel is irresistibly attractive. For instance, time travel offers the edifying spectacle of "moderns" traveling into the past to remake the world closer to the heart's desire. Mark Twain's *A Connecticut Yankee in King Arthur's Court* (1889) contrasts industrial ingenuity with feudal romance, to darkly hilarious effect. L. Sprague de Camp's novel *Lest Darkness Fall* (1941) has an American archaeologist rescuing Imperial Rome in its decline, an act the hero carries out with such luminous attention to techno-historical detail that it resembles a World Bank bailout of an underdeveloped country.

Time tourism, a distinct subgenre, is a perennial SF theme. It is exemplified in Ray Bradbury's *A Sound of Thunder* (1952), in which a tiny misstep by dinosaur hunters grimly affects the consequent course of history. In Robert Silverberg's *Up the Line* (1969), voyeuristic thrill seekers from the future infest the past.

Another variant on the time travel theme involves physical objects that become displaced in time. C.M. Kornbluth's *The Little Black Bag* (1950) concerns a doctor's bag from the future. Warring groups of time travelers battle one another up and down the time streams in Poul Anderson's *Guardians of Time* (1960) and Fritz Leiber's *The Change War* (1978). Barrington J. Bayley's *Fall of Chronopolis* (1974) achieves the technicolour proportions of "time opera." In John Kessel's *Corrupting Dr. Nice* (1997), cynical exploiters from the future invade the past wholesale, kidnapping major historical figures and crassly employing them as underlings and talk-show hosts.

A one-way trip into the future is the staple of the suspended-animation story, the device behind the Buck Rogers stories and a host of consequent tales in which a hero of the present-day escapes the customary time-bound limits of human mortality. In Martin Amis's *Time's Arrow* (1991), the flow of time is entirely reversed, but life seems just as precarious as people solemnly march to a final end in their mother's wombs.

The long-lived British television series *Dr. Who* (1963–89, and again from 2005) involved an eccentric time traveler whose exotic mode of transport was disguised as a common telephone booth. Periodically portrayed by different actors, Dr. Who exhibited a popularity so perennial that he indeed seemed timeless. The popularity of the notion can be seen in any number of time-travel films, including *The Time Machine* (1960 and 2002), *Slaughterhouse-Five* (1972), *Time Bandits* (1981), *Back to the Future* (1985), *Terminator* (1984), and *Twelve Monkeys* (1995).

ALTERNATE HISTORIES AND PARALLEL UNIVERSES

Stories centred on time-travel paradoxes developed as a separate school of science fiction. If a human being broke free from the conventional chains of causality, intriguing metaphysical puzzles ensued. The classic SF version of these puzzles is the challenge posed by a man who travels back in time and kills his own grandfather, thus ensuring that he, the time traveler, can never be born in the first place. Time-travel paradoxes were usually resolved as ingeniously as locked-room murder mysteries.

Murray Leinster's *Sidewise in Time* (1934) expanded the possibilities by suggesting a vast multiplicity of "histories," all occurring at the same "time." Under the scheme Leister proposed, one need not limit oneself to one past or one future but might travel between many alternate worlds existing in parallel. This new SF convention of a "multiverse" opened a vast potential canvas for fictional exploitation, with humanity's universe just one undistinguished universe among many.

Narratives set in the future offered at least some potential connection to the real world. By contrast, the "parallel universe" was entirely conjectural and hypothetical. Initially, readers found parallel worlds an amusing but inconsequential conceit, just as they had once found works set within the future academic or absurd. They soon realized, however, that the notion of uchronia (or "no-times") offered certain pleasures all its own, such as the ability to deploy actual historical figures as fictional characters. Well-known settings and events could be mutated and distorted at will.

The passage of time had a complex, uchronic effect on science fiction itself. Despite the passing of the year 1984 itself, a number of concepts presented in *Nineteen Eighty-four*—such as omnipresent video surveillance—were not so far-fetched at the turn of the 21st century, and Orwell's political concerns remain painfully relevant. In addition to representing the uchronic effect of some works of science fiction, *Nineteen Eighty-four* is an excellent example of a uchronic novel. It is neither futuristic nor historical, existing in a peculiar uchronic netherworld. As time passes, growing numbers of SF classics fall into this conceptual category. It is a small step from this category to parallel worlds and alternate histories. Those concepts no longer seem abstract and improbable, but they have become part of the heritage of science fiction.

Even historical fiction has dealt with the "what if" posed by uchronias. In 1907 G.M. Trevelyan wrote an essay speculating on the consequences of a Napoleonic victory at Waterloo. Trevelyan's work inspired J.C. Squires's anthology *If It*

Had Happened Otherwise (1931), in which such period worthies as Winston Churchill, André Maurois, and G.K. Chesterton speculated on counterfactual historical turning points. This was an intellectual parlour game of the type that science fiction liked to play.

Alternate histories existed well outside the customary bounds of science fiction, such as Len Deighton's thriller *SS-GB* (1978), about the grim role of Nazi occupiers in Britain, and Vladimir Nabokov's involved and elegant *Ada* (1969). Alternate histories tend to cluster around particularly dramatic and colourful junctures of history, with World War II and the American Civil War as particular favourites. Some ventured farther out, postulating a global Roman Empire or a world in which dinosaurs avoided extinction.

The film *It's a Wonderful Life* (1946)—based on the story *The Greatest Gift* (1943) by Philip Van Doren Stern—is a perennial sentimental favourite. In the film, a man in despair learns that his life does matter when he sees that, without his presence, his hometown becomes an evil dystopia. It is an ultimate compliment to the individual when the universe rewrites itself around a fantasy of self-worth.

In some deep sense, all works of fiction must be alternate histories and parallel worlds, for their protagonists and described events do not in fact exist. As the tradition of fiction grew longer and deeper, presenting works ever more distant from the reader's cultural framework, readers seemed more willing to accept work that was radically detached from local truisms of time and space.

HIGH TECHNOLOGIES

Leo Marx, author of the techno-social study *The Machine in the Garden* (1964), coined the useful term *technological sublime* to indicate a quasi-spiritual haze given off by any particularly visible and impressive technological advance. Science fiction dotes on the sublime, which ruptures the everyday and lifts the human spirit to the plateaus of high imagination. Common models of the technological sublime include railroads, photography, aviation, giant dams, rural electrification (a particular Soviet favourite), atomic power and atomic weapons, space flight, television, computers, virtual reality, and the "information superhighway." The most sublime of all technologies are, in reality, not technologies at all but rather technological concepts—time machines, interplanetary starships, and androids.

Humans quickly lose a sense of awe over the technological advancements that have been fully integrated into the fabric of everyday life. Technologies such as immunization, plumbing, recycling, and the birth control pill have had a profound cultural effect, but they are not considered sublime nor are they generally subjects for science fiction. The reason for this is not directly related to the scientific principles involved or any inherent difficulties of the engineering. It is entirely a social judgment, with distinctly metaphysical overtones. Science fiction is one of the arenas in which these judgments are cast.

Space flight is one high technology to which science fiction has shown a passionate allegiance. For the most part, the space shuttle remains sublime, even though it is three decades old and in its final years of operation. Were space shuttles as common as 747s, they would quickly lose their sublime affect.

Outer space and cyberspace—a science fiction term applied to computer networks and simulated spaces—are conceptual cousins, offering the same high-tech thrill through different instruments in different historical periods. Yet with cybertechnology rapidly achieving mass acceptance and becoming commonplace in many parts of the world, its SF allure is fading fast. Science fiction therefore has been once again making tentative overtures to biotechnology, although a relationship has existed at least since Mary Shelley's *Frankenstein* was published. Unlike computers, biotechnology is deeply rooted in ancient and highly conservative pursuits such as medicine and agriculture. Social resistance to gene-altered crops, animals, and especially human children is widespread.

The sheer novelty of computers masked their particular affinity for pornography, swindling, organized crime, and terrorist conspiracy until they were widely present in the home. By contrast, the potential social impact of cloning was easy to recognize and led to a spate of SF works, including Aldous Huxley's *Brave New World* (1932), with its tank-born castes of workers. Czech "biopunk" stories of the 1980s used genetic parables to indict the moral warping of Czech society under Warsaw Pact oppression. Biologically altered "posthumans" are becoming an SF staple. First visualized as menacing monsters or Nietzschean supermen, the genetically altered were increasingly seen as people with unconventional personal problems.

Although many of the technologies that were first envisioned by science fiction have become reality—and become mundane aspects of mainstream fictional works—scientific knowledge is growing exponentially, leaving plenty of room for further speculation about its future impact on society and individuals. It is hard to imagine any contemporary society's being fully immune to the prognosticating lure of science fiction.

SCIENCE FICTION: TERMS AND CONCEPTS

The reader of science fiction may run across many unfamiliar creatures and worlds, yet science fiction differs from fantasy in a significant way, as can be seen in the work of Harry Potter's creator, J.K. Rowling. Also presented here is a cursory explanation of two of the best-known awards in the field.

FANTASY

The imaginative fiction that is dependent for effect on strangeness of setting (such as other worlds or times) and of characters (such as supernatural or unnatural beings) is called fantasy (and sometimes spelled phantasy). Examples include William Shakespeare's *A Midsummer Night's Dream*, Jonathan Swift's *Gulliver's Travels*, J.R.R. Tolkien's *The Lord of the Rings*, and T.H. White's *The Once and Future King*. The wildly popular Harry Potter novels by J.K. Rowling are perhaps the best-known examples of fantasy in the 21st century. Science fiction can be seen as a form of fantasy, but the terms are not interchangeable, because science fiction usually is set in the future and is based on some aspect of science or technology, while fantasy is set in an imaginary world and usually features the magic of mythical beings.

J.K. ROWLING

(b. July 31, 1965, Chipping Sodbury, near Bristol, Eng.)

The British author Joanne Kathleen Rowling is best known as the creator of the popular and critically acclaimed Harry Potter series, about a young sorcerer in training.

After graduating from the University of Exeter in 1986, Rowling began working for Amnesty International in London, where she started to write the Harry Potter adventures. In the early 1990s she traveled to Portugal to teach English as a foreign language, but, after a brief marriage and the birth of her daughter, she returned to the United Kingdom, settling in Edinburgh. Living on public assistance between stints as a French teacher, she continued to write.

Rowling's first book in the series, Harry Potter and the Philosopher's Stone *(1997; also published as* Harry Potter and the Sorcerer's Stone*), was an immediate success. Featuring vivid descriptions and an imaginative story line, it followed the adventures of the unlikely hero Harry Potter, a lonely orphan who discovers that he is actually a wizard and enrolls in the Hogwarts School of Witchcraft and Wizardry. The book received numerous awards, including the British Book Award. Succeeding volumes—*Harry Potter and the Chamber of Secrets *(1998),* Harry Potter and the Prisoner of Azkaban *(1999),* Harry Potter and the Goblet of Fire *(2000),* Harry Potter and the Order of the Phoenix *(2003), and* Harry Potter and the Half-Blood Prince *(2005)—also were best sellers, available in more than 200 countries and some 60 languages. The seventh and final installment in the series,* Harry Potter and the Deathly Hallows, *was released in 2007.*

Other works include the companion books Fantastic Beasts & Where to Find Them *and* Quidditch Through the Ages, *both of which were published in 2001, with proceeds going to charity. The series sparked great enthusiasm among children and was credited with generating a new interest in reading. A film version of the first Harry Potter book was released in 2001 and became one of the top-grossing movies in the world. Other volumes were also made into highly successful films. In 2008 Rowling followed her successful Harry Potter series with* The Tales of Beedle the Bard, *a collection of fairy tales. Rowling was appointed OBE (Officer of the British Empire) in March 2001. In 2009 she was named a chevalier of the French Legion of Honour.*

HUGO AWARDS

The Hugo Awards consist of several annual awards presented by the World Science Fiction Society (WSFS). They are granted for notable achievement in science fiction or science fantasy writing. Established in 1953, the Hugo Awards were named in honour of Hugo Gernsback (1884–1967), the founder of *Amazing Stories*, the first magazine exclusively for science fiction.

Gernsback received a technical education in Luxembourg and Germany. He traveled to the United States in 1904 to market an improved dry battery that he had invented and then formed a radio supply house. In 1908 he founded *Modern Electrics* (later absorbed by *Popular Science*), a pioneer magazine for radio enthusiasts. In 1911 the magazine published a serialized story by Gernsback that later became the novel *Ralph 124C 41+* (1925). Set in the 27th century, its plot was a rather formulaic pulp adventure, but the richly imagined future, filled with fantastic inventions and spaceship travel, established many of the conventions that came to characterize the genre we now know as science fiction.

In 1926 Gernsback began publishing *Amazing Stories*, one of the first magazines devoted exclusively to what he referred to as "scientifiction." The stories were often crudely written, but the very existence of the magazine and its successors, including *Wonder Stories*, encouraged the development and refinement of the genre.

NEBULA AWARDS

The annual Nebula Awards are presented by the Science Fiction and Fantasy Writers of America (SFWA). Although the SFWA is open to writers, editors, illustrators, agents, and others, only "active members" (published writers) are eligible to vote for the awards, which are currently given for best novel, novella, novelette, short story, and script. The first Nebula Awards were given in 1965, and Frank Herbert's *Dune* won the award for best novel. The Nebula Awards are generally considered more prestigious than the Hugo Awards, which are voted by science fiction fans.

CHAPTER 3

FABLE, PARABLE, AND ALLEGORY

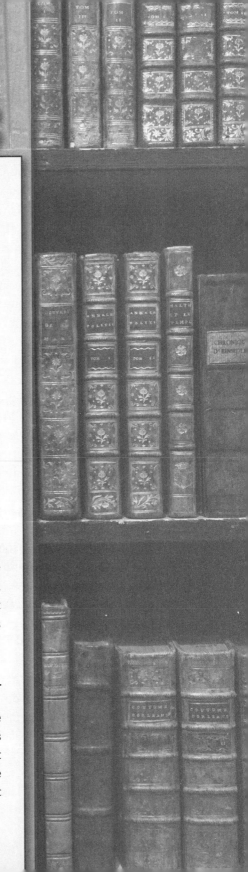

Fable, parable, and allegory are related types of imaginative literature or spoken utterance constructed in such a way that readers or listeners are encouraged to look for meanings hidden beneath the literal surface of the fiction. A story is told or perhaps enacted whose details—when interpreted—are found to correspond to the details of some other system of relations (its hidden, allegorical sense). The poet, for example, may describe the ascent of a hill in such a way that each physical step corresponds to a new stage in the soul's progress toward a higher level of existence.

Many forms of literature elicit this kind of searching interpretation, and the generic term for the cluster is *allegory*. Under it may be grouped fables, parables, and other symbolic shapings. Allegory may involve either a creative or an interpretive process: either the act of building up the allegorical structure and giving "body" to the surface narrative or the act of breaking down this structure to see what themes or ideas run parallel to it.

ALLEGORY AND MYTH

The fate of allegory, in all its many variations, is tied to the development of myth and mythology. Every culture embodies its basic assumptions in stories whose mythic structures reflect the society's prevailing attitudes toward life. If the attitudes are disengaged from the structure, the allegorical meaning implicit in the structure is revealed. The systematic discipline of interpreting the real meaning of a text (called the hermeneutic process) plays a major role in the teaching and defense of sacred wisdom, because religions have traditionally preserved and handed down the old beliefs by telling exemplary stories. These sometimes appear to conflict with a system of morality that has in the meantime developed, and so their "correct" meaning can only be something other than the literal narration of events. Every culture puts pressure on its authors to assert its central beliefs, which are often reflected in literature without the author's necessarily being aware that he is an allegorist. Equally, determined critics may sometimes find allegorical meaning in texts with less than total justification—instances might include the mystical interpretation of the Hebrew Bible's Song of Solomon, an erotic marriage poem, or the frequent allegorizing of classical and modern literature in the light of Freud's psychoanalytic discoveries. Some awareness of the author's intention seems necessary to curb unduly fanciful commentary.

THE ALLEGORICAL MODE

The range of allegorical literature is so wide that to consider allegory as a fixed literary genre is less useful than to regard it as a dimension, or mode, of controlled indirectness and double meaning (which, in fact, all literature possesses to some degree). Critics usually reserve the term *allegory* itself for works of considerable length, complexity, or unique shape.

JOHN BUNYAN

(b. November 1628, Elstow, Bedfordshire, Eng.—d. Aug. 31, 1688, London)

The English minister and author John Bunyan wrote one of the great allegorical tales of all time, The Pilgrim's Progress, *in two parts (1678, 1684). Bunyan encountered the seething religious life of various left-wing sects while serving in Oliver Cromwell's army in the English Civil Wars. He underwent a period of spiritual crisis, converted to Puritanism (a Calvinist religious reform movement), and became a preacher. After the Restoration of the monarchy in England, he was jailed for 12 years as a Nonconformist—one who refused to conform to the doctrines and practices of the Church of England. During his confinement he wrote his spiritual autobiography,* Grace Abounding *(1666). He is best known, however, for* The Pilgrim's Progress, *a religious allegory expressing the Puritan religious outlook. A symbolic vision of the character Christian's pilgrimage through life, it was at one time second only to the Bible in popularity among ordinary readers. Despite his ministerial responsibilities, he published numerous works in his last 10 years.*

Thus, the following varied works might be called allegories: the biblical parable of the sower; *Everyman*, the medieval morality play; *The Pilgrim's Progress*, by John Bunyan; Jonathan Swift's *Gulliver's Travels*; *The Scarlet Letter*, by Nathaniel Hawthorne; William Wordsworth's "Ode: Intimations of Immortality"; Nikolay Gogol's *Dead Souls*; *The Picture of*

Dorian Gray, by Oscar Wilde; and the plays *Six Characters in Search of an Author*, by Luigi Pirandello; *Waiting for Godot*, by Samuel Beckett; and *Who's Afraid of Virginia Woolf?*, by Edward Albee. No one genre can take in such modal range.

FABLE

Fable and parable are short, simple forms of naive allegory. The fable is usually a tale about animals who are personified and behave as though they were humans. The device of personification is also extended to trees, winds, streams, stones, and other natural objects. The earliest of these tales also included humans and gods as characters, but fable tends to concentrate on animating the inanimate. A feature that isolates fable from the ordinary folktale, which it resembles, is that a moral—a rule of behaviour—is woven into the story.

PARABLE

Like fable, the parable also tells a simple story. But, whereas fables tend to personify animal characters—often giving the same impression as does an animated cartoon—the typical parable uses human agents. Parables generally show less interest in the storytelling and more in the analogy they draw between a particular instance of human behaviour (the true neighbourly kindness shown by the good Samaritan in the Bible story, for example) and human behaviour at large. Parable and fable have their roots in preliterate

oral cultures, and both are means of handing down traditional folk wisdom. Their styles differ, however. Fables tend toward detailed, sharply observed social realism (which eventually leads to satire), while the simpler narrative surface of parables gives them a mysterious tone and makes them especially useful for teaching spiritual values.

DERIVATION OF THE TERMS

The original meanings of these critical terms themselves suggest the direction of their development. Fable (from the Latin *fabula*, meaning "a telling") puts the emphasis on narrative (and in the medieval and Renaissance periods was often used when speaking of "the plot" of a narrative). Parable (from Greek *parabolē*, meaning a "setting beside") suggests a juxtaposition that compares and contrasts this story with that idea. Allegory (from Greek *allos* and *agoreuein*, meaning an "other-speaking") suggests a more expanded use of deceptive and oblique language. (In early Greek, though, the term *allegory* itself was not used. Instead, the idea of a hidden, underlying meaning is indicated by the word *hyponoia*—literally, "underthought"—and this term is used of the allegorical interpretation of the Greek poet Homer.)

OBJECTIVES OF THE FABLE

Fables teach a general principle of conduct by presenting a specific example of behaviour. Thus, to define the moral that "People who rush into things without using judgment run into strange and unexpected dangers," Aesop—the traditional "father" of the fable form—told the following story:

> There was a dog who was fond of eating eggs. Mistaking a shellfish for an egg one day, he opened his mouth wide and swallowed it down in one gulp. The weight of it in his stomach caused him intense pain. "Serve me right," he said, "for thinking that anything round must be an egg."

By a slight change of emphasis, the fabulist could have been able to draw a moral about the dangerous effects of gluttony.

Because the moral is embodied in the plot of the fable, an explicit statement of the moral need not be given, though it usually is. Many of these moral tag lines have taken on the status of proverb because they so clearly express commonly held social attitudes.

The Aesopian fables emphasize the social interactions of human beings, and the morals they draw tend to embody advice on the best way to deal with the competitive realities of life. With some irony, fables view the world in terms of its power structures. One of the shortest Aesopian fables says: "A vixen sneered at a lioness because she never bore more than one cub. 'Only one,' she replied, 'but a lion.' " Foxes and wolves, which the poet Samuel Taylor Coleridge called "Everyman's metaphor" for cunning

and cruelty, appear often as characters in fables chiefly because, in the human world, such predatory cunning and cruelty are able to get around restraints of justice and authority. The mere fact that fables unmask the "beast in me," as James Thurber, the 20th-century American humorist and fabulist, put it, suggests their satiric force. Subversive topical satire in tsarist and Soviet Russia is often called "Aesopism"; all comic strips that project a message (such as the Charles Schulz creation "Peanuts" and Walt Kelly's "Pogo") have affinities with Aesop's method.

OBJECTIVES OF THE PARABLE

Parables do not analyze social systems so much as they remind the listener of his or her beliefs. The moral and spiritual stress of the form falls upon memory rather than on the critical faculty. The audience hearing the parable is assumed to share a communal truth but perhaps to have set it aside or forgotten it. The rhetorical appeal of a parable is directed primarily toward an elite, in that a final core of its truth is known only to an inner circle, however simple its narrative may appear on the surface (a number of the parables that Christ used for teaching, for example, conveyed figuratively the meaning of the elusive concept Kingdom of Heaven).

ALLEGORY

Allegory, as the basic process of arousing in the reader or listener a response to levels of meaning, provides writers with the structure of fables, parables, and other related forms. By awakening the impulse to question appearances and by bringing order to mythological interpretation, allegory imparts cultural values. A measure of allegory is present in literature whenever it emphasizes thematic content, ideas rather than events. Generally, the allegorical mode flourishes under authoritarian conditions. Thus it found sustenance during the age of medieval Christendom, when Christian dogma sought universal sway over the Western mind. As such, allegory was a means of freedom under conditions of strong restraint. In general, realism, mimetic playfulness, and the resistance to authority tend to counteract the allegorical process, by loosening its stratified forms. This unbinding of symbolic hierarchies has forced allegory to seek new structures in the modern period. Nevertheless, through allegorical understanding, the great myths continue to be reread and reinterpreted, as the human significance of the new interpretations is passed down from one generation to the next. The abiding impression left by the allegorical mode is one of indirect, ambiguous, even enigmatic symbolism, which inevitably calls for interpretation.

DIVERSITY OF FORMS

Because an allegorical purpose can inform works of literature in a wide range of genres, it is not surprising to find that the largest allegories are epic in scope. A quest forms the narrative thread of both the Greek epic *Odyssey* and the Latin, *Aeneid*, and it is an allegory of the quest for heroic perfection. Thus, allegory is aligned with the epic form. Romances, both prose and verse, are inevitably allegorical, although their forms vary in detail with the prevailing cultural ideals of the age. By comparison, the forms of fable and parable are relatively stable—yet even they may play down the moral idea or the mysterious element and emphasize instead the narrative interest, which then results in an elaboration of the form. (Such an elaboration may be seen in a given tale, as told by successive fabulists, such as a fable of the town mouse and the country mouse. With each retelling, the story is absorbed into a new matrix of interpretation.)

Shifts from naive to sophisticated intent are accompanied by shifts in form. The early authors of fable, following Aesop, wrote in verse. In the 10th century, however, there appeared collected fables, entitled *Romulus*, written in prose (and books such as this brought down into the medieval and modern era a rich tradition of prose fables). This collection in turn was converted back into elegiac verse. Later masters of fable wrote in verse, but modern favourites—such as Joel Chandler Harris, author of "Uncle Remus" stories, Beatrix Potter, creator of Peter Rabbit, or James Thurber in *Fables for Our Time*—employ their own distinctive prose. Again, while for parables prose narrative may be the norm, they have also been told in verse (as in the

Children's book author Beatrix Potter hit upon the characteristic voice of Peter Rabbit in a letter she wrote to a sick boy, in which she described the adventures of four young rabbits. Hulton Archive/Getty Images

emblematic poetry of the 17th-century English Metaphysical poets such as George Herbert, Francis Quarles, and Henry Vaughan).

Loosening the allegorical forms further, some authors have combined prose with verse. Boethius's *Consolation of Philosophy* (c. 524 CE) and Dante's *The New Life* (c. 1293) interrupt the prose discourse with short poems. Verse and prose then interact to give a new thematic perspective. A related mixing of elements appears in Menippean satire (those writings deriving from the 3rd-century-BCE Cynic philosopher Menippus of Gadara), as exemplified in Swift's *Tale of a Tub* (1704). There a relatively simple allegory of Reformation history (the *Tale* proper) is interrupted by a series of digressions that comment allegorically on the story into which they break.

Even the lyric poem can be adapted to yield allegorical themes. It was made to do so, for example, in the visionary and rhapsodic odes written during the high Romantic period after the late 18th century throughout Europe.

The lesson seems to be that every literary genre is adaptable to the allegorical search for multiplicity of meaning.

DIVERSITY OF MEDIA

In the broadest sense, allegorical procedures are linguistic. Allegory is a manipulation of the language of symbols. Verbally, this mode underwent a major shift in medium along with the shift from oral to written literature: allegories that had initially been delivered in oral form (Christ's parables, for example) were written down by scribes and then transcribed by subsequent generations. Much more remarkable transformations, however, take place when the verbal medium is replaced by nonverbal or partially verbal media.

The drama is the chief of such replacements. The enactment of myth in the beginning had close ties with religious ritual, and in the drama of Classical Greece both comedy and tragedy, by preserving ritual forms, lean toward allegory. Old Comedy, as represented by most of Aristophanes' plays, contains a curious blending of elements—allusions to men of the day, stories suggesting ideas other than the obvious literal sense, religious ceremony, parodies of the graver mysteries, personified abstractions, and stock types of character. Aeschylus's *Prometheus Bound* uses allegory for tragic ends, while Euripides' tragedies make a continuous interpretive commentary on the hidden meaning of the basic myths. Allegory is simplified in Roman drama, submitting heroic deeds to the control of the fickle, often malignant goddess Fortuna. Christian symbolism is responsible for the structure of the medieval morality plays, in which human dilemmas are presented through the conflicts of personified abstractions such as the "Virtues" and their "Vice" opponents. The allegory in Renaissance drama is often more atmospheric than structural—though even Shakespeare writes allegorical romances, such as *Cymbeline*, *Pericles*, and *The Winter's Tale* (and allowed his tragedy of *Coriolanus* to grow out of the "fable of the belly," which embodies a commonplace of Renaissance political wisdom and is recounted by one of the characters in the play). In 1598 Ben Jonson introduced the comedy of humours, which was dependent on the biological theory that the humours of the body (blood, phlegm, black bile, yellow bile) affect personality: in Jonson's play *Epicoene; or, The Silent Woman* (1609), the character Morose is possessed by the demon of ill humour. Comic allegory of this kind evolved into the Restoration comedy of manners and through that channel entered modern drama with Wilde, Shaw, and Pirandello. Ibsen, the master of realistic drama, himself used a free-style allegory in *Peer Gynt*, while the surrealism of modern dramatists—such as Ionesco, Genet, and Beckett in the Theatre of the Absurd—serves to reinforce the real meaning of their plays.

The degree to which the cinema has been allegorical in its methods has never been surveyed in detail. Any such survey would certainly reveal that many basic techniques in film montage builds up multiple layers of meaning. (Animated cartoons, too, continue the tradition of Aesopian fable.)

From time immemorial men have carved religious monuments and have drawn and painted sacred icons. Triumphal arches and chariots have symbolized glory and victory. Religious art makes wide use of allegory, both in its subject matter and in its imagery (such as the cross, the fish, the lamb). Even in poetry there can be an interaction of visual and verbal levels, sometimes achieved by patterning the stanza form. George Herbert's "Easter Wings," for instance, has two stanzas set out by the typographer to resemble the shape of a dove's wings. Such devices belong to the Renaissance tradition of the "emblem," which combines a motto with a simple symbolic picture (often a woodcut or engraving) and a concise explanation of the picture motto.

While allegory thrives on the visual, it has also been well able to embrace the empty form of pure mathematics. Number symbolism is very old: early Christian systems of cosmology were often based on the number three, referring to the doctrine of the Trinity (and in fact recalling earlier Hebraic and even Hellenic numerology). Musical symbolism has been discovered in the compositions of the 18th-century Baroque composers such as Johann Sebastian Bach. The most evanescent form of allegory, musical imagery and patterns, is also the closest to pure religious vision, because it merges the physical aspects of harmony (based on number) with the sublime and metaphysical effect on its hearers. The final extension of media occurs in the combination of spectacle, drama, dance, and music that is achieved by grand opera, which is at its most allegorical in the total artwork of Richard Wagner in the second half of the 19th century. His *Ring* cycle of operas is a complete mythography and allegory, with words and music making two levels of meaning and the whole unified by a type of musical emblem, which Wagner called the leitmotif.

ALLEGORY AND COSMOLOGY

The allegorical mode has been of major importance in representing the cosmos: the earliest Greek philosophers, for example, speculated on the nature of the universe in allegorical terms. In the Hebrew Bible's oblique interpretation of the universe, too, the world is seen as a symbolic system. The symbolic stories that explain the cosmos are ritualized to ensure that they encode a message. Held together by a system of magical causality, events in allegories are often surrounded by an occult atmosphere of charms, spells, talismans, genies, and magic rites. Science becomes science fiction or a fantastic setting blurs reality so that objects and events become metamorphically unstable. Allegorical fictions are often psychological dramas whose scene is the mind. Then their protagonists are personified mental drives. Symbolic climate is most prominent in romance, whose heroic quests project an aura of erotic mysticism, perfect courtesy, and moral fervour that creates a sublime heightening of tone and a picturesque sense of good order.

The cosmic and demonic character of allegorical thinking is most fully reflected in the period of its greatest vogue, the High Middle Ages. During this period poets and priests alike were able to read with increasingly elaborate allegorical technique until their methods perhaps overgrew themselves. A belief had been inherited in the Great Chain of Being, the Platonic principle of cosmic unity and fullness, according to which the lowest forms of being were linked with the highest in an ascending order. On the basis of this ladderlike conception were built systems of rising transcendency, starting from a material basis and rising to a spiritual pinnacle. The early Church Fathers sometimes used a threefold method of interpreting texts, encompassing literal, moral, and spiritual meanings. This was refined and commonly believed to have achieved its final form in the medieval allegorist's "fourfold theory of interpretation." This method also began every reading with a search for the literal sense of the passage. It moved up to a level of ideal interpretation in general, which was the allegorical level proper. (This was an affirmation that the true Christian believer was right to go beyond literal truth.) Still higher above the literal and the allegorical levels, the reader came to the tropological level, which told him where his moral duty lay. Finally, because Christian thought was apocalyptic and visionary, the fourfold method reached its apogee at the anagogic level, at which the reader was led to meditate on the final cosmic destiny of all Christians and of himself as a Christian hoping for eternal salvation.

While modern scholars have shown that such thinking played its part in the poetry of the Middle Ages and even the Italian poet Dante discussed the theological relations between his poems and such a method of exegesis, the main arena for the extreme elaboration of this allegory was in the discussion and the teaching of sacred Scriptures. As such, the fourfold method is of highest import, and it should be observed that it did not need to be applied in a rigid four-stage way. It could be reduced, and commonly was reduced, to a two-stage method of interpretation. Then the reader sought simply a literal and a spiritual meaning. But it could also be expanded. The passion for numerology, combined with the inner drive of allegory toward infinite extension, led to a proliferation of levels. If four levels were good, then five or eight or nine might be better.

DEVELOPMENT OF THE FABLE IN THE WEST

The origins of fable are lost in the mists of time. Fables appear independently in ancient Indian and Mediterranean cultures. The Western tradition begins effectively with Aesop (6th century BCE), of whom little or nothing is known for certain. Before him, however, the Greek poet Hesiod (8th century BCE) recounts the fable of the hawk and the nightingale, while fragments of similar tales survive in Archilochus, the 7th-century-BCE warrior-poet. Within 100 years of the first Aesopian inventions, the name of Aesop was firmly identified with the genre, as if he, not a collective folk, were its originator. Like the Greek philosopher Socrates, Aesop was reputed to have been ugly but wise. Legend connected him with the island of Samos. The historian Herodotus believed him to have been a slave.

Modern editions list approximately 200 "Aesop" fables, but there is no way of knowing who invented which tales or what their original occasions might have been. Aesop had already receded into legend when Demetrius of Phaleron, a rhetorician, compiled an edition of Aesop's fables in the 4th century BCE. The poetic resources of the form developed slowly. A versified Latin collection made by Phaedrus, a freed slave in the house of the Roman emperor Augustus, included fables invented by the poet, along with the traditional favourites, which he retold with many elaborations and considerable grace. (Phaedrus may also have been the first to write topically allusive fables, satirizing Roman politics.) A similar extension of range marks the work of the Hellenized Roman Babrius, writing in the 2nd century CE. Among the Classical authors who advanced upon Aesopian formulas may be named the Roman poet Horace, the Greek biographer Plutarch, and the great satirist Lucian of Samosata.

BEAST EPIC

In the Middle Ages, along with every other type of allegory, fable flourished. Toward the end of the 12th century, Marie de France made a collection of more than 100 tales, mingling beast fables with stories of Greek and Roman worthies. In another compilation, Christine de Pisan's Othéa manuscript illuminations provide keys to the interpretation of the stories and support the appended moral tag line. Expanded, the form of the fable could grow into what is called the beast epic, a lengthy, episodic animal story, replete with hero, villain, victim, and endless epic endeavour. (One motive for thus enlarging upon fable was the desire to parody epic grandeur: the beast epic mocks its own genre.) Most famous of these works is a 12th-century collection of related satiric tales called *Renard the Fox*, whose hero is a fox symbolizing human cunning. *Renard the Fox* includes the story of the fox and Chantecler (Chanticleer), a cock, a tale soon afterward told in German, Dutch, and English versions (in *The Canterbury Tales*, Geoffrey Chaucer took it as the basis for his "Nun's Priest's Tale"). Soon *Renard the Fox* had achieved universal favour throughout Europe. The Renaissance poet Edmund Spenser also made use of this kind of material; in his "Mother Hubberd's Tale," published in 1591, a fox and an ape go off to visit the court, only to discover that life is no better there than in the provinces. More sage and serious, John Dryden's poem of "The Hind and Panther" (1687) revived the beast epic as a framework for theological debate. Bernard de Mandeville's *Fable of the Bees* (first published 1705 as *The Grumbling Hive; or, Knaves Turn'd Honest*) illustrated the rapacious nature of humans in society through the age-old metaphor of the kingdom of the bees. In modern times, children's literature has made use of animal fable but often trivialized it. But the form has been taken seriously, as, for example, by the political satirist George Orwell, who, in his novel *Animal Farm* (1945), used it to attack totalitarianism.

GEORGE ORWELL

(b. 1903, Motihari, Bengal, India—d. Jan. 21, 1950, London, Eng.)

The British novelist, essayist, and critic George Orwell was born Eric Arthur Blair. Although he never entirely abandoned his original name, his nom de plume became so closely attached to him that few people other than relatives knew his real name. Instead of accepting a scholarship to a university, Orwell went to Burma to serve in the Indian Imperial Police (1922–27), an experience that changed him into a literary and political rebel. On returning to Europe, he lived in self-imposed poverty, gaining material for Down and Out in Paris and London *(1933), and became a socialist. He went to Spain to report on the Spanish Civil War and stayed to join the Republican militia. His war experiences, which gave him a lifelong dread of communism (he would later provide British intelligence services with lists of his fellow British communists), are recounted in* Homage to Catalonia *(1938). His novels typically portray a sensitive, conscientious, emotionally isolated individual at odds with an oppressive or dishonest social environment. His most famous works are the anti-Soviet satirical fable* Animal Farm *(1945) and* Nineteen Eighty-four *(1949), a dystopic vision of totalitarianism whose influence was widely felt in the postwar decades. His literary essays are also admired.*

INFLUENCE OF JEAN DE LA FONTAINE

The fable has usually been of limited length, however, and the form reached its zenith in 17th-century France, at the court of Louis XIV, especially in the work of Jean de La Fontaine. He published his *Fables* in two segments: the first, his initial volume of 1668, and the second, an accretion of "Books" of fables appearing over the next 25 years. The 1668 *Fables* follow the Aesopian pattern, but the later ones branch out to satirize the court, the bureaucrats attending it, the church, the rising bourgeoisie—indeed the whole human scene. La Fontaine's great theme was the folly of human vanity. He was a skeptic, not unkind but full of the sense of human frailty and ambition. His satiric themes permitted him an enlargement of poetic diction. He could be eloquent in mocking eloquence or in contrast use a severely simple style. (His range of tone and style was admirably reflected in a version of his works made by 20th-century American poet Marianne Moore.) La Fontaine's example gave new impetus to the genre throughout Europe, and during the Romantic period a vogue for Aesopian fable spread to Russia, where its great practitioner was Ivan Andreyevich Krylov. The 19th century saw the rise of literature written specifically for children, in whom fable found a new audience. Among the most celebrated authors who wrote for them are Lewis Carroll, Charles Kingsley, Rudyard Kipling, Kenneth Grahame,

Hilaire Belloc, and Beatrix Potter. There is no clear division between such authors and the "adult" fabulist, such as Hans Christian Andersen, Lewis Carroll, Oscar Wilde, Saint-Exupéry, or J.R.R. Tolkien. In the 20th century there were the outstanding *Fables for Our Time*, written by James Thurber and apparently directed toward an adult audience (although a sardonic parent might well read the *Fables* to his children).

DEVELOPMENT OF THE PARABLE IN THE WEST

In the West the conventions of parable were largely established through the New Testament record of the teachings of Jesus Christ. It contains a sufficient number of his parables, with their occasions, to show that to some extent his disciples were chosen as his initiates and followers because they "had ears to hear" the true meaning of his parables. (It has already been noted that the parable can be fully understood only by an elite, made up of those who can decipher its inner core of truth.) Despite a bias toward simplicity and away from rhetorical elaboration, the parable loses little in the way of allegorical richness: the speaker can exploit an enigmatic brevity that is akin to the style of presenting a complex riddle. Parable is thus an immensely useful preaching device: while theologians in the period of the early Christian church were developing glosses on Jesus' enigmatic stories, preachers were inventing their own to drive home straightforward lessons in good Christian conduct. For centuries, therefore, the model of parable that had been laid down by Jesus flourished on Sundays in churches all over the Western world. Pious tales were collected in handbooks: the *Gesta Romanorum*, the *Alphabet of Thales*, the *Book of the Knight of La Tour Landry*, and many more. Infinitely varied in subject matter, these exemplary tales used a plain but lively style, presenting stories of magicians, necromancers, prophets, chivalrous knights and ladies, great emperors—a combination bound to appeal to congregations, if not to theologians. An important offshoot of the parable and exemplary tale was the saint's life. Here, too, massive compilations were possible. The most celebrated was *The Golden Legend* of the 15th century, which included approximately 200 stories of saintly virtue and martyrdom.

As long as preaching remained a major religious activity, the tradition of parable preserved its strong didactic strain. Its more paradoxical aspect gained renewed lustre in theological and literary spheres when the 19th-century Danish philosopher Søren Kierkegaard began to use parables in his treatises on Christian faith and action. In *Fear and Trembling* he retold the story of Abraham and Isaac. In *Repetition* he treated episodes in his own life in the manner of parable. Such usage led to strange new literary forms of discourse, and his writing influenced, among others, the Austro-Czech novelist Franz Kafka and the French "absurdist" philosopher, novelist, and playwright Albert Camus. Kafka's parables, full of

doubt and anxiety, meditate on the infinite chasm between humanity and God and on the intermediate role played by the law. His vision, powerfully expressed in parables of novel length (*The Castle*, *The Trial*, *Amerika*), was one of the more enigmatic of the 20th century.

DEVELOPMENT OF THE ALLEGORY IN THE WEST

The early history of Western allegory is intricate and encompasses an interplay between the two prevailing world views—the Hellenic and the Judeo-Christian—as theologians and philosophers attempted to extract a higher meaning from these two bodies of traditional myth.

In terms of allegory, the Greco-Roman and Judeo-Christian cultures both have a common starting point: a creation myth. The book of Genesis in the Torah roughly parallels the story of the creation as told by the Greek poet Hesiod in his *Theogony* (and the later Roman version of the same event given in Ovid's *Metamorphoses*). The two traditions thus start with an adequate source of cosmic imagery, and both envisage a universe full of mysterious signs and symbolic strata. But thereafter the two cultures diverge. This is most apparent in the way that the style of the body of poetry attributed to Homer—the ancient Greek "Bible"—differs from the narrative in the Hebrew Bible. The Greek poet presented his heroes against an articulated narrative scene, a context full enough for the listener (and, later, the reader) to ignore secondary levels of significance. By contrast, the Jewish authors of the Hebrew Bible generally emptied the narrative foreground, leaving the reader to fill the scenic vacuum with a deepening, thickening allegorical interpretation.

Hebrew Bible (Old Testament)

The Hebrew Bible, including its prophetic books, has a core of historical record focusing on the trials of the tribes of Israel. In their own view an elect nation, the Israelites believe their history spells out a providential design. The Prophets understand the earliest texts, Genesis and Exodus, in terms of this providential scheme. Hebraic texts are interpreted as typological: that is, they view serious myth as a theoretical history in which all events are types—portents, foreshadowing the destiny of the chosen people. Christian exegesis (the critical interpretation of Scripture) inherits the same approach.

Typological allegory looks for hidden meaning in the lives of actual individuals who, as types or figures of later historical persons, serve a prophetic function by prefiguring those later persons. Adam, for example (regarded as a historical person), is thought to prefigure Jesus in his human aspect, Joshua to prefigure the victorious militant Jesus. This critical approach to Scripture is helped by the fact of monotheism, which makes it easier to detect the workings of a divine plan. The splendours of nature hymned in the Psalms provide a gloss upon the "glory of God." The Law (the Torah) structures the social aspect of sacred history and, as reformulated by Christ, provides the chief link between Old and New Testaments. Christ appeals to the authority of "the Law and the Prophets" but assumes the ultimate prophetic role himself, creating the New Law and the New Covenant—or Testament—with the same one God of old.

The Greeks

Hellenic tradition after Homer stands in sharp contrast to this concentration on the fulfilling of a divine plan. The analytic, essentially scientific histories of Herodotus and Thucydides precluded much confident belief in visionary providence. The Greeks rather believed history to be structured in cycles, as distinct from the more purposive linearity of Jewish historicism.

Nevertheless, allegory did find a place in the Hellenic world. Its main arena was in philosophic speculation, centring on the interpretation of Homer. Some philosophers attacked and others defended the Homeric mythology. A pious defense argued that the stories—about the monstrous love affairs of the supreme god Zeus, quarrels of the other Olympian gods, scurrility of the heroes, and the like—implied something beyond their literal sense. The defense sometimes took a scientific, physical form. In this case, Homeric turmoil was seen as reflecting the conflict between the elements. Or

Homer was moralized; the goddess Pallas Athene, for example, who in physical allegory stood for the ether, in moral allegory was taken to represent reflective wisdom because she was born out of the forehead of her father, Zeus. Moral and physical interpretation is often intermingled.

Plato, the Idealist philosopher, occupies a central position with regard to Greek allegory. His own myths imply that our world is a mere shadow of the ideal and eternal world of forms (the Platonic ideas), which has real, independent existence, and that the true philosopher must therefore be an allegorist in reverse. He must regard phenomena—things and events—as a text to be interpreted upward, giving them final value only insofar as they reveal, however obscurely, their ideal reality in the world of forms. Using this inverted allegorical mode, Plato attacked Homeric narrative, whose beauty beguiles men into looking away from the truly philosophic life. Plato went further. He attacked other fashionable philosophic allegorists because they did not lead up to the reality but limited speculation to the sphere of moral and physical necessity. Platonic allegory envisaged the system of the universe as an ascending ladder of forms, a Great Chain of Being, and was summed up in terms of myth in his *Timaeus*. Plato and Platonic thought became, through the influence of this and other texts on Plotinus (died 269/270) and through him on Porphyry (died *c.* 304), a pagan mainstay of later Christian allegory. Medieval translations of Dionysius the Areopagite (before 6th century CE) were equally influential descendants of Platonic vision.

A second and equally influential Hellenic tradition of allegory was created by the Stoic philosophers, who held that the local gods of the Mediterranean peoples were signs of a divinely ordered natural destiny. Stoic allegory thus emphasized the role of fate, which, because all were subject to it, could become a common bond between peoples of different nations. A later aspect of moral exegesis in the Stoic manner was the notion that myths of the gods really represent, in elevated form, the actions of great men. In the 2nd century BCE, under Stoic influence, the Sicilian writer Euhemerus argued that theology had an earthly source. His allegory of history was the converse of Jewish typology—which found the origin of the divine in the omnipotence of the one God—for Euhemerus found the origin of mythological gods in human kings and heroes, divinized by their peoples. His theories enjoyed at least an aesthetic revival during the Renaissance.

BLENDING OF RIVAL SYSTEMS: THE MIDDLE AGES

At the time of the birth of Jesus, ideological conditions within the Mediterranean world accelerated the mingling of Hellenic and Jewish traditions. Philo Judaeus laid the groundwork. Clement of Alexandria and Origen followed him. The craft of allegorical syncretism—that is, making rival systems accommodate one another through the transformation of their disparate elements—was already a developed art by the time St. Paul and the author of The Gospel According to John wove the complex strands of the Judeo-Christian synthesis. Over centuries of quarrelling, the timeless philosophy of the Greek allegorists was accommodated to the time-laden typology of the Hebrew Prophets and their Christian successors and at length achieved a hybrid unity that permitted great allegories of Western Christendom to be written.

As a hybrid method, allegory could draw on two archetypal story lines: the war and the quest of Homer's *Iliad* and *Odyssey*, which was paralleled by the struggles and wanderings of the children of Israel. Throughout the Middle Ages the figure of the wandering Aeneas (who, in the second half of Virgil's Latin epic, *Aeneid*, fought bloody battles) was seen as a type in a system of hidden Christianity. Virgil's fourth *Eclogue*, a prophetic vision of the birth of a child who would usher in the "golden age," was read as a prophecy of the birth of Jesus. Seen by many Christian commentators as the ideal allegorist, Virgil himself was hailed as a proto-Christian prophet. The blending of rival systems of allegory from widely assorted cultures became the rule for later allegory. Adapting the Latin writer Apuleius's fable of Cupid and Psyche, Edmund Spenser combined its elements with ancient Middle Eastern lore, Egyptian wisdom, and dashes of critical interpretation of the Hebrew Bible to convert the enclosed garden of the biblical Song of Solomon into the gardens of Adonis in *The Faerie Queene*, Book III. The pagan gods survived unharmed throughout the Middle Ages if wearing Christian costumes, because Christians were taught that pagan worthies could be read as figures of Christian rulers. The labours of Hercules, for instance, stood for the wanderings and trials of all Christians. The Hellenic theme of heroic warfare took a Christianized form, available to allegory, when in the 4th century the poet and hymn writer Prudentius internalized war as the inner struggle of the Christian, suspended between virtue and vice. For complete triumph in explaining the significance of the world, Christianity needed one further element: a world-historical theory large enough to contain all other theories of meaning. This it found in the belief that God was the author of the world. His creation wrote the world. The world, read as a text, provided a platform for transforming the piecemeal, post-Classical syncretism into some semblance of order. Firmly established in the West, Christianity, for all its strains of discord, slowly achieved a measure of coherence. St. Thomas Aquinas could write its *Summa*. Theocentric, authoritarian, spiritualist, and word-oriented, the medieval model of allegory lent itself to the creation of the most wonderful of all allegorical poems, Dante's *Divine Comedy*, completed shortly before his death in 1321.

Before this could happen, however, the Christian worldview was subjected to an important pressure during the 12th century. It may be called the pressure to externalize. Alain de Lille, Bernard of Sylvestris, John of Salisbury, and other forerunners of the movement known as European humanism "discovered" nature. Delighting in the wonders of God's cosmic text, they brought theological speculation down to earth. Romances of love and chivalry placed heroes and heroines against the freshness of spring. Everywhere nature shone, sparkling with the beauty of earthly life. The externalization and naturalizing of Christian belief flowers most obviously in *The Romance of the Rose*, begun in the 13th century by Guillaume de Lorris and completed, in vastly complicated form, by Jean de Meun. The *Romance* personifies the experiences of courtly love, recounting the pursuit of an ideal lady by an ideal knight, set in an enclosed garden and castle, which permits Guillaume to dwell on the beauty of nature. With Jean de Meun the interest in nature is made explicit, and the poem ends in a series of lengthy digressive discourses, several of them spoken by Dame Nature herself. In medieval English poetry, this same love of spring and seasonal pleasures is apparent everywhere—certainly in the poems of Geoffrey Chaucer, who, besides creating several allegories of his own, translated *The Romance of the Rose* into English.

Dante's *Divine Comedy* has physical immediacy and contains an immense amount of historical detail. He anchors his poem in a real world, accepting Christian typology as historical fact and adopting an ordered system of cosmology (based on the number three, proceeding from the Trinity). Dante's passion for numerology does not, however, block a closeness to nature that had perhaps not been equalled in poetry since Homer. He enfolds Classical thought into his epic by making Virgil one of its main protagonists—again to prefigure Christian heroism. Perhaps only William Langland, the author of *The Vision of Piers Plowman*, could be said to rival Dante's cosmic range. *Piers Plowman* is a simpler apocalyptic vision than the *Comedy*, but it has an existential immediacy, arising from its concern for the poor, which gives it great natural power.

THE RENAISSANCE

Romance and romantic forms provide the main vehicle for the entrance of allegory into the literature of the Renaissance period. The old Arthurian legends carry a new sophistication and polish in the epics of the Italians Matteo Boiardo, Ludovico Ariosto, and Torquato Tasso and in the work of Edmund Spenser. By interlacing several simultaneous stories in one larger narrative, the literary technique known as *entrelacement* allowed digression—yet kept an ebbing, flowing kind of unity—while presenting opportunities for moral and ironic commentary. But although the forms and themes of romance were medieval in origin, the new age was forced to accommodate altered values. The Middle Ages had externalized the Christian model. The

Renaissance now internalized it, largely by emphasizing the centrality of human understanding. This process of internalization had begun slowly. In rough outline it can be discerned in the belief that biological humours affected personality, in the adaptations of Platonic Idealism from which arose a new emphasis on imagination, in the rise of an introspective, soliloquizing drama in England. It can further be discerned in the gradual adoption of more self-conscious theories of being: Shakespeare's Hamlet, finding himself by thinking out his situation, prefigures the first modern philosopher, René Descartes, whose starting point for argument was "I think, therefore I am." Christopher Marlowe's characterization of Dr. Faustus epitomizes the new age. Pursuing power in the form of knowledge, he is led to discover the demons of allegory within himself. He is an essential figure for later European literature, archetypal in Germany for both Goethe and Thomas Mann and influential everywhere.

THE MODERN PERIOD

With the Baroque and Neoclassical periods, allegory began to turn away from cosmology and toward rhetorical ambiguity. John Milton allegorized sin and death in his epic poem *Paradise Lost*, but allegory for him seems chiefly to lie in the ambiguous diction and syntax employed in the poem. Instead of flashing allegorical emblems before the reader, Milton generates a questioning attitude that searches out allegory more as a mysterious form than a visible content. His central allegorical theme is perhaps the analogy he draws between poetry, music, and ideas of cosmic order. This theme, which generates allegory at once, recurs in later English poetry right up to T.S. Eliot's *Four Quartets* (1943).

The social and religious attitudes of the Enlightenment in the 18th century could be expressed coolly and without ambiguity—and thus there was little need for spiritual allegory in the period's literature. Oblique symbolism was used mainly for satiric purposes. John Dryden and Alexander Pope were masters of verse satire, Jonathan Swift of prose satire. Voltaire and the French writers of the Enlightenment similarly employed a wit whose aim was to cast doubt on inherited pieties and attitudes. A new vogue for the encyclopaedia allowed a close, critical commentary on the ancient myths, but the criticism was rationalist and opposed to demonology.

Under such conditions the allegorical mode might have dried up entirely. Yet the new Romantic age of the late 18th and early 19th centuries revived the old cosmologies once more, and poetic forms quickly reflected the change, with the Romantic poets and their precursors (Blake, William Collins, Edward Young, Thomas Gray, and others) managing to reinstate the high destiny of the allegorical imagination. The Romantics went back to nature. Poets took note of exactly

Writers of the Romantic period had a keen appreciation for the beauties of nature, finding in it both creative inspiration and a context in which to examine personal emotion. Shutterstock.com

what they saw when they went out walking, and their awareness of nature and its manifestations found its way into their poetry. Appropriate poetic forms for expressing this sensibility tended to be open, rhapsodic, and autobiographical—qualities notably present in William Wordsworth and in Samuel Taylor Coleridge, for example. Percy Bysshe Shelley is the most strikingly allegorical of English Romantics. He not only followed the Platonic tradition of Spenser and the Renaissance—with ode, elegy, and brief romance—but he also invented forms

of his own, such as *Epipsychidion*, a rhapsodic meditation, and he was working on a great Dantesque vision, *The Triumph of Life*, when he died. Visionary masterpieces came from Germany, where Novalis and Friedrich Hölderlin hymned the powers of nature in odes of mythic overtone and resonance. French Romanticism, merging gradually with the theory and practice of the Symbolist movement (dealing in impressions and intuitions rather than in descriptions), in turn followed the same path. The pantheist cosmology of Victor Hugo, the central writer of the somewhat delayed French Romantic movement, created an allegory of occult forces and demonic hero worship. It is fair to say that, in its most flexible and visionary forms, allegory flourished throughout the Romantic period.

There also developed a novelistic mode of allegory by which prose authors brought fate, necessity, the demonic, and the cosmological into their narratives. Émile Zola used a theory of genetics, Charles Dickens the idea of ecological doom, Leo Tolstoy the belief in historical destiny, and Fyodor Dostoyevsky the fatalism of madness and neurosis. Nikolay Gogol revived the art of the grotesque, picturing absurdities in the scene of tsarist Russia. Even the arch-naturalist playwright Anton Chekhov made an emblem of the cherry orchard and the sea gull in his plays of those titles.

However its dates are established, the modern period is exceedingly complex in its mythmaking. Psychoanalytic theory has been both a critical and a creative resource. Modern allegory has remained internalized in the Renaissance tradition. In the free play of American letters, where Nathaniel Hawthorne, Herman Melville, Edgar Allan Poe, and Henry James (particularly in his later novels) had essayed an allegorical mode, the future of its use is uncertain. T.S. Eliot's enigmatic style in a long poem, "Ash Wednesday," may be related to his search for a Dantesque dramatic style, for which he also tried in plays, most obviously *Murder in the Cathedral* (a morality play) and *The Cocktail Party* (a philosophic farce). More clearly popular authors such as George Orwell and William Golding used the most familiar allegorical conventions. D.H. Lawrence shaped novels such as *The Plumed Serpent* to project a thematic, cultural polemic. W.H. Auden's operatic librettos reflect once more the allegorical potential of this mixture of media.

Modern allegory has in fact no set pattern or model, although Surrealism has provided a dominant style of discontinuous fragmentary expression. The only rule seems to be that there is no rule. Science fiction, an ancient field dating back at least to the earliest philosophers of Greece, has set no limits on the speculations it will entertain. The allegorical author now even questions the allegorical process itself, criticizing the very notions of cosmos, demon, and magic. It may be that modern allegory has completed a vast circle begun by the first conflict between ways of interpreting myth, as revealed in Homer and the Jewish prophets.

ALLEGORICAL LITERATURE IN THE EAST

The oral tradition of fable in India may well predate that of Greece, having origins that may date as far back as the 5th century BCE. Undoubtedly there was mutual influence from very early times, for indirect contacts between Greece and India (by trade routes) had existed long before the time of Alexander the Great.

China and Japan also have notable examples of the form.

INDIA

The fable was apparently first used in India as a vehicle of Buddhist instruction. Some of the *Jatakas*, birth stories of the Buddha, which relate some of his experiences in previous animal incarnations, resemble Greek fables and are used to point a moral. They may date from as far back as the 5th century BCE, though the written records are much later.

The most important compilation is *The Fables of Bidpai*, or the *Panchatantra* ("Five Chapters"), a Sanskrit collection of beast fables. The original has not survived, but it has been transmitted (via a lost Pahlavi version) as the mid-8th-century Arabic *Kalīlah wa Dimnah*. Kalīlah and Dimnah are two jackals, counselors to the lion king, and the work is a frame story containing numerous fables designed to teach political wisdom or cunning. From the Arabic this was translated into many languages, including Hebrew, which rendition John of Capua used to make a Latin version in the 13th century. This, the *Directorium humanae vitae* ("Guide for Human Life"), was the chief means by which Eastern fables became current in Europe. In *The Fables of Bidpai*, animals act like humans in animal form, and little attention is paid to their supposed animal characteristics. It is in this respect that they differ most from the fables of Aesop, in which animals behave as animals.

CHINA

Chinese philosophers from the Qin dynasty (221–206 BCE) onward often used extended metaphors (from which fable is the logical development) to make their points. This is believed to reflect the fact that, as "realistic" thinkers, the Chinese generally did not favour more abstract argument. Thus simple allegory helped to stimulate audience interest and to increase the force of an argument. A century earlier, Mencius, a Confucian philosopher, had used the following little allegory in illustrating his theory that an effort has to be made if natural goodness is to be recovered:

> *A man will begin searching when his dog or chicken is missing; but he does not go searching for the good character he was born with after it is lost. Is this not regrettable?*

The same writer also used a parable to bring home his point that mental training could not be hurried, but was a gradual process:

> *A man in Song sowed seeds in a field. The seedlings grew so slowly, however, that one day he took a walk through the field pulling at each one of the seedlings. On returning home he announced that he was exhausted, but that he had helped the seedlings'*

growth. His son, hurrying to the field, found the seedlings dead.

Tales such as this were often borrowed from folklore, but others were probably original creations, including a striking story that opens the *Zhuangzi*, a summa of Daoist thought. It makes the point that ordinary people frequently deplore the actions of a man of genius because they are unable to understand his vision, which is not answerable to the laws of "common sense":

A giant fish, living at the northern end of the world, transformed itself into a bird so that it could make the arduous flight to the southernmost sea. Smaller birds, measuring his ambition against their own capabilities, laughed at the impossibility of it.

But the full development of fable, as it is understood in the West, was hindered by the fact that Chinese ways of thinking prohibited them from accepting the notion of animals that thought and behaved as humans. Actual events from the past were thought to be more instructive than fictitious stories, and this led to the development of a large body of legendary tales and supernatural stories. Between the 4th and 6th centuries, however, Chinese Buddhists adapted fables from Buddhist India in a work known as *Bore jing*, and they also began to make use of traditional Chinese stories that could further understanding of Buddhist doctrines.

JAPAN

In Japan the *Kojiki* (712; "Records of Ancient Matters") and the *Nihon shoki* (8th century; "Chronicles of Japan"), both official histories of Japan, were studded with fables, many of them on the theme of a small intelligent animal getting the better of a large stupid one. The same is true of the *fudoki* (local gazetteers dating from 713 and later). The form reached its height in the Kamakura period (1192–1333). Toward the end of the Muromachi period (1338–1573), Jesuit missionaries introduced the fables of Aesop to Japan, and the influence of these can be traced in stories written between then and the 19th century.

FABLE, ALLEGORY, AND PARABLE: TERMS AND CONCEPTS

Two representative genres related to fable, allegory, and parable are the bestiary and the dream allegory. Both were prevalent in the Middle Ages, though one modern version of the former type is *The Book of Imaginary Beings* by Jorge Luis Borges.

BESTIARY

The bestiary is a literary genre of the European Middle Ages consisting of a collection of stories, each based on a description of certain qualities of an animal, plant, or inanimate object (such as a stone). These stories presented Christian allegories for moral and religious instruction and admonition.

The numerous manuscripts of medieval bestiaries ultimately are derived from the Greek *Physiologus*, a text compiled by an unknown author before the middle of the 2nd century CE. It consists of stories based on natural science as it was then understood by someone called Physiologus (Latin meaning "Naturalist"), about whom nothing further is known, and from the compiler's own religious ideas.

The *Physiologus* consists of 48 sections, each dealing with one creature, plant, or stone and each linked to a biblical text. It probably originated in Alexandria and, in some manuscripts, is ascribed to one or other of the 4th-century bishops Basil and Epiphanius, though it must be older. The stories may derive from popular fables about animals and plants. Some Indian influence is clear—for example, in the introduction of the elephant and of the Peridexion tree, actually called Indian in the *Physiologus*. India may also be the source of the story of the unicorn, which became very popular in the West.

The popularity of the *Physiologus*, which circulated in the early Middle Ages almost as widely as the Bible, is clear from the existence of many early translations. It was translated into Latin (first in the 4th or 5th century), Ethiopian, Syriac, Arabic, Coptic, and Armenian. Early translations from the Greek also were made into Georgian and into Slavic languages.

Translations were made from Latin into Anglo-Saxon before 1000. In the 11th century an otherwise unknown Thetbaldus made a metrical Latin version of 13 sections of the *Physiologus*. This was translated, with alterations, in the only surviving Middle English *Bestiary*, dating from the 13th century. It, and other lost Middle English and Anglo-Norman versions, influenced the development of the beast fable. Early translations into Flemish and German influenced the satiric beast epic. Bestiaries were popular in France and the Low Countries in the 13th century, and a 14th-century French *Bestiaire d'amour* applied the allegory to love. An Italian translation of the *Physiologus*, known as the *Bestiario toscano*, was made in the 13th century.

Many medieval bestiaries were illustrated, and the earliest known of these manuscripts is from the 9th century. Illustrations accompanying other medieval manuscripts are often based on illustrations in the *Physiologus*, as are sculptures and carvings (especially in churches) and frescoes and paintings well into the Renaissance period.

The religious sections of the *Physiologus* (and of the bestiaries that were derived from it) are concerned primarily with abstinence and chastity. They also warn against heresies. The frequently abstruse stories to which these admonitions were added were often based on

Decorated initial for the story about the unicorn in a late 12th-century Latin bestiary (Harley MS. 4751, folio 6v); in the British Library. Reproduced by permission of the British Library Board

misconceptions about the facts of natural history (e.g., the stag is described as drowning its enemy, the snake, in its den; and the ichneumon as crawling into the jaws of the crocodile and then devouring its intestines). Many attributes that have become traditionally associated with real or mythical creatures derive from the bestiaries (e.g., the phoenix's burning itself to be born again, the parental love of the pelican, and the hedgehog's collecting its stores for the winter with its prickles). These have become part of folklore and have passed into literature and art, influencing the development of allegory, symbolism, and imagery, though their source in the bestiary may be frequently overlooked.

DREAM ALLEGORY

An allegorical tale presented in the narrative framework of a dream is called a dream allegory, or dream vision. Especially popular in the Middle Ages, the device made more acceptable the fantastic and sometimes bizarre world of personifications and symbolic objects characteristic of medieval allegory. Well-known examples of the dream allegory include the first part of *Roman de la rose* (13th century); Chaucer's *Book of the Duchess* (1369/70); *Pearl* (late 14th century); *Piers Plowman* (c. 1362–c. 1387), attributed to William Langland; William Dunbar's *The Thistle and the Rose* and *The Golden Targe* (early 16th century); and Bunyan's *Pilgrim's Progress*.

EMBLEM BOOK

The emblem book is a collection of symbolic pictures, usually accompanied by mottoes and expositions in verse and often also by a prose commentary. Derived from the medieval allegory and bestiary, the emblem book developed as a pictorial-literary genre in 16th-century Italy and became popular throughout western Europe in the 17th century.

The father of emblem literature was the 16th-century Italian lawyer and humanist Andrea Alciato, whose *Emblemata* (1531; written in Latin) appeared in translation and in more than 150 editions. The Plantin press specialized in emblem literature, publishing at Antwerp in 1564 the *Emblemata* of the Hungarian physician and historian Johannes Sambucus; in 1565, that of the Dutch physician Hadrianus Junius (Adriaen de Jonghe); and, at Leiden, the early English emblem book, Geoffrey Whitney's *Choice of Emblemes* (1585), an anthology of emblems from Alciato, Junius, and others. English emblem books were either printed in the Netherlands or made by combining English text with foreign engravings, as in the English edition of the *Amorum Emblemata, Figuris Aeneis Incisa* (1608) of Octavius Vaenius (Otto van Veen), an important early Dutch emblem book.

The Netherlands became the centre of the vogue. Vaenius's *Amorum Emblemata* presented metaphors from Ovid and other Latin erotic poets with pictorial representation. The Dutch emblem books were widely translated, plagiarized, and reprinted with different text or engravings. From polyglot editions, begun by Heinsius's verses in Dutch and Latin and later in French, publication of emblem books became an international enterprise, and books of love emblems were exchanged by lovers and formed pretty little encyclopaedias of those "questions of love" that had been the erudite pastime of the academies throughout the Renaissance. Meanwhile, the Dutch emblematists had turned to religious emblems, serving Calvinists as well as Jesuits, who used them for propaganda. In Vaenius's *Amoris Divini Emblemata* (1615), quotations from St. Augustine replace those of Ovid, and Cupid reappears as the soul's preceptor.

The only English emblem book to achieve widespread popularity was the *Emblemes* (1635) of Francis Quarles, with plates from the *Pia Desideria* and from *Typus Mundi* (1627), popular Jesuit emblem books.

EXEMPLUM

An exemplum (plural exempla) is a short tale originally incorporated by a medieval preacher into his sermon to emphasize a moral or illustrate a point of doctrine. Fables, folktales, and legends were gathered into collections, such as *Exempla* (c. 1200) by Jacques de Vitry, for the use of preachers. Such exempla often provided the germ or plot for medieval secular tales in verse or prose. The influence of exempla can be seen in Geoffrey Chaucer's *Canterbury Tales* (1387–1400) in the haunting "Pardoner's Tale."

PERSONIFICATION

Personification is the attribution of human characteristics to an abstract quality, animal, or inanimate object. An example of this figure of speech is "The Moon doth with delight / Look round her when the heavens are bare" (William Wordsworth, "Ode: Intimations of Immortality from Recollections of Early Childhood," 1807). Another is "Death lays his icy hand on kings" (James Shirley, "The Glories of Our Blood and State," 1659). Personification has been used in European poetry since Homer and is particularly common in allegory. For example, the medieval morality play *Everyman* (c. 1500) and the Christian prose allegory *Pilgrim's Progress* (1678) by John Bunyan contain characters such as Death, Fellowship, Knowledge, Giant Despair, Sloth, Hypocrisy, and Piety. Personification became almost an automatic mannerism in 18th-century Neoclassical poetry, as exemplified by these lines from Thomas Gray's "An Elegy Written in a Country Church Yard":

> *Here rests his head upon the lap of earth*
> *A youth to Fortune and to Fame unknown:*
> *Fair science frowned not on his humble birth,*
> *And Melancholy marked him for her own.*

PROVERB

Proverbs are succinct and pithy sayings in general use, expressing commonly held ideas and beliefs. They are part of every spoken language and are related to such other forms of folk literature as riddles and fables that have originated in oral tradition. Comparisons of proverbs found in various parts of the world show that the same kernel of wisdom may be gleaned under different cultural conditions and languages. The biblical proverb "An eye for an eye, a tooth for a tooth," for example, has an equivalent among the Nandi of East Africa: "A goat's hide buys a goat's hide, and a gourd, a gourd." Both form part of codes of behaviour and exemplify the proverb's use for the transmission of tribal wisdom and rules of conduct. Often, the same proverb may be found in many variants. In Europe this may result from the international currency of Latin proverbs in the Middle Ages. The proverb known in English as "A bird in the hand is worth two in the bush" originated in medieval Latin, and variants of it are found in Romanian, Italian, Portuguese, Spanish, German, and Icelandic. Many biblical proverbs have parallels in ancient Greece. "A soft answer turneth away wrath" was known to Aeschylus as well as to Solomon, and "Physician, heal thyself" (Luke 4:23) was also known to the Greeks.

Certain stylistic similarities have been found in proverbs from the same part of the world. Middle Eastern proverbs, for instance, make frequent use of hyperbole and colourful pictorial forms of expression. Typical is the proverbial Egyptian description of a lucky man: "Fling him in the Nile and he will come up with a fish in his mouth." Classical Latin proverbs are typically pithy and terse (e.g., *Praemonitus, praemunitis*; "forewarned is forearmed"). Many languages use rhyme, alliteration, and wordplay in their proverbs, as in the Scots "Many a mickle makes a muckle" ("Many small things make one big thing"). Folk proverbs are commonly illustrated with homely imagery—household objects, farm animals and pets, and the events of daily life.

Proverbs come from many sources, most of them anonymous and all of them difficult to trace. Their first appearance in literary form is often an adaptation of an oral saying. Abraham Lincoln is said to have invented the saying about not swapping horses in the middle of the river, but he may only have used a proverb already current. Popular usage sometimes creates new proverbs from old ones. For example, the biblical proverb, "The love of money is the root of all evil" has become "Money is the root of all evil." Many still-current proverbs refer to obsolete customs. The common "If the cap fits, wear it," for instance, refers to the medieval fool's cap. Proverbs sometimes embody superstitions ("Marry in May, repent alway"), weather lore ("Rain before seven, fine before eleven"), or medical advice ("Early to bed, early to rise, / Makes a man healthy, wealthy, and wise").

Most literate societies have valued their proverbs and collected them for posterity. There are ancient Egyptian collections dating from as early as 2500 BCE. Sumerian inscriptions give grammatical rules in proverbial form. Proverbs were used in ancient China for ethical instruction, and the Vedic writings of India used them to expound philosophical ideas. The biblical book of Proverbs, traditionally associated with Solomon, actually includes sayings from earlier compilations.

One of the earliest English proverb collections is the so-called *Proverbs of Alfred* (c. 1150–80), containing religious and moral precepts. The use of proverbs in monasteries to teach novices Latin, in schools of rhetoric, and in sermons, homilies, and didactic works made them widely known and led to their preservation in manuscripts.

The use of proverbs in literature and oratory was at its height in England in the 16th and 17th centuries. John Heywood wrote a dialogue in proverbs (1546; later enlarged) and Michael Drayton a sonnet. In the 16th century a speech in proverbs was made in the House of Commons.

In North America the best-known use of proverbs is probably in *Poor Richard's*, an almanac published annually between 1732 and 1757 by Benjamin Franklin. Many of Poor Richard's sayings were traditional European proverbs reworked by Franklin and given an American context when appropriate.

The study of folklore in the 20th century brought renewed interest in the proverb as a reflection of folk culture.

REYNARD THE FOX

Reynard the Fox is the hero of several medieval European cycles of versified animal tales that satirize contemporary human society. Though he is sly, amoral, cowardly, and self-seeking, he is still a sympathetic hero, whose cunning is a necessity for survival. He symbolizes the triumph of craft over brute strength, usually personified by Isengrim, the greedy and dull-witted wolf. Some cyclic stories collected around him, such as the wolf or bear fishing with his tail through a hole in the ice, are found all over the world. Others, like the sick lion cured by the wolf's skin, derive by oral transmission from Greco-Roman sources. The cycle arose in the area between Flanders and Germany in the 10th and 11th centuries, when clerks began to forge Latin beast epics out of popular tales. The name "Ysengrimus" was first used as the title of a poem in Latin elegiac couplets by Nivard of Ghent in 1152, and some stories were soon recounted in French octosyllabic couplets. The Middle High German poem "Fuchs Reinhard" (c. 1180) by Heinrich (der Glîchesaere?), a masterpiece of 2,000 lines, freely adapted from a lost French original, is another early version of the cycle.

The main literary tradition of Reynard the Fox, however, descends from the extant French "branches" of the *Roman de Renart* (about 30 in number, totaling nearly 40,000 lines of verse). These French branches are probably elaborations of the same kernel poem that was used by Heinrich in the earlier German version. The facetious portrayal of rustic life, the camel as a papal legate speaking broken French, the animals riding on horses and recounting elaborate dreams, suggest the atmosphere of 13th-century France and foreshadow the more sophisticated "Nun's Priest's Tale" of Geoffrey Chaucer. Because of the popularity of these tales the nickname *renard* has replaced the old word *goupil* ("fox") throughout France. The Flemish adaptations of these French tales by Aenout and Willem (*c.* 1250) were the sources of the Dutch and Low German prose manuscripts and chapbooks, which in turn were used by the English printer William Caxton and subsequent imitators down to J.W. von Goethe's *Reineke Fuchs* (1794).

CHAPTER 4

ROMANCE

Romance is a literary form, usually characterized by its treatment of chivalry, that came into being in France in the mid-12th century. It had antecedents in many prose works from classical antiquity (the so-called Greek romances), but as a distinctive genre it was developed in the context of the aristocratic courts of such patrons as Eleanor of Aquitaine.

The Old French word *romanz* originally meant "the speech of the people," or "the vulgar tongue," from a popular Latin word, *Romanice*, meaning written in the vernacular (in contrast to the written form of literary Latin). Its meaning then shifted from the language in which the work was written to the work itself. Thus, an adaptation of Geoffrey of Monmouth's *Historia regum Britanniae* (1135–39; *History of the Kings of Britain*), made by the Anglo-Norman Wace of Jersey in 1155, was known as *Li Romanz de Brut*, while an anonymous adaptation (of slightly later date) of Virgil's *Aeneid* was known as *Li Romanz d'Enéas*. It is difficult to tell whether in such cases *li romanz* still meant "the French version" or had already come to mean "the story." It soon specialized in the latter sense, however, and was applied to narrative compositions similar in character to those imitated from Latin sources but totally different in origin. And, as the nature of these compositions changed, the word itself acquired an increasingly wide spectrum of meanings. In modern French a *roman* is just a novel, whatever its content and structure, whereas in modern English the word *romance* (derived from

Old French *romanz*) can mean either a medieval narrative composition or a love affair, or, again, a story about a love affair, generally one of a rather idyllic or idealized type, sometimes marked by strange or unexpected incidents and developments; and "to romance" has come to mean "to make up a story that has no connection with reality."

For a proper understanding of these changes it is essential to know something of the history of the literary form to which, since the Middle Ages, the term has been applied. The account that follows is intended to elucidate historically some of the ways in which the word is used in English and in other European languages.

THE COMPONENT ELEMENTS

The romances of love, chivalry, and adventure produced in 12th-century France have analogues elsewhere, notably in what are sometimes known as the Greek romances—narrative works in prose by Greek writers from the 1st century BCE to the 3rd century CE. The first known, the fragmentary Ninus romance, in telling the story of the love of Ninus, mythical founder of Nineveh, anticipates the medieval *roman d'antiquité*. A number of works by writers of the 2nd and 3rd centuries CE—Chariton, Xenophon of Ephesus, Heliodorus, Achilles Tatius, and Longus—introduce a theme that was to reappear in the *roman d'aventure*: that of faithful lovers parted by accident or design and reunited only after numerous

adventures. Direct connection, however, can be proved only in the case of the tale of *Apollonius of Tyre*, presumably deriving from a lost Greek original but known through a 3rd- or 4th-century Latin version. This too is a story of separation, adventure, and reunion, and, like the others (except for Longus's pastoral *Daphnis and Chloë*), it has a quasi-historical setting. It became one of the most popular and widespread stories in European literature during the Middle Ages and later provided Shakespeare with the theme of *Pericles*.

STYLE AND SUBJECT MATTER

But the real debt of 12th-century romance to classical antiquity was incurred in a sphere outside that of subject matter. During the present century, scholars have laid ever-increasing emphasis on the impact of late classical antiquity upon the culture of medieval Europe, especially on that of medieval France. In particular, it is necessary to note the place that rhetoric (the systematic study of oratory) had assumed in the educational system of the late Roman Empire. Originally conceived as part of the training for public speaking, essential for the lawyer and politician, it had by this time become a literary exercise, the art of adorning or expanding a set theme: combined with grammar and enshrined in the educational system inherited by the Christian Church, rhetoric became an important factor in the birth of romance. Twelfth-century romance was, at the outset, the creation of "clerks"—professional writers who had been trained in grammar (that is to say, the study of the Latin language and the interpretation of Latin authors) and in rhetoric in the cathedral schools. They were skilled in the art of exposition, by which a subject matter was not only developed systematically but also given such meaning as the author thought appropriate. The "romance style" was, apparently, first used by the authors of three *romans d'antiquité*, all composed in the period 1150–65: *Roman de Thebes*, an adaptation of the epic *Thebaïs* by the late Latin poet Statius; *Roman d'Enéas*, adapted from Virgil's *Aeneid*; and *Roman de Troie*, a retelling by Benoît de Sainte-Maure of the tale of Troy, based not on Homer (who was unknown in western Europe, where Greek was not normally read) but on 4th- and 5th-century Latin versions. In all three, style and subject matter are closely interconnected. Elaborate set descriptions, in which the various features of what is described are gone through, item by item, and eulogized, result in the action's taking place in lavish surroundings, resplendent with gold, silver, marble, fine textiles, and precious stones. To these embellishments are added astonishing works of architecture and quaint technological marvels that recall the Seven Wonders of the World and the reputed glories of Byzantium. *Troie* and *Enéas* have, moreover, a strong love interest, inspired by the Roman poet Ovid's conception of love as a restless malady. This concept produced the first portrayal in Western literature of the doubts, hesitations, and self-torment of young lovers, as exemplified in the Achilles–Polyxena story in *Troie* and in the Aeneas–Lavinia story in *Enéas*. Yet even more important is the way in which this new theme is introduced: the rhetorical devices appropriate to expounding an argument are here employed to allow a character in love to explore his own feelings, to describe his attitude to the loved one, and to explain whatever action he is about to take.

DEVELOPING PSYCHOLOGICAL AWARENESS

As W.P. Ker, a pioneer in the study of medieval epic and romance, observed in his *Epic and Romance* (1897), the advent of romance is "something as momentous and as far-reaching as that to which the name Renaissance is generally applied." The Old French poets who composed the chansons de geste (as the Old French epics are called) had been content to tell a story. They were concerned with statement, not with motivation, and their characters could act without explicitly justifying their actions. Thus, in what is one of the earliest and certainly the finest of the chansons de geste, *La Chanson de Roland* (c. 1100), the hero's decision to fight on against odds (to let the rear guard of Charlemagne's army be destroyed by the Saracen hordes in the hopeless and heroic Battle of Roncesvalles rather than sound his horn to call back Charlemagne) is not treated as a matter for discussion and analysis: the anonymous poet seems to take it for granted that the reader is not primarily concerned with the reason why things happened as they did. The new techniques of elucidating and elaborating material, developed by romance writers in the 12th century, produced a method whereby actions, motives, states of mind, were scrutinized and debated. The story of how Troilus fell in love with Briseïs and how, when taken to the Grecian camp, she deserted him for Diomedes (as related, and presumably invented, by Benoît de Sainte-Maure in his *Roman de Troie*) is not one of marvelous adventures in some exotic fairyland setting: it is clearly a theme of considerable psychological interest, and for this reason it attracted three of the greatest writers of all time: Boccaccio in his *Il filostrato* (c. 1338), Chaucer in his *Troilus and Criseyde* (before 1385), and Shakespeare in his *Troilus and Cressida* (c. 1601–02). With the 12th-century pioneers of what came to be called romance, the beginnings of the analytical method found in the modern novel can easily be recognized.

SOURCES AND PARALLELS

Where exactly medieval romance writers found their material when they were not simply copying classical or pseudo-classical models is still a highly controversial issue. Parallels to certain famous stories, such as that of Tristan and Iseult, have been found in regions as wide apart as Persia and Ireland: in the mid-11th-century Persian epic of *Wis and Ramin* and in the Old Irish *Diarmaid and Gráinne*. While in the latter case it is possible to argue in favour of a genetic link between the two traditions, the former is more likely to be a case of parallel development because of the inner logic of the theme as well as certain similarities in the ideological and social background of the two works. Failure to maintain the essential distinction between source and parallel has greatly hindered the understanding of the true nature of medieval romance and has led to the production of a vast critical literature the relevance of which to the study of the genre is at best questionable.

GEOFFREY OF MONMOUTH

(d. 1155)

Geoffrey of Monmouth, the medieval British chronicler and bishop of St. Asaph, introduced Arthurian legend into European literature. Geoffrey was probably an Oxford cleric for most of his life. His mostly fictional History of the Kings of Britain *(c. 1135–39) traced the descent of British princes from the Trojans. It established the story of Arthur and introduced the figure of the enchanter Merlin, whose story Geoffrey related in the* Vita Merlini *(c. 1148–51?). Though denounced from the first by other historians, the* History *was one of the most popular books of the Middle Ages and had an enormous influence on later chroniclers.*

THE MARVELOUS

The marvelous is by no means an essential ingredient of "romance" in the sense in which it has been defined. Yet to most English readers the term *romance* carries implications of the wonderful, the miraculous, the exaggerated, and the wholly ideal. Ker regarded much of the literature of the Middle Ages as "romantic" in this sense—the only types of narrative free from such "romanticizing" tendencies being the historical and family narrative, or Icelanders' sagas developed in classical Icelandic literature at the end of the 12th and in the early 13th century. *La Chanson de Roland* indulges freely in the fantastic and the unreal: hence Charlemagne's patriarchal age and preternatural strength (he is more than 200 years old when he conquers Spain); or the colossal numbers of those slain by the French; or, again, the monstrous races of men following the Saracen banners. Pious legends and saints' lives favour the marvelous, as do stories of apocryphal adventures like those of Irish St. Brendan (*c.* 486–578) who, as hero of a legend first written down in the 9th century, *Navigatio Brendani*, and later widely translated and adapted, wanders among strange islands on his way to the earthly paradise. The great 12th-century *Roman d'Alexandre*, a *roman d'antiquité* based on and developing the early Greek romance of Alexander the Great (the Alexander romance), was begun in the first years of the century by Alberic

A bust of Charlemagne, one character in La Chanson de Roland. *This work clearly employs the fantastic: Charlemagne is 200 years old and preternaturally strong when he conquers Spain.* Imagno/Hulton Archive/Getty Images

de Briançon and later continued by other poets. It introduces fantastic elements, more especially technological wonders and the marvels of India: the springs of rejuvenation, the flower-maidens growing in a forest, the cynocephali (dog-headed men), the bathyscaphe that takes Alexander to the bottom of the ocean, and the car in which he is drawn through the air by griffins on his celestial journey.

THE SETTING

The fact that so many medieval romances are set in distant times and remote places is not an essential feature of romance but rather a reflection of its origins. As has been seen, the Old French word *romanz* early came to mean "historical work in the vernacular." All the *romans d'antiquité* have a historical or pseudohistorical theme, whether they evoke Greece, Troy, or the legendary world of Alexander. While making some attempt to give antiquity an exotic aspect by means of marvels or technological wonders, however, medieval writers were quite unable to create a convincing historical setting. Thus in all important matters of social life and organization they projected the western European world of the 12th century back into the past. Similarly, historical and contemporary geography were not kept separate. The result is often a confused jumble, as, for example, in the Anglo-Norman Hue de Rotelande's *Protesilaus*, in which the characters have Greek names. The action takes place in Burgundy, Crete, Calabria, and Apulia; and Theseus is described as "king of Denmark." This lavish use of exotic personal and geographical names and a certain irresponsibility about settings was still to be found in some of Shakespeare's romantic comedies: the "seacoast of Bohemia" in *The Winter's Tale* is thoroughly medieval in its antecedents. In the medieval period, myth and folktale and straightforward fact were on an equal footing. Not that any marvel or preternatural happening taking place in secular (as opposed to biblical) history was necessarily to be believed: it was simply that the remote times and regions were convenient locations for picturesque and marvelous incidents. It is, indeed, at precisely this point that the transition begins from the concept of romance as "past history in the vernacular" to that of "a wholly fictitious story."

MEDIEVAL VERSE ROMANCES

The body of stories and medieval romances known as "the matter of Britain" centre on the legendary King Arthur. Medieval writers, especially the French, variously treated stories of Arthur's birth, the adventures of his knights, and the adulterous love between his knight Sir Lancelot and his queen, Guinevere. This last situation and the quest for the Holy Grail (the vessel used by Christ at the Last Supper and given to Joseph of Arimathea) brought about the dissolution of the knightly fellowship, the death of Arthur, and the destruction of his kingdom.

Arthur's story, offered by Geoffrey of Monmouth, was taken up and developed by the French poet Chrétien de Troyes, the initiator of the sophisticated courtly romance. Deeply versed in contemporary rhetoric, he treated love in a humorously detached fashion, bringing folklore themes and love situations together in an Arthurian world of adventure. Above all, in this genre, love was an abiding theme.

ARTHURIAN ROMANCE AND THE MATTER OF BRITAIN

In his *History of the Kings of Britain*, Geoffrey of Monmouth "invented history" by drawing on classical authors, the Bible, and Celtic tradition to create the story of a British kingdom, to some extent paralleling that of Israel. He described the rise of the British people to glory in the reigns of Uther Pendragon and Arthur, then the decline and final destruction of the kingdom, with the exile of the British survivors and their last king, Cadwalader. Romances that have Arthur or some of his knights as main characters were classified as *matière de Bretagne* by Jehan Bodel (fl. 1200) in a well-known poem. There is in this "matter of Britain" a certain amount of material ultimately based on the belief—probably Celtic in origin—in an otherworld, where human men can both challenge the inhabitants and enjoy the love of fairy women. Such themes appear in a highly rationalized form in the lays (*lais*) of the late 12th-century French poet

William Hatherell's The Battle Between King Arthur and Sir Mordred. *King Arthur and his companions are the main subjects of what Jehan Bodel called the "matter of Britain"* (matiere de Bretagne). Mansell/Time & Life Pictures/Getty Images

Marie de France, although she mentions Arthur and his queen only in one, the lay of *Lanval*.

THE INFLUENCE OF CHRÉTIEN DE TROYES

It was Chrétien de Troyes who in five romances (*Erec, Cligès, Lancelot, Yvain,* and *Perceval*) fashioned a new type of narrative based on the matter of Britain. The internal debate and self-analysis of the *roman d'antiquité* is here used with artistry. At times, what seems to matter most to the poet is not the plot but the thematic pattern he imposes upon it and the significance he succeeds in conveying, either in individual scenes in which the action is interpreted by the characters in long monologues or through the work as a whole. In addition to this, he attempts what he himself calls a *conjointure*—that is, the organization into a coherent whole of a series of episodes. The adventures begin and end at the court of King Arthur. The marvels that bring together material from a number of sources are not always meant to be believed, however, especially because they are somehow dovetailed into the normal incidents of life at a feudal court. Whatever Chrétien's intentions may have been, he inaugurated what may be called a Latin tradition of romance—clear, hard, bright, adorned with rhetoric, in which neither the courtly sentiment nor the enchantments are seriously meant. Chrétien had only one faithful follower, the trouvère Raoul de Houdenc (fl. 1200-30), author of *Méraugis de Portlesguez.*

CHRÉTIEN DE TROYES

(fl. 1165–80)

The French poet Chrétien de Troyes was critical in the development of Arthurian legend. Little is known of his life. He is the author of the five Arthurian romances Erec; Cligès; Lancelot, ou Le Chevalier de la charrette; Yvain, ou Le Chevalier au lion; *and* Perceval, ou Le Conte du Graal. *He may also possibly have written a non-Arthurian tale,* Guillaume d'Angleterre. *Written in the vernacular, his romances were derived from the writings of Geoffrey of Monmouth. They combine separate adventures into well-knit stories.* Erec *is the tale of the submissive wife who proves her love for her husband by disobeying his commands;* Cligès, *that of the victim of a marriage made under constraint who feigns death and wakens to a new and happy life with her lover;* Lancelot, *an exaggerated but perhaps parodic treatment of the lover who is servile to the god of love and to his imperious mistress Guinevere, wife of his overlord Arthur; and* Yvain, *a brilliant extravaganza, combining the theme of a widow's too hasty marriage to her husband's slayer with that of the new husband's fall from grace and final restoration to favour.* Perceval, *which Chrétien left unfinished, unites the religious theme of the Holy Grail with fantastic adventure. They were imitated almost immediately by other French poets and were translated and adapted frequently as the romance continued to develop as a narrative form.* Erec, *for example, supplied some of the material for the 14th-century poem* Sir Gawayne and the Grene Knight.

He shared Chrétien's taste for love casuistry, rhetorical adornment, and fantastic adventure. For both authors, elements of rhetoric and self-analysis remain important, although the dose of rhetoric varies from one romance to another. Even in Chrétien's *Perceval, ou Le Conte du Graal* ("Perceval, or the Romance of the Grail")—the work in which the Holy Grail appears for the first time in European literature—the stress is on narrative incident interspersed with predictions of future happenings and retrospective explanations. Arthurian romances of the period 1170–1250 are *romans d'aventure*, exploiting the strange, the supernatural, and the magical in the Arthurian tradition. A number (for example, *La Mule sans frein* ["The Mule Without a Bridle"], c. 1200, and *L'Âtre périlleux* ["The Perilous Churchyard"], c. 1250) have as their hero Arthur's nephew Gawain, who in the earlier Arthurian verse romances is a type of the ideal knight.

Love as a Major Theme

The treatment of love varies greatly from one romance to another. It is helpful to distinguish sharply here between two kinds of theme: the one, whether borrowed from classical antiquity (such as the story of Hero and Leander or that of Pyramus and Thisbe, taken from Ovid's *Metamorphoses*) or of much more recent origin, ending tragically; the other ending with marriage, reconciliation, or the reunion of separated lovers. It is noteworthy that "romance," as applied to a love affair in real life, has in modern English the connotation of a happy ending. This is also true of most Old French love romances in verse: the tragic ending is rare and is usually linked with the theme of the lover who, finding his or her partner dead, joins the beloved in death, either by suicide or from grief.

The Tristan Story

The greatest tragic love story found as a romance theme is that of Tristan and Iseult. It was given the form in which it has become known to succeeding generations in approximately 1150–60 by an otherwise unknown Old French poet whose work, although lost, can be reconstructed in its essentials from surviving early versions based upon it. Probably closest in spirit to the original is the fragmentary version of c. 1170–90 by the Norman poet Béroul. From this it can be inferred that the archetypal poem told the story of an all-absorbing passion caused by a magic potion, a passion stronger than death yet unable to triumph over the feudal order to which the heroes belong. The story ended with Iseult's death in the embrace of her dying lover and with the symbol of two trees growing from the graves of the lovers and intertwining their branches so closely that they could never be separated. Most later versions, including a courtly version by an Anglo-Norman poet known only as Thomas, attempt to resolve the tragic conflict in favour of the sovereignty of passion and to turn the magic potion into a mere symbol.

Gottfried von Strassburg's German version, *Tristan und Isolde* (c. 1210), based on Thomas, is one of the great courtly romances of the Middle Ages. Although love is set up as the supreme value and as the object of the lovers' worship, the mellifluous and limpid verse translates the story into the idyllic mode. Another tragic and somewhat unreal story is that told in the anonymous *Chastelaine de Vergi* (c. 1250), one of the gems of medieval poetry, in which the heroine dies of grief because, under pressure, her lover has revealed their secret and adulterous love to the duke of Burgundy. The latter tells it to his own wife, who allows the heroine to believe that her lover has betrayed her. The theme of the dead lover's heart served up by the jealous husband to the lady—tragic, sophisticated, and farfetched—appears in the anonymous *Chastelain de Couci* (c. 1280) and again in *Daz Herzmaere* by the late 13th-century German poet Konrad von Würzburg. The theme of the outwitting of the jealous husband, common in the fabliaux (short verse tales containing realistic, even coarse detail and written to amuse), is frequently found in 13th-century romance and in lighter lyric verse. It occurs both in the *Chastelain de Couci* and in the Provençal romance *Flamenca* (c. 1234), in which it is treated comically.

THE THEME OF SEPARATION AND REUNION

But the theme that has left the deepest impress on romance is that of a happy resolution, after many trials and manifold dangers, of lovers' difficulties. As has been seen, this theme was derived from late classical Greek romance by way of *Apollonius of Tyre* and its numerous translations and variants. A somewhat similar theme, used for pious edification, is that of the legendary St. Eustace, reputedly a high officer under the Roman emperor Trajan, who lost his position, property, and family only to regain them after many tribulations, trials, and dangers. The St. Eustace theme appears in *Guillaume d'Angleterre*, a pious tale rather than a romance proper, which some have attributed to Chrétien de Troyes.

A variant on the theme of separation and reunion is found in the romance of *Floire et Blancheflor* (c. 1170), in which Floire, son of the Saracen "king" of Spain, is parted by his parents from Blancheflor, daughter of a Christian slave of noble birth, who is sold to foreign slave dealers. He traces her to a tower where maidens destined for the sultan's harem are kept, and the two are reunited when he gains access to her there by hiding in a basket of flowers. This romance was translated into Middle High German, Middle Dutch, Norse, and Middle English (as *Floris and Blancheflur*, 1250) and in the early 13th century was imitated in *Aucassin et Nicolette*, which is a chantefable (a story told in alternating sections of sung verse and recited prose) thought by some critics to share a common source with *Floire et Blancheflor*. In it, the roles and nationality, or religion, of the main characters are reversed. Nicolette, a Saracen slave converted to Christianity, who proves to be daughter of the king of Carthage, disguises herself as a minstrel to return to Aucassin, son of Count Gavin of Beaucaire. Jean Renart's *L'Escoufle* (c. 1200–02) uses the theme of lovers who, accidentally separated while fleeing together from the emperor's court, are eventually reunited. The highly esteemed and influential *Guillaume de Palerne* (c. 1200) combines the theme of escaping lovers with that of the "grateful animal" (here a werewolf, which later resumes human shape as a king's son) assisting the lovers in their successful flight. The popular *Partenopeus de Blois* (c. 1180), of which 10 French manuscripts and many translated versions are known, resembles the Cupid and Psyche story told in the Roman writer Apuleius's *The Golden Ass* (2nd century CE), although there is probably no direct connection. In the early 13th-century *Galeran de Bretagne*, Galeran loves Fresne, a foundling brought up in a convent. Their correspondence discovered, Fresne is sent away but appears in Galeran's land just in time to prevent him from marrying her twin sister, Fleurie.

The theme of a knight who undertakes adventures to prove to his lady that he is worthy of her love is represented by a variety of romances including the *Ipomedon* (1174–90) of Hue de Rotelande and the anonymous mid–13th-century Anglo-Norman *Gui de Warewic*. Finally, there are many examples of the "persecuted heroine" theme. In one variety a person having knowledge of some "corporal sign"—a birthmark or mole—on a lady wagers with her husband that he will seduce her and offer proof that he has done so (sometimes called the "Imogen theme" from its use in Shakespeare's *Cymbeline*). The deceit is finally exposed and the lady's honour vindicated. In the early 13th-century *Guillaume de Dôle* by Jean Renart, the birthmark is a rose; and in the *Roman de Violette*, written after 1225 by Gerbert de Montreuil, it is a violet. Philippe de Beaumanoir's *La Manekine* (c. 1270), Jean Maillart's *La Contesse d'Anjou* (1361), and Chaucer's *Man of Law's Tale* (after 1387) all treat the theme of the tribulations of a wife falsely accused and banished but, after many adventures, reunited with her husband.

MEDIEVAL PROSE ROMANCES

Prose romances of the 13th century further examined the legend of Arthur. An early prose romance centring on Lancelot seems to have become the kernel of a cyclic work known as the Prose *Lancelot*, or Vulgate cycle (c. 1225).

ARTHURIAN THEMES

The Arthurian prose romances arose out of the attempt, made first by Robert de Boron in the verse romances *Joseph d'Arimathie, ou le Roman de l'estoire dou Graal* and *Merlin* (c. 1190–1200), to combine the fictional history of the Holy Grail with the chronicle of the reign of King Arthur. Robert gave his story an allegorical meaning, related to the person and work of Christ. A severe condemnation of secular chivalry and courtly love characterize the Grail branch of the Prose Lancelot-Grail, or Vulgate, cycle as well as some parts of the post-Vulgate "romance of the Grail" (after 1225). In the one case, Lancelot (here representing fallen human nature) and, in the other, Balain (who strikes the Dolorous Stroke) are contrasted with Galahad, a type of the Redeemer. The conflict between earthly chivalry and the demands of religion is absent from the *Perlesvaus* (after 1230?), in which the hero Perlesvaus (that is, Perceval) has Christological overtones and in which the task of knighthood is to uphold and advance Christianity. A 13th-century prose *Tristan* (*Tristan de Léonois*), fundamentally an adaptation of the Tristan story to an Arthurian setting, complicates the love theme of the original with the theme of a love rivalry between Tristan and the converted Saracen Palamède and represents the action as a conflict between the treacherous villain King Mark and the "good" knight Tristan.

In the 14th century, when chivalry enjoyed a new vogue as a social ideal and the great orders of secular chivalry were founded, the romance writers, to judge from what is known of the voluminous *Perceforest* (written c. 1330 and still unpublished in its entirety), evolved an acceptable compromise between the knight's duty to his king, to his lady, and to God. Chivalry as an exalted ideal of conduct finds its highest expression in the anonymous Middle English *Sir Gawayne and the Grene Knight* (c. 1370), whose fantastic beheading scene (presumably taken from a lost French prose romance source) is made to illustrate the fidelity to the pledged word, the trust in God, and the unshakable courage that should characterize the knight.

STRUCTURE

The Vulgate *Lancelot-Grail* cycle displays a peculiar technique of interweaving that enables the author (or authors) to bring together a large number of originally independent themes. The story of Lancelot, of Arthur's kingdom, and the coming of Galahad (Lancelot's son) are all interconnected by the device of episodes that diverge, subdivide, join, and separate again, making the work a kind of interlocking whole, devoid of unity in the modern sense but forming as impregnable a structure as any revolving around a single centre. One of its most important features is its capacity for absorbing contrasting themes, such as the story of Lancelot's love for Guinevere, Arthur's queen, and the Quest of the Grail. Another feature is its ability to grow through continuations or elaborations of earlier themes insufficiently developed. The great proliferation of prose romances at the end of the Middle Ages would have been impossible without this peculiarity of structure. Unlike any work that is wholly true to the Aristotelian principle of indivisibility and isolation (or organic unity), the prose romances satisfy the first condition, but not the second: internal cohesion goes with a tendency to seek connections with other similar compositions and to absorb an increasingly vast number of new themes. Thus the Prose *Tristan* brings together the stories of Tristan and Iseult, the rise and fall of Arthur's kingdom, and the Grail Quest. It early gave rise to an offshoot, the romance of *Palamède* (before 1240), which deals with the older generation of Arthur's knights. A similar example of "extension backward" is the *Perceforest*, which associates the beginnings of knighthood in Britain with both Brutus the Trojan (reputedly Aeneas's grandson and the legendary founder of Britain) and Alexander the Great and makes its hero, Perceforest, live long before the Christian era.

LATER DEVELOPMENTS

The Arthurian prose romances were influential in both Italy and Spain. This circumstance favoured the development in these countries of works best described as *romans d'aventure*, with their constantly growing interest in tournaments, enchantments, single combat between knights, love intrigues, and rambling adventures. In Italy, early prose compilations of Old French epic material from the Charlemagne cycle were subsequently assimilated to the other great bodies of medieval French narrative fiction and infused with the spirit of Arthurian prose romance. The great Italian heroic and romantic epics, Matteo

Boiardo's *Orlando innamorato* (1483) and Ludovico Ariosto's *Orlando furioso* (1516), are based on this fusion. The serious themes of the Holy Grail and death of Arthur left no mark in Italy. The romantic idealism of Boiardo and Ariosto exploits instead the worldly adventures and the love sentiment of Arthurian prose romance, recounted lightly and with a sophisticated humour.

In Spain the significant development is the appearance, as early as the 14th, or even the 13th, century, of a native prose romance, the *Amadís de Gaula*. Arthurian in spirit but not in setting and with a freely invented episodic content, this work, in the form given to it by Garci Rodríguez de Montalvo in its first known edition of 1508, captured the imagination of the polite society of western Europe by its blend of heroic and incredible feats of arms and tender sentiment and by its exaltation of an idealized and refined concept of chivalry. Quickly translated and adapted into French, Italian, Dutch, and English and followed by numerous sequels and imitations in Spanish and Portuguese, it remained influential for more than four centuries, greatly affecting the outlook and sensibility of Western society. Cervantes parodied the fashion inspired by *Amadís* in *Don Quixote* (1605). However, his admiration for the work itself caused him to introduce many of its features into his own masterpiece, so that the spirit and the character of chivalric romance may be said to have entered into the first great modern novel.

More important still for the development of the novel form was the use made by romance writers of the technique of multiple thematic structure and "interweaving" earlier mentioned. Like the great examples of Romanesque ornamental art, both sculptural and pictorial, the cyclic romances of the late Middle Ages, while showing a strong sense of cohesion, bear no trace whatever of the classical concept of subordination to a single theme: an excellent proof, if proof were needed, of the limited relevance of this concept in literary aesthetics. Even those romances which, like the *Amadís* and its ancestor, the French prose *Lancelot*, had one great figure as the centre of action, cannot be said to have progressed in any way toward the notion of the unity of theme.

THE SPREAD AND POPULARITY OF ROMANCE LITERATURE

This is as true of medieval romances as of their descendants, including the French and the English 18th-century novel and the pastoral romance, which, at the time of the Renaissance, revived the classical traditions of pastoral poetry and led to the appearance, in 1504, of the *Arcadia* by the Italian poet Jacopo Sannazzaro and, about 1559, of the *Diana* by the Spanish poet and novelist Jorge de Montemayor. Both works were widely influential in translation, and each has claims to be regarded as the first pastoral romance, but in spirit *Diana* is the true inheritor of the romance tradition, giving

it, in alliance with the pastoral, a new impetus and direction.

Medieval romance began in the 12th century when clerks, working for aristocratic patrons—often ladies of royal birth such as Eleanor of Aquitaine and her daughters, Marie de Champagne and Matilda, wife of Henry the Lion, duke of Saxony—began to write for a leisured and refined society. Like the courtly lyric, romance was a vehicle of a new aristocratic culture which, based in France, spread to other parts of western Europe. Translations and adaptations of French romances appear early in German: the *Roman d'Enéas*, in a version written by Heinrich von Veldeke before 1186, and the archetypal Tristan romance in Eilhart von Oberge's *Tristant* of c. 1170–80. In England many French romances were adapted, sometimes quite freely, into English verse and prose from the late 13th to the 15th century. But by far the most important English contribution to the development and popularization of romance was the adaptation of a number of French Arthurian romances completed by Sir Thomas Malory in 1469–70 and published in 1485 by William Caxton under the title of *Le Morte Darthur*. In the Scandinavian countries the connection with the Angevin rulers of England led to importation of French romances in the reign (1217–63) of Haakon of Norway.

THE DECLINE OF ROMANCE

As has been seen, in the later Middle Ages the prose romances were influential in France, Italy, and Spain, as well as in England. The advent of the printed book made them available to a still wider audience. But although they continued in vogue into the 16th century, with the spread of the ideals of the New Learning, the greater range and depth of vernacular literature, and the rise of the Neoclassical critics, the essentially medieval image of the perfect knight was bound to change into that of the scholar-courtier, who, as presented by the Italian Baldassare Castiglione in his *Il cortegiano* (written 1513–18, published 1528; *The Courtier*), embodies the highest moral ideals of the Renaissance. The new Spanish romances continued to enjoy international popularity until well into the 17th century and in France gave rise to compendious sentimental romances with an adventurous, pastoral, or pseudo-historical colouring popular with Parisian salon society until *c.* 1660. But the French intellectual climate, especially after the beginning of the so-called classical period in the 1660s, was unfavourable to the success of romance as a "noble" genre. Before disappearing, however, the romances lent the French form of their name to such *romans* as Antoine Furetière's *Le Roman bourgeois* (1666) and Paul Scarron's *Le Roman comique* (1651–57). These preserved something of the outward form of romance but little of its spirit. And while they transmitted the name to the kind of narrative fiction that succeeded them, they were in no sense intermediaries between its old and its new connotations.

The great critical issue dominating the thought of western Europe from about 1660 onward was that of "truth" in literature. Romance, as being "unnatural" and unreasonable, was condemned. Only in England and Germany did it find a home with poets and novelists. Thus, while Robert Boyle, the natural philosopher, in his *Occasional Discourses* (1666) was inveighing against gentlemen whose libraries contained nothing more substantial than "romances," Milton, in *Paradise Lost*, could still invoke "what resounds/In fable or romance of Uther's son ..."

THE 18TH-CENTURY ROMANTIC REVIVAL

The 18th century in both England and Germany saw a strong reaction against the rationalistic canons of French classicism—a reaction that found its positive counterpart in such romantic material as had survived from medieval times. The Gothic romances, of which Horace Walpole's *Castle of Otranto* (1764; dated 1765) is the most famous, are perhaps less important than the ideas underlying the defense of romance by Richard Hurd in his *Letters on Chivalry and Romance* (1762). To Hurd, romance is not truth but a delightful and necessary holiday from common sense. This definition of romance (to which both Ariosto and Chrétien de Troyes would no doubt have subscribed) inspired on the one hand the romantic epic *Oberon* (1780) and on the other the historical romances of Sir Walter Scott. But influential though Scott's romantic novels may have been in every corner of Europe (including the Latin countries), it was the German and English Romantics who, with a richer theory of the imagination than Hurd's, recaptured something of the spirit of romance—the German Romantics by turning to their own medieval past; the English, by turning to the tradition perpetuated by Edmund Spenser and Shakespeare. In the 19th century, Nathaniel Hawthorne and Herman Melville adapted the European romance to address the distinct needs of a young American republic and literature.

ROMANCE: TERMS AND CONCEPTS

Though written in verse, chansons de geste (a French phrase meaning "songs of deeds") are related to the romance genre. They form the core of the Charlemagne legends. Also useful in any discussion of the literature of romance is an understanding of the highly conventionalized code known as courtly love. And finally, an early form related to the medieval romance is the adventure tale called the Hellenistic romance.

ALEXANDER ROMANCE

The Alexander romances are a body of legends about the career of Alexander the Great, told and retold with varying emphasis and purpose by succeeding ages and civilizations.

The chief source of all Alexander romance literature was a folk epic written in Greek by a Hellenized Egyptian in Alexandria during the 2nd century CE. Surviving translations and copies make its reconstruction possible. It portrayed Alexander as a national messianic hero, the natural son of an Egyptian wizard-king by the wife of Philip II of Macedon. Magic and marvels played a subsidiary part in the epic—in the story of Alexander's birth, for example, and in his meeting with the Amazons in India. In later romances, however, marvels and exotic anecdotes predominated and gradually eclipsed the historical personality. Minor episodes in the original were filled out, often through "letters" supposedly written by or to Alexander, and an independent legend about his capture of the wild peoples of Gog and Magog was incorporated into several texts of many vernacular versions. An account of the Alexander legends was included in a 9th-century Old English translation of Orosius's history of the world. In the 11th century, a Middle Irish Alexander romance appeared, and about 1100, the Middle High German *Annolied*. During the 12th century, Alexander appeared as a pattern of knightly chivalry in a succession of great poems, beginning with the *Roman d'Alexandre* by Albéric de Briançon. This work inspired the *Alexanderlied* by the German poet Lamprecht der Pfaffe. An Anglo-Norman poet, Thomas of Kent, wrote the *Roman de toute chevalerie* toward the end of the 12th century, and about 1275 this was remodeled to become the Middle English romance of *King Alisaunder*. Italian Alexander romances began to appear during the 14th century, closely followed by versions in Swedish, Danish, Scots, and (dating from a little earlier) in the Slavic languages.

Eastern accounts of Alexander's fabled career paid a good deal of attention to the Gog and Magog episode, a version of this story being included in the Qur'ān. The Arabs, expanding Syrian versions of the legend, passed them on to the many peoples with whom they came in contact. Through them, the Persian poets, notably Nezāmī in the 12th century, gave the stories new form.

Alexander romance literature declined in the late 12th century, and, with the revival of classical scholarship during the Renaissance, historical accounts displaced the Alexander romances.

CHANSON DE GESTE

The Old French epic poems that form the core of the Charlemagne legends consist of more than 80 chansons, most of them thousands of lines long, that have survived in manuscripts dating from the 12th to the 15th century. They deal chiefly with events of the 8th and 9th centuries during the reigns of Charlemagne and his successors. In general, the poems contain a core of historical truth overlaid with legendary accretions. Whether they were composed under the inspiration of the events they narrate and survived for generations in oral tradition or were the independent compositions of professional poets of a later date is still disputed. A few poems have authors' names, but most are anonymous.

Chansons de geste are composed in lines of 10 or 12 syllables grouped into *laisses* (irregular stanzas) based on assonance or, later, rhyme. They range in length from approximately 1,500 to more than 18,000 lines. Their fictional background is the struggle of Christian France against a conventionalized polytheistic or idolatrous "Muslim" enemy. Portrayed as the champion of Christendom, the emperor Charlemagne is surrounded by his court of Twelve Noble Peers, among whom are Roland, Oliver (Olivier), Ogier the Dane, and Archbishop Turpin.

Besides the stories grouped around Charlemagne, there is a subordinate cycle of 24 poems dealing with Guillaume d'Orange, a loyal and long-suffering supporter of Charlemagne's weak son, Louis the Pious. Another cycle deals with the wars of such powerful barons as Doon de Mayence, Girart de Roussillon, Ogier the Dane, or Raoul de Cambrai against the crown or against each other.

The earlier chansons are heroic in spirit and theme. They focus on great battles or feuds and on the legal and moral niceties of feudal allegiances. After the 13th century, elements of romance and courtly love came to be introduced, and the austere early poems were supplemented by *enfances* (youthful exploits) of the heroes and fictitious adventures of their ancestors and descendants. The masterpiece and probably the earliest of the chansons de geste is the 4,000-line *La Chanson de Roland*. Appearing at the threshold of French epic literature, *Roland* was the formative influence on the rest of the chansons de geste. The chansons, in turn, spread throughout Europe and strongly influenced Spanish heroic poetry. The mid-12th-century Spanish epic *Cantar de mío Cid* ("Song of My Cid"), in particular, is indebted to them. In Italy stories about Orlando and Rinaldo (Roland and Oliver) were extremely popular and formed the basis for the Renaissance epics *Orlando innamorato* by Matteo Boiardo (1495) and *Orlando furioso* by Ludovico Ariosto (1532). In the 13th century the German poet Wolfram von Eschenbach based his incomplete epic *Willehalm* on the life of William of Orange, and the chansons were recorded in prose in the Icelandic *Karlamagnús saga*. Charlemagne legends, referred to as "the matter of France," were long staple subjects of romance. In the 20th century the chansons continued to enjoy a strange afterlife in folk ballads of the Brazilian backlands, called *literatura de la corda* ("literature on a string") because, in pamphlet form, they were formerly hung from strings and sold in marketplaces. Frequently in these ballads, through a misunderstanding of a Portuguese homonym, Charlemagne is surrounded by a company of 24 knights (i.e., "Twelve Noble Pairs").

CHANTEFABLE

A medieval tale of adventure told in alternating sections of sung verse and recited prose is called a chantefable. The word itself was used—and perhaps coined—by the anonymous author of the 13th-century French work *Aucassin et Nicolette* in its concluding lines: "No cantefable prent fin" ("Our chantefable is drawing to a close"). The work is the sole surviving example of the genre. The word is from the Old French (Picard dialect) *cantefable,* literally, "(it) sings (and it) narrates."

COURTLY LOVE

In the later Middle Ages, a highly conventionalized code of courtly love prescribed the behaviour of ladies and their lovers. Known in French as *amour courtois,* this code also provided the theme of an extensive courtly medieval literature that began with the troubadour poetry of Aquitaine and Provence in southern France toward the end of the 11th century. It constituted a revolution in thought and feeling, the effects of which are still apparent in Western culture.

The courtly lover existed to serve his lady. His love was invariably adulterous, marriage at that time being usually the result of business interest or the seal of a power alliance. Ultimately, the lover saw himself as serving the all-powerful god of love and worshiping his lady-saint. Faithlessness was the mortal sin.

The philosophy found little precedent in other, older cultures. Conditions in the castle civilization of 11th-century southern France, however, were favourable to a change of attitude toward women. Castles themselves housed many men, few women; poets, wishing to idealize physical passion, looked beyond the marriage state. The Roman poet Ovid undoubtedly provided inspiration in the developing concept of courtly love. His *Ars amatoria* had pictured a lover as the slave of passion—sighing, trembling, growing pale and sleepless, even dying for love. The Ovidian lover's adoration was calculated to win sensual rewards. The courtly lover, however, while displaying the same outward signs of passion, was fired by respect for his lady. This idealistic outlook may be explained partly by contemporary religious devotions, both orthodox and heretical, especially regarding the Virgin Mary, and partly by France's exposure to Arab mystical philosophy (gained through contacts with Islam during the Crusades), which embodied concepts of love—as a delightful disease, as demanding of faithful service—that were to characterize courtly love.

Courtly love may therefore be regarded as the complex product of numerous factors—social, erotic, religious, and philosophical. The idea spread swiftly across Europe, and a decisive influence in this transmission was Eleanor of Aquitaine, wife first to Louis VII of France and then to Henry II of England, who inspired some of the best poetry of Bernard de Ventadour, among the last (12th century) and finest of troubadour poets. Her daughter Marie of Champagne encouraged the composition of Chrétien de Troyes's *Lancelot*, a courtly romance whose hero obeys every imperious (and unreasonable) demand of the heroine. Soon afterward the doctrine was "codified" in a three-book treatise by André le Chapelain. In the 13th century, a long allegorical poem, the *Roman de la rose*, expressed the concept of a lover suspended between happiness and despair.

Courtly love soon pervaded the literatures of Europe. The German minnesinger lyrics and court epics such as Gottfried von Strassburg's *Tristan und Isolde* (c. 1210) are evidence of its power. Italian poetry embodied the courtly ideals as early as the 12th century, and during the 14th century their essence was distilled in Francesco Petrarch's sonnets to Laura. But perhaps more significantly, Dante had earlier managed to fuse courtly love and mystical vision: his Beatrice was, in life, his earthly inspiration; in *The Divine Comedy* she became his spiritual guide to the mysteries of Paradise. Courtly love was also a vital influential force on most medieval literature in England, but there it came to be adopted as part of the courtship ritual leading to marriage. This development, discussed in C.S. Lewis's *Allegory of Love* (1936, rev. ed., 1951), became more pronounced in later romances.

HELLENISTIC ROMANCE

The Hellenistic romance, also called Greek romance, is an adventure tale, usually with a quasi-historical setting, in which a virtuous heroine and her valiant lover are separated by a series of misadventures (e.g., jealous quarrels, kidnapping, shipwrecks, or bandits) but are eventually reunited and live happily together. Five complete romances have survived in ancient Greek (in the presumed chronological order): Chariton's *Chaereas and Callirhoë* (1st century CE); Xenophon of Ephesus's *Anthia and Habrocomes*, or *Ephesiaca* (2nd century CE; "The Ephesian Story"); Achilles Tatius's *Leucippe and Clitophon* (2nd century CE); Longus's *Daphnis and Chloe* (2nd century CE; sometimes called "The Pastoral Story"); and Heliodorus's *Theagenes and Charicles*, or *Ethiopica* (4th century CE; "The Ethiopian Story"). Written under the Roman Empire, all five are extended fictional narratives whose protagonists are two young lovers.

Testimonies from other authors and the growing number of papyrus discoveries show that the romance originated during the latter part of the Hellenistic Age (323–30 BCE). Besides the five known complete romances, the titles (and sometimes plots) of at least 20 others have been identified. The oldest (1st century BCE) is *Ninus*, which is named for the protagonist, the Assyrian king Ninus, whose consort was Semiramis (Sammu-ramat). Others include Antonius Diogenes's *Hyper Thoulēn apista* (1st century CE; "The Wonders Beyond Thule"), which describes incredible adventures in the far north; Iamblichus's *Babyloniaca* (2nd century CE; "Babylonian Stories"), a tale of exotic adventures and magic; and Lollianus's *Phoenicica* (2nd century CE; "Phoenician Stories"), which is characterized by crude and direct realism and includes a scene of cannibalism.

The Greek romance furnished many motifs and themes to Latin narrative fiction, of which the most important examples are Petronius's *Satyricon* (1st century CE) and Apuleius's *The Golden Ass* (2nd century CE). The Greek romance, as it evolved through these Latin works, was the ancestor of the modern novel.

ROMANCE OF ʿANTAR

The tales of chivalry centred on the Arab desert poet and warrior ʿAntarah ibn Shaddād, one of the poets of the celebrated pre-Islamic collection *Al-Muʿallaqāt*, are collectively known as the *Romance of ʿAntar*.

Though the work itself credits the 9th-century philologist al-Aṣmaʿī with its authorship, it was composed anonymously between the 11th and the 12th century. Written in rhymed prose (*sajʿ*) interspersed with 10,000 poetic verses, the *Romance* is commonly divided into 32 books, each leaving the conclusion of a tale in suspense. It relates the fabulous childhood of ʿAntar, son of an Arab king by an African slave girl—hence regarded as

The stories that make up the Romance of 'Antar *are divided into 32 books, each ending with suspense.* Thomas J. Abercrombie/National Geographic Image Collection/Getty Images

illegitimate by his people—and the adventures he undertakes to attain the hand of his cousin 'Ablah in marriage. These take him beyond Arabia and his own time period to Iraq, Iran, Syria, Spain, North Africa, Egypt, Constantinople, Rome, and the Sudan. They bring him in contact with a Byzantine emperor and with Frankish, Spanish, and Roman kings. Though childless by 'Ablah, 'Antar fathers several children, including two Crusaders, Ghadanfar (by the sister of the king of Rome) and Jufrān (by a Frankish princess).

The *Romance of 'Antar* evolved out of a Bedouin tradition that stressed nobility of character and desert chivalry and of which 'Antar was made the epitome. With the advent of Islam, it assumed a new outlook that reinterpreted 'Antar as a precursor of the new religion. A strong Persian hand in the later authorship of the *Romance*—demonstrated by the detailed knowledge of Persian history and court life—then shows 'Antar in Iran. Lastly, the *Romance* incorporated European elements that were encountered among the Crusaders.

CHAPTER 5

SAGA

Any type of medieval Icelandic prose story or history, irrespective of the kind or nature of the narrative or the purposes for which it was written, is called a saga. Used in this general sense, the term applies to a wide range of literary works, including those of hagiography (biography of saints), historiography, and secular fiction in a variety of modes. Lives of the saints and other stories for edification are entitled sagas, as are the Norse versions of French romances and the Icelandic adaptations of various Latin histories. Chronicles and other factual records of the history of Scandinavia and Iceland down to the 14th century are also included under the blanket term *saga literature*. In a stricter sense, however, the term *saga* is confined to legendary and historical fictions, in which the author has attempted an imaginative reconstruction of the past and organized the subject matter according to certain aesthetic principles.

The origin and evolution of saga writing in Iceland are largely matters for speculation. A common pastime on Icelandic farms, from the 12th century down to modern times, was the reading aloud of stories to entertain the household, known as *sagnaskemmtun* ("saga entertainment"). It seems to have replaced the traditional art of storytelling. All kinds of written narratives were used in *sagnaskemmtun*: secular, sacred, historical, and legendary. The Icelandic church took a sympathetic view of the writing and reading of sagas, and many of the authors whose identity is still known were monks or priests.

NONFICTIONAL SAGA LITERATURE

Nonfictional saga literature is sorted into two types: translations and native histories. European narratives were known in Iceland in the 12th and 13th centuries. They undoubtedly served as models for Icelandic writers when they set out to form a coherent picture of early Scandinavian history.

TRANSLATIONS

From the 12th century onward, translations of lives of the saints and the apostles and accounts of the Holy Virgin testify to the skill of Icelandic prose writers in handling the vernacular for narrative purposes. Histories were also adapted and translated from Latin, based on those of the 7th- and 8th-century Anglo-Saxon writer Bede the Venerable, the 7th-century Spanish historian St. Isidore of Sevilla, and others; on fictitious accounts of the Trojan wars, notably, one of the 5th century attributed to Dares Phrygius and one of the 4th century attributed to Dictys Cretensis; on the 12th-century British chronicler Geoffrey of Monmouth; and on the 1st-century Roman historians Sallust and Lucan. In the 13th century, Abbot Brandr Jónsson wrote a history of the Jews based on the Vulgate, on the 10th-century biblical scholar Peter Comestor, and on other sources.

Tristrams saga *(the story of Tristan and Iseult) was probably one of the earliest sagas translated into Norwegian.* Ron Scherl/Redferns/Getty Images

In the 13th century, saga literature was also enriched by Norwegian prose translations of French romance literature. These soon found their way into Iceland, where they were popular and a strong influence on native storywriting. Probably the earliest, *Tristrams saga* (the story of Tristan and Iseult), was translated in 1226. Most of the themes of French romance appear in Icelandic versions (e.g., *Karlamagnús saga* was based on Charlemagne legends).

NATIVE HISTORICAL ACCOUNTS

Icelandic historians seem to have started writing about their country's past toward the end of the 11th century. Saemundr Sigfússon, trained as a priest in France, wrote a Latin history of the kings of Norway, now lost but referred to by later authors. The first Icelander to use the vernacular for historical accounts was Ari Þorgilsson, whose *Íslendingabók* (or *Libellus Islandorum* [*The Book of the Icelanders*]) survives. It is a concise description of the course of Icelandic history from the beginning of the settlement (c. 870) to 1118. Ari seems to have written this book about 1125, but before that date he may already have compiled (in collaboration with Kolskeggr Ásbjarnarson) the so-called *Landnámabók* ("Book of Settlements"), which lists the names and land claims of about 400 settlers. Because this work survives only in 13th- and 14th-century versions, it is impossible to tell how much of it is Ari's. Both books gave the Icelanders a clear picture of the beginning of their society. Both works served to stimulate public interest in the period during which events recounted in the sagas of Icelanders are supposed to have taken place. Other factual accounts of the history of Iceland followed later: *Kristni saga* describes Iceland's conversion to Christianity about the end of the 10th century and the emergence of a national church. *Hungrvaka* ("The Appetizer") contains accounts of the lives of the first five bishops of Skálholt, from the mid-11th century to the third quarter of the 12th century. The biographies of other prominent bishops are in the *Biskupa sǫgur*. Though some of these have a strong hagiographical flavour, others are soberly written and of great historical value. The period c. 1100–1264 is also dealt with in several secular histories, known collectively as *Sturlunga saga*, the most important of which is the *Íslendinga saga* ("The Icelanders' Saga") of Sturla Þórðarson, who describes in memorable detail the bitter personal and political feuds that marked the final episode in the history of the Icelandic commonwealth (c. 1200–64).

LEGENDARY AND HISTORICAL FICTION

In the strictest sense, sagas are fictional narratives. Using the distinctive features of the hero as principal guideline, medieval Icelandic narrative fiction can be classified into one of three categories: kings' sagas, legendary sagas, or sagas of Icelanders.

KINGS' SAGAS

After Sæmundr Sigfússon (1056–1133), Icelandic and Norwegian authors continued to explore the history of Scandinavia in terms of rulers and royal families, some of them writing in Latin and others in the vernacular. Broadly speaking, the kings' sagas fall into two distinct groups: contemporary (or near contemporary) biographies and histories of remoter periods. To the first group belonged a now-lost work, written about 1170 by an Icelander called Eiríkr Oddsson, dealing with several 12th-century kings of Norway. *Sverris saga* describes the life of King Sverrir (reigned 1184–1202). The first part was written by Abbot Karl Jónsson under the supervision of the king himself, but it was completed (probably by the abbot) in Iceland after Sverrir's death. Sturla Þórðarson wrote two royal biographies: *Hákonar saga* on King Haakon Haakonsson (c. 1204–63) and *Magnús saga* on his son and successor, Magnus VI Lawmender (Lagabøte; reigned 1263–80); of the latter only fragments survive. In writing these sagas Sturla used written documents as source material and, like Abbot Karl before him, he also relied on the accounts of eyewitnesses. Works on the history of the earlier kings of Norway include two Latin chronicles of Norwegian provenance, one of which was compiled c. 1180, and two vernacular histories, also written in Norway, the so-called *Ágrip* (c. 1190) and *Fagrskinna* (c. 1230). The Icelandic *Morkinskinna* (c. 1220) deals with the kings of Norway from 1047 to 1177. It tells some brilliant stories of Icelandic poets and adventurers who visited the royal courts of Scandinavia.

The kings' sagas reached their zenith in the *Heimskringla*, or *Noregs konunga sǫgur* ("History of the Kings of Norway"), of Snorri Sturluson, which describes the history of the royal house of Norway from legendary times down to 1177. Snorri was a leading 13th-century Icelandic poet, who used as sources all the court poetry from the 9th century onward that was available to him. He also used many earlier histories of the kings of Norway and other written sources. *Heimskringla* is a supreme literary achievement that ranks Snorri Sturluson with the great writers of medieval Europe. He interpreted history in terms of personalities rather than politics, and many of his character portrayals are superbly drawn. Two of the early kings of Norway, Olaf Tryggvason (reigned 995–1000) and Olaf Haraldsson (Olaf the Saint; reigned 1015–30), received special attention from Icelandic antiquarians and authors. Only fragments of a 12th-century *Ólafs saga helga* ("St. Olaf's Saga") survive, and a 13th-century biography of the same king by Styrmir Kárason is also largely lost. (Snorri Sturluson wrote a brilliant saga of St. Olaf, rejecting some of the grosser hagiographical elements in his sources. This work forms the central part of his *Heimskringla*.) About 1190 a Benedictine monk, Oddr Snorrason, wrote a Latin life of Olaf Tryggvason, of which an Icelandic version still survives. A brother in the same monastery, Gunnlaugr Leifsson, expanded this biography, and his work was incorporated into later versions of *Ólafs saga Tryggvasonar*. Closely related to the lives of the kings of Norway are *Færeyinga saga*, describing the resistance of Faeroese leaders to Norwegian interference during the first part of the 11th century, and *Orkneyinga saga*, dealing with the rulers of the earldom of Orkney from roughly 900 to the end of the 12th century. These two works were probably written about 1200. The history of the kings of Denmark from *c.* 940 to 1187 is told in *Knýtlinga saga*.

LEGENDARY SAGAS

The learned men of medieval Iceland took great pride in their pagan past and copied traditional poems on mythological and legendary themes. In due course some of these narrative poems served as the basis for sagas in prose. In his *Edda* (probably written *c.* 1225), Snorri Sturluson tells several memorable stories, based on ancient mythological poems, about the old gods of the North, including such masterpieces as the tragic death of Balder and the comic tale of Thor's journey to giantland. Snorri's book also contains a summary of the legendary Nibelungen cycle. (A much fuller treatment of the same theme is to be found in *Vǫlsunga saga* and *Þiðriks saga* the latter composed in Norway about 1250 and based on German sources.) Other Icelandic stories based on early poetic tradition include *Heiðreks saga*; *Hrólfs saga kraka*, which

has a certain affinity with the Old English poem *Beowulf*; *Hálfs saga og Hálfsrekka*; *Gautreks saga*; and *Ásmundar saga kappabana*, which tells the same story as the Old High German *Hildebrandslied*, that of a duel of honour between a father and a son. The term *legendary sagas* also covers a number of stories the antecedents and models of which are not exclusively native. These sagas are set in what might be called the legendary heroic age at one level and also vaguely in the more recent Viking age at the other, the action taking place in Scandinavia and other parts of the Viking world, from Russia to Ireland, but occasionally also in the world of myth and fantasy. It is mostly through valour and heroic exploits that the typical hero's personality is realized. He is, however, often a composite character, for some of his features are borrowed from a later and more refined ethos than that of early Scandinavia. He is in fact the synthesis of Viking ideals on the one hand and of codes of courtly chivalry on the other. Of individual stories the following are notable: *Egils saga einhenda ok Ásmundar berserkjabana*, which skillfully employs the flashback device; *Bósa saga ok Herrauðs*, exceptional for its erotic elements; *Friðþjófs saga ins frækna*, a romantic love story; *Hrólfs saga Gautrekssonar*; *Göngu-Hrólfs saga*; and *Hálfdanar saga Eysteinssonar*. There are many more. The legendary sagas are essentially romantic literature, offering an idealized picture of the remote past, and many of them are strongly influenced by French romance literature. In these sagas the main emphasis is on a lively narrative, entertainment being their primary aim and function. Some of the themes in the legendary sagas are also treated in the *Gesta Danorum* of the 12th-century Danish historian Saxo Grammaticus, who states that some of his informants for the legendary history of Denmark were Icelanders.

SAGAS OF ICELANDERS

In the late 12th century, Icelandic authors began to fictionalize the early part of their history (*c.* 900–1050), and a new literary genre was born: the sagas of Icelanders. Whereas the ethos of the kings' sagas and of the legendary sagas is aristocratic and their principal heroes warlike leaders, the sagas of Icelanders describe characters who are essentially farmers or farmers' sons or at least people who were socially not far above the author's public, and their conduct and motivation are measurable in terms of the author's own ethos. These authors constantly aimed at geographic, social, and cultural verisimilitude. They made it their business to depict life in Iceland as they had experienced it or as they imagined it had actually been in the past. Though a good deal of the subject matter was evidently derived from oral tradition and thus of historical value for the period described, some of the best sagas are largely fictional. Their relevance to the authors' own times mattered perhaps no less than their incidental information about the past. An important aim of

this literature was to encourage people to attain a better understanding of their social environment and a truer knowledge of themselves through studying the real and imagined fates of their forbears. A spirit of humanism, sometimes coloured by a fatalistic heroic outlook, pervades the narrative. The edificatory role, however, was never allowed to get out of hand or dominate the literary art. Giving aesthetic pleasure remained the saga writer's primary aim and duty.

Nothing is known of the authorship of the sagas of Icelanders, and it has proved impossible to assign a definite date to many of them. It seems improbable that in their present form any of them could have been written before *c.* 1200. The period *c.* 1230–90 has been described as the golden age of saga writing because such masterpieces as *Egils saga, Víga-Glúms saga, Gísla saga Súrssonar, Eyrbyggja saga, Hrafnkels saga Freysgoda, Bandamanna saga, Hænsna-Þóris saga,* and *Njáls saga* appear to have been written during that time. Although a number of sagas date from the 14th century, only one, *Grettis saga,* can be ranked with the classical ones.

The sagas of Icelanders can be subdivided into several categories according to the social and ethical status of the principal heroes. In some, the hero is a poet who sets out from the rural society of his native land in search of fame and adventure to become the retainer of the king of Norway or some other foreign ruler. Another feature of these stories is that the hero is also a lover.

To this group belong some of the early-13th-century sagas, including *Kormáks saga*, *Hallfreðar saga vandræðaskálds*, and *Bjarnar saga hítdælakappa*. In *Gunnlaugs saga ormstungu*, which may have been written after the middle of the 13th century, the love theme is treated more romantically than in the others. *Fóstbræþa saga* ("The Blood-Brothers' Saga") describes two contrasting heroes: one a poet and lover, the other a ruthless killer. *Egils saga* offers a brilliant study of a complex personality: a ruthless Viking who is also a sensitive poet, a rebel against authority from early childhood who ends his life as a defenseless, blind old man. In several sagas the hero becomes an outlaw fighting a hopeless battle against the social forces that have rejected him. To this group belong *Harðar saga ok Hólmverja* and *Droplaugarsona saga*. But the greatest of the outlaw sagas are *Gísla saga Súrssonar*, describing a man who murders his own brother-in-law and whose sister reveals his dark secret, and *Grettis saga*, which deals with a hero of great talents and courage who is constantly fighting against heavy odds and is treacherously slain by an unscrupulous enemy.

Most sagas of Icelanders, however, are concerned with people who are fully integrated members of society, either as ordinary farmers or as farmers who also act as chieftains. *Hrafnkels saga* describes a chieftain who murders his shepherd, is then tortured and humiliated for his crime, and finally takes cruel revenge on one of his tormentors. The hero who gives his name to *Hænsna-Þóris saga* is a man of humble background who makes money as a peddler and becomes a wealthy but unpopular landowner. His egotism creates trouble in the neighbourhood, and after he has set fire to one of the farmsteads, killing the farmer and the entire household, he is prosecuted and later put to death. *Qlkofra þáttr* (the term *þáttr* is often used for a short story) and *Bandamanna saga* ("The Confederates' Saga") satirize chieftains who fail in their duty to guard the integrity of the law and try to turn other people's mistakes into profit for themselves. The central plot in *Laxdæla saga* is a love triangle, in which the jealous heroine forces her husband to kill his best friend. *Eyrbyggja saga* describes a complex series of feuds between several interrelated families. *Hávarðar saga Ísfirðings* is about an old farmer who takes revenge on his son's killer, the local chieftain. *Víga-Glúms saga* tells of a ruthless chieftain who commits several killings and swears an ambiguous oath in order to cover his guilt. And *Vatnsdæla saga* is the story of a noble chieftain whose last act is to help his killer escape.

In the sagas of Icelanders, justice, rather than courage, is often the primary virtue, as might be expected in a literature that places the success of an individual below the welfare of society at large. This theme is an underlying one in *Njáls saga*, the greatest of all the sagas.

Njáls Saga

The Icelanders' saga known as Njáls *(or* Njála) saga *is one of the longest and finest of its type. A story of great complexity and richness, it offers a host of brilliantly executed character portrayals and a profound understanding of human strengths and weaknesses. Its structure is highly complex, but at its core is the tragedy of an influential farmer and sage who devotes his life to a hopeless struggle against the destructive forces of society but ends it inexorably when his enemies set fire to his house, killing his wife and sons with him. (This act provides the saga's variant name,* Burnt Njáll.) *Set in a society where blood ties impose inescapable obligations and honour demands vengeance for past injuries, it presents the most comprehensive picture of Icelandic life in the heroic age. Its overriding mood is tragic pessimism. Its vividly drawn characters, who range from comic to sinister, include two heroes—Gunnar (Gunther), a brave, guileless, generous youth, and Njál, a wise and prudent man endowed with prophetic gifts.*

SAGA: TERMS AND CONCEPTS

Specialized terms and concepts that the reader might find while studying sagas include a particular class of saga known as *fornaldarsarsǫgur norðurlanda* ("ancient sagas of the northern lands"), or, more commonly, *fornaldarsǫgur.* (Note that some sources use the phonetic symbol -ö- rather than -ǫ- in the spelling of this and other Old Norse words.) Other terms that may require further examination are heroic prose and legend.

FORNALDARSǪGUR

The Old Norse term *fornaldarsarsǫgur* means "sagas of antiquity," and it refers to a class of Icelandic sagas dealing with the ancient myths and hero legends of Germania, with the adventures of Vikings, or with other exotic adventures in foreign lands. These stories take place on the European continent before the settlement of Iceland. Though the existing *fornaldarsarsǫgur* were written in 1250–1350, after the Icelanders' family sagas (written 1200–20), they are thought to be of earlier oral composition. Despite their fantastic content, they are written in the terse, objective style of the family sagas.

These heroic sagas do not have the same literary value as the Icelanders' sagas, but, because they are based on lost heroic poetry, they are of great antiquarian interest. The most important in this respect is the *Vǫlsunga saga* (c. 1270). This story of Sigurd, grandson of Vǫlsung, is the Northern version of the story of Siegfried and of the destruction of the Burgundians told in the Middle German epic *Nibelungenlied.* It differs in many particulars from the *Nibelungenlied.*

HERO

Broadly, the term *hero* refers to the main male character in a literary work, but it is also used in a specialized sense for any figure celebrated in the ancient legends of a people or in such early heroic epics as *Gilgamesh*, the *Iliad, Beowulf,* or *La Chanson de Roland.*

These legendary heroes belong to a princely class existing in an early stage of the history of a people, and they transcend ordinary men in skill, strength, and courage. They are usually born to their role. Some, like the Greek Achilles and the Irish Cú Chulainn (Cuchulain), are of semidivine origin, unusual beauty, and extraordinary precocity. A few, like the Anglo-Saxon Beowulf and the Russian Ilya of Murom, are dark horses, slow to develop.

War or dangerous adventure is the hero's normal occupation. He is surrounded by noble peers and is magnanimous to his followers and ruthless to his enemies. In addition to his prowess in battle, he is resourceful and skillful in many crafts; he can build a house, sail a boat, and, if shipwrecked, is an expert swimmer. He is sometimes, like Odysseus, cunning and wise in counsel, but a hero is not usually given to much subtlety. He is a man of action rather than thought and lives by a personal code of honour that admits of no qualification. His responses are usually instinctive, predictable, and inevitable. He accepts challenge and sometimes even courts disaster. Thus baldly stated, the hero's ethos seems oversimple by the standards of a later age. He is childlike in his boasting and rivalry, his love of presents and rewards, and his concern for his reputation. He is sometimes foolhardy and wrong-headed, risking his life—and the lives of others—for trifles. Roland, for instance, dies because he is too proud to sound his horn for help when he is overwhelmed in battle. Yet the hero still exerts an attraction for sophisticated readers and remains a seminal influence in literature.

The appearance of heroes in literature marks a revolution in thought that occurred when poets and their audiences turned their attention away from immortal gods to mortal men, who suffer pain and death, but in defiance of this live gallantly and fully, and create, through their own efforts, a moment's glory that survives in the memory of their descendants. They are the first human beings in literature, and the novelty of their experiences has a perennial freshness.

HEROIC PROSE

Narrative prose tales are the counterpart of heroic poetry in subject, outlook, and dramatic style. Whether composed orally or written down, the stories are meant to be recited, and they employ many of the formulaic expressions of oral tradition. A remarkable body of this prose is the early Irish Ulaid (Ulster) cycle of stories, recorded between the 8th and 11th centuries, featuring the hero Cú Chulainn (Cuchulain) and his associates. A 12th-century group of Irish stories is the Fenian cycle, focusing on the hero Finn MacCumhaill (MacCool), his son, the poet Oisín (Ossian), and his elite corps of warriors and hunters, the Fianna Éireann.

The 13th-century Icelandic sagas provide other examples. Both the "heroic sagas"—such as the *Vǫlsunga saga* and the *Þiðriks saga*, based on ancient Germanic oral tradition of the 4th to 6th century and containing many lines from lost heroic lays, or narrative poems— and the "Icelander sagas," which deal with native Icelandic families who live by the grim and complicated code of the blood feud, are examples of heroic prose.

Hero Finn MacCumhaill (MacCool) is featured in a 12th-century cycle of Irish tales. Hulton Archive/Getty Images

LEGEND

In the 21st century, a legend is defined as a traditional story or a group of stories told about a particular person or place. In an earlier era the term referred specifically to a tale about a saint. Legends resemble folktales in content. They may include supernatural beings, elements of mythology, or explanations of natural phenomena, but they are associated with a particular locality or person and are told as a matter of history.

Some legends are the unique property of the place or person that they depict, such as the story of young George Washington, the future first president of the United States, who confesses to chopping down the cherry tree. But many local legends are actually well-known folktales that have become attached to some particular person or place. For example, a widely distributed folktale of an excellent marksman who is forced to shoot an apple, hazelnut, or some other object from his son's head has become associated with the Swiss hero William Tell. Another popular tale, of a younger son whose only inheritance is a cat, which he sells for a fortune in a land overrun with mice, has become associated with Richard Whittington, thrice lord mayor of London in the early 15th century. The story told about King Lear is essentially the folktale "Love Like Salt."

Local legends sometimes travel. Though the Pied Piper of Hamelin is famous through literary treatment, many other European towns have a similar legend of a piper who lured their children away.

SCÉLA

In Irish- (Gaelic-) language literature, scéla (singular scél) are the early prose and verse legends of gods and folk heroes, most of which originated during or before the 11th century. Scéla were divided into primary and secondary types. The primary, or most important, were classified according to the actions they celebrated: destructions, cattle raids, navigations, elopements, violent deaths, conflagrations, and others. In modern times these tales have been grouped into cycles according to the characters and periods with which they deal. The first is the mythological cycle, dealing with immortal beings. A second is the Ulster (Ulaid) cycle, dealing with the Ulster heroes during the reign of King Conor (Conchobar mac Nessa) in the 1st century BCE. The events of the Ulster cycle are set in the 1st century BCE and reflect the customs of a pre-Christian aristocracy who fight from chariots, take heads as trophies, and are influenced by Druids. The third grouping is the Fenian cycle, dealing mainly with the deeds of Finn MacCumhaill's war band during the reign of Cormac mac Art in the 3rd century. Interspersed in the narratives are passages of verse, usually speeches, that are often older than the prose. Because of the verse sections, it is thought that these stories may derive from a lost body of heroic poetry. Among the Irish tales only the Ulaid story "The Cattle Raid of Cooley" has the scope of an epic, but it survives in a much mutilated text. The formulaic and poetic language of the Irish cycles is admirably preserved in the Irish playwright Lady Gregory's retelling of the stories Cuchulain of Muirthemne *(1902) and* Gods and Fighting Men *(1904).*

VIKINGS

Also called Norsemen, or Northmen, the Vikings were Scandinavian seafaring warriors who raided and colonized wide areas of Europe from the 9th to the 11th century and whose disruptive influence profoundly affected European history. These pagan Danish, Norwegian, and Swedish warriors were probably prompted to undertake their raids by a combination of factors ranging from overpopulation at home to the relative helplessness of victims abroad.

The Vikings were made up of landowning chieftains and clan heads, their retainers, freemen, and any energetic young clan members who sought adventure and booty overseas. At home these Scandinavians were independent farmers, but at sea they were raiders and pillagers. During the Viking period the Scandinavian countries seem to have possessed a practically inexhaustible surplus of manpower, and leaders of ability, who could organize groups of warriors into conquering bands and armies, were seldom lacking. These bands would negotiate the seas in their longships and mount hit-and-run raids at cities and towns along the coasts of Europe. Their burning, plundering, and killing earned them the name *vikingr*, meaning "pirate" in the early Scandinavian languages.

The exact ethnic composition of the Viking armies is unknown in particular cases, but the Vikings' expansion in the Baltic lands and in Russia can reasonably be attributed to the Swedes. Conversely, the nonmilitary colonization of the Orkney Islands, Faroe Islands, and Iceland was clearly accomplished by the Norwegians.

ENGLAND

In England desultory raiding occurred in the late 8th century but began more earnestly in 865, when a force led by the sons of Ragnar Lodbrok—Healfdene, Inwaer, and perhaps Hubba—conquered the ancient kingdoms of East Anglia and Northumbria and reduced Mercia to a fraction of its former size. Yet it was unable to subdue the Wessex of Alfred the Great, with whom in 878 a truce was made, which became the basis of a treaty in or soon after 886. This recognized that much of England was in Danish hands. Although hard pressed by fresh armies of Vikings from 892 to 899, Alfred was finally victorious over them, and the spirit of Wessex was so little broken that his son Edward the Elder was able to commence the reconquest of Danish England. Before his death in 924 the small Danish states on old Mercian and East Anglian territory had fallen before him. The more remote Northumbria resisted longer, largely under Viking leaders

from Ireland, but the Scandinavian power there was finally liquidated by Edred in 954. Viking raids on England began again in 980, and the country ultimately became part of the empire of Canute. Nevertheless, the native house was peacefully restored in 1042, and the Viking threat ended with the ineffective passes made by Canute II in the reign of William I. The Scandinavian conquests in England left deep marks on the areas affected—in social structure, dialect, place-names, and personal names.

THE WESTERN SEAS AND IRELAND

In the western seas, Scandinavian expansion touched practically every possible point. Settlers poured into Iceland from at least about 900, and from Iceland colonies were founded in Greenland and attempted in North America. The same period saw settlements arise in the Orkney, Faroe, and Shetland islands, the Hebrides, and the Isle of Man.

Scandinavian invasions of Ireland are recorded from 795, when Rechru, an island not identified, was ravaged. Thenceforth fighting was incessant, and, although the natives often more than held their own, Scandinavian kingdoms arose at Dublin, Limerick, and Waterford. The kings of Dublin for a time felt strong enough for foreign adventure, and in the early 10th century several of them ruled in both Dublin and Northumberland. The likelihood that Ireland would be unified under Scandinavian leadership passed with the Battle of Clontarf in 1014, when the Irish Scandinavians, supported by the earl of Orkney and some native Irish, suffered disastrous defeat. Yet in the 12th century the English invaders of Ireland found the Scandinavians still dominant (though Christianized) at Dublin, Waterford, Limerick, Wexford, and Cork.

The Carolingian Empire and France

Viking settlement was never achieved in the well-defended Carolingian empire on the scale evidenced in the British Isles, and Scandinavian influence on continental languages and institutions is, outside Normandy, very slight. Sporadic raiding did occur, however, until the end of the Viking period. And, in the 10th century, settlements on the Seine River became the germ of the duchy of Normandy, the only permanent Viking achievement in what had been the empire of Charlemagne.

Farther south than France—in the Iberian Peninsula and on the Mediterranean coasts—the Vikings raided from time to time but accomplished little of permanence.

Norsemen intermittently raided the Carolingian empire throughout the end of the Viking period. Apic/Hulton Archive/Getty Images

EASTERN EUROPE

The eastern Viking expansion was probably a less violent process than that on the Atlantic coasts. Although there was, no doubt, plenty of sporadic raiding in the Baltic and although "to go on the east-Viking" was an expression meaning to indulge in such activity, no Viking kingdom was founded with the sword in that area.

The greatest eastern movement of the Scandinavians was that which carried them into the heart of Russia. The extent of this penetration is difficult to assess, for, although the Scandinavians were at one time dominant at Novgorod, Kiev, and other centres, they were rapidly absorbed by the Slavonic population, to which, however, they gave their name Rus, "Russians." The Rus were clearly in the main traders, and two of their commercial treaties with the Greeks are preserved in the *Primary Chronicle* under 912 and 945. The Rus signatories have indubitably Scandinavian names. Occasionally, however, the Rus attempted voyages of plunder like their kinsmen in the west. Their existence as a separate people did not continue past 1050 at the latest.

The first half of the 11th century appears to have seen a new Viking movement toward the east. A number of Swedish runic stones record the names of men who went with Yngvarr on his journeys. These journeys were to the east, but only legendary accounts of their precise direction and intention survive. A further activity of the Scandinavians in the east was service as mercenaries in Constantinople (Istanbul), where they formed the Varangian Guard of the Byzantine emperor.

After the 11th century the Viking chief became a figure of the past. Norway and Sweden had no more force for external adventure, and Denmark became a conquering power, able to absorb the more unruly elements of its population into its own royal armies. Olaf II Haraldsson of Norway, before he became king in 1015, was practically the last Viking chief in the old independent tradition.

CHAPTER 6

SHORT STORY

T he short story is a brief fictional prose narrative that is shorter than a novel and that usually deals with only a few characters. It is usually concerned with a single effect conveyed in only one or a few significant episodes or scenes. The form encourages economy of setting, concise narrative, and the omission of a complex plot. Character is disclosed in action and dramatic encounter but is seldom fully developed. Despite its relatively limited scope, though, a short story is often judged by its ability to provide a "complete" or satisfying treatment of its characters and subject.

Before the 19th century the short story was not generally regarded as a distinct literary form. But although in this sense it may seem to be a uniquely modern genre, the fact is that short prose fiction is nearly as old as language itself. Throughout history humankind has enjoyed various types of brief narratives: jests, anecdotes, studied digressions, short allegorical romances, moralizing fairy tales, short myths, and abbreviated historical legends. None of these constitutes a short story as defined in the 19th century and beyond, but they do make up a large part of the milieu from which the modern short story emerged.

ANALYSIS OF THE GENRE

As a genre, the short story has received relatively little critical attention, and the most valuable studies of the form that exist are often limited by region or era. One recent attempt to account for the genre has been offered by the Irish short story writer Frank O'Connor, who suggests that stories are a means for "submerged population groups" to address a dominating community. Most other theoretical discussions, however, are predicated in one way or another on Edgar Allan Poe's thesis that stories must have a compact, unified effect.

By far, most criticism on the short story focusses on techniques of writing. Many, and often the best of the technical works, advise the young reader—alerting him to the variety of devices and tactics employed by the skilled writer. However, many such works are no more than treatises on "how to write stories" for the young writer, and not serious critical material.

The prevalence in the 19th century of two words, *sketch* and *tale*, affords one way of looking at the genre. In the United States alone there were virtually hundreds of books claiming to be collections of sketches (Washington Irving's *Sketch Book*, William Dean Howells's *Suburban Sketches*) or collections of tales (Poe's *Tales of the Grotesque and Arabesque*, Herman Melville's *Piazza Tales*). These two terms establish the polarities of the milieu out of which the modern short story grew.

The tale is much older than the sketch. Basically, the tale is a manifestation of a culture's unaging desire to name and conceptualize its place in the cosmos. It provides a culture's narrative framework for such things as its vision of itself and its homeland or for expressing its conception of its ancestors and its gods. Usually filled with cryptic and uniquely deployed motifs, personages, and symbols, tales are frequently fully understood only by members of the particular culture to which they belong. Simply, tales are intracultural. Seldom created to address an outside culture, a tale is a medium through which a culture speaks to itself and thus perpetuates its own values and stabilizes its own identity. The old speak to the young through tales.

The sketch, by contrast, is intercultural, depicting some phenomenon of one culture for the benefit or pleasure of a second culture. Factual and journalistic, in essence the sketch is generally more analytic or descriptive and less narrative or dramatic than the tale. Moreover, the sketch by nature is *suggestive*, incomplete. The tale is often *hyperbolic*, overstated.

The primary mode of the sketch is written; that of the tale, spoken. This difference alone accounts for their strikingly different effects. The sketch writer can have, or pretend to have, his eye on his subject. The tale, recounted at court or campfire—or at some place similarly removed in time from the event—is nearly always a recreation of the past. The tale-teller is an agent of *time*, bringing together a culture's past and its present. The sketch writer is more an agent of *space*, bringing an aspect of one culture to the attention of a second.

A campfire's dramatic lighting and heightened sense of the not-quite-visible lurking nearby gives the skilled storyteller an additional power to manipulate the listeners' emotions and make the fantastic seem possible. SuperStock/Getty Images

It is only a slight oversimplification to suggest that the tale was the only kind of short fiction until the 16th century, when a rising middle class interest in social realism on the one hand and in exotic lands on the other put a premium on sketches of subcultures and foreign regions. In the 19th century certain writers one might call the "fathers" of the modern story—Nikolay Gogol, Hawthorne, E.T.A. Hoffmann, Heinrich von Kleist, Prosper Mérimée, Poe—combined elements of the tale with elements of the sketch. Each writer worked in his own way, but the general effect was to mitigate some of the fantasy and stultifying conventionality of the tale and, at the same time, to liberate the sketch from its bondage to strict factuality. The modern short story, then, ranges between the highly imaginative tale and the photographic sketch and in some ways draws on both.

The short stories of Ernest Hemingway, for example, may often gain their force from an exploitation of traditional mythic symbols (water, fish, groin wounds), but they are more closely related to the sketch than to the tale. Indeed, Hemingway was able at times to submit his apparently factual stories as newspaper copy. In contrast, the stories of Hemingway's contemporary William Faulkner more closely resemble the tale. Faulkner seldom seems to understate, and his stories carry a heavy flavour of the past. Both his language and his subject matter are rich in traditional material. A Southerner might well suspect that only a reader steeped in sympathetic knowledge of the traditional South could fully understand Faulkner. Faulkner may seem, at times, to be a Southerner speaking to and for Southerners. But, as, by virtue of their imaginative and symbolic qualities, Hemingway's narratives are more than journalistic sketches, so, by virtue of their explorative and analytic qualities, Faulkner's narratives are more than Southern tales.

Whether or not one sees the modern short story as a fusion of sketch and tale, it is hardly disputable that today the short story is a distinct and autonomous, though still developing, genre.

ORIGINS

The evolution of the short story first began before humans could write. To aid in the construction and memorization of tales, the early storyteller often relied on stock phrases, fixed rhythms, and rhyme. Consequently, many of the oldest narratives in the world, such as the famous Babylonian tale the *Epic of Gilgamesh* (c. 2000 BCE), are in verse. Indeed, most major stories from the ancient Middle East were in verse: "The War of the Gods," "The Story of Adapa" (both Babylonian), "The Heavenly Bow," and "The King Who Forgot" (both Canaanite). These tales were inscribed in cuneiform on clay during the 2nd millennium BCE.

FROM EGYPT TO INDIA

The earliest tales extant from Egypt were composed on papyrus at a comparable date. The ancient Egyptians seem to have written their narratives largely in prose, apparently reserving verse for their religious hymns and working songs. One of the earliest surviving Egyptian tales, "The Shipwrecked Sailor" (*c.* 2000 BCE), is clearly intended to be a consoling and inspiring story to reassure its aristocratic audience that apparent misfortune can in the end become good fortune. Also recorded during the 12th dynasty were the success story of the exile Sinuhe and the moralizing tale called "King Cheops [Khufu] and the Magicians." The provocative and profusely detailed story "The Tale of Two Brothers" (or "Anpu and Bata") was written down during the New Kingdom, probably about 1250 BCE. Of all the early Egyptian tales, most of which are baldly didactic, this story is perhaps the richest in folk motifs and the most intricate in plot.

The earliest tales from India are not as old as those from Egypt and the Middle East. The *Brahmanas* (*c.* 700 BCE) function mostly as theological appendixes to the Four Vedas, but a few are composed as short, instructional parables. Perhaps more interesting as stories are the later tales in the Pali language, *The Jataka*. Although these tales have a religious frame that attempts to recast them as Buddhist ethical teachings, their actual concern is generally with secular behaviour and practical wisdom. Another, nearly contemporaneous collection of Indian tales, *The Panchatantra* (*c.* 500 CE), has been one of the world's most popular books. This anthology of amusing

and moralistic animal tales, akin to those of "Aesop" in Greece, was translated into Middle Persian in the 6th century; Arabic in the 8th century; and Hebrew, Greek, and Latin soon thereafter. Sir Thomas North's English translation appeared in 1570. Another noteworthy collection is *Kathasaritsagara* ("Ocean of Rivers of Tales"), a series of tales assembled and recounted in narrative verse in the 11th century by the Sanskrit writer Samadeva. Most of these tales come from much older material, and they vary from the fantastic story of a transformed swan to a more probable tale of a loyal but misunderstood servant.

During the 2nd, 3rd, and 4th centuries BCE, the Hebrews first wrote down some of their sophisticated narratives, versions of which are now a part of the Hebrew Bible and the Apocrypha. The book of Tobit displays an unprecedented sense of ironic humour. Judith creates an unrelenting and suspenseful tension as it builds to its bloody climax. The story of Susanna, the most compact and least fantastic in the Apocrypha, develops a three-sided conflict involving the innocent beauty of Susanna, the lechery of the elders, and the triumphant wisdom of Daniel. The biblical books of Ruth, Esther, and Jonah hardly need mentioning: they may well be the most famous stories in the Judeo-Christian world.

Nearly all the ancient tales, whether from Israel, India, Egypt, or the Middle East, were fundamentally didactic. Some of these ancient stories preached by presenting an ideal for readers to imitate.

Others tagged with a "moral" were more direct. Most stories, however, preached by illustrating the success and joy that was available to the "good" person and by conveying a sense of the terror and misery that was in store for the wayward.

THE GREEKS

The early Greeks contributed greatly to the scope and art of short fiction. As in India, the moralizing animal fable was a common form. Many of these tales were collected as "Aesop's fables" in the 6th century BCE. Brief mythological stories of the gods' adventures in love and war were also popular in the pre-Attic age. Apollodorus of Athens compiled a handbook of epitomes, or abstracts, of these tales around the 2nd century BCE, but the tales themselves are no longer extant in their original form. They appear, though somewhat transformed, in the longer poetical works of Hesiod, Homer, and the tragedians. Short tales found their way into long prose forms as well, as in Hellanicus's *Persika* (5th century BCE, extant only in fragments).

Herodotus, the "father of history," saw himself as a maker and reciter of *logoi* (things for telling, tales). His long *History* is interspersed with such fictionalized digressions as the stories of Polycrates and his emerald ring, of Candaules's attractive wife, and of Rhampsinitus's stolen treasure. Xenophon's philosophical history, the *Cyropaedia* (4th century BCE), contains the famous story of the soldier Abradates and his lovely and loyal wife Panthea, perhaps the first Western love story. The *Cyropaedia* also contains other narrative interpolations: the story of Pheraules, who freely gave away his wealth; the tale of Gobryas's murdered son; and various anecdotes describing the life of the Persian soldier.

Moreover, the Greeks are usually credited with originating the romance, a long form of prose fiction with stylized plots of love, catastrophe, and reunion. The early Greek romances frequently took shape as a series of short tales. The *Love Romances* of Parthenius of Nicaea, who wrote during the reign of Augustus Caesar, is a collection of 36 prose stories of unhappy lovers. *The Milesian Tales* (no longer extant) was an extremely popular collection of erotic and ribald stories composed by Aristides of Miletus in the 2nd century BCE and translated almost immediately into Latin. As the variety of these short narratives suggests, the Greeks were less insistent than earlier cultures that short fiction be predominantly didactic.

By comparison the contribution of the Romans to short narrative was small. Ovid's long poem, *Metamorphoses*, is basically a reshaping of more than 100 short, popular tales into a thematic pattern. The other major fictional narratives to come out of Rome are the aforementioned novel-length works by Petronius (*Satyricon*, 1st century CE) and Apuleius (*The Golden Ass*, 2nd century CE). Like Ovid these men used potential short-story material as episodes within a larger whole. The Roman love of rhetoric, it seems, encouraged the development of longer and more comprehensive forms of expression. Regardless, the trend away from didacticism inaugurated by the Greeks was not reversed.

MIDDLE AGES, RENAISSANCE, AND AFTER

In the centuries that followed, short stories took a variety of forms. These were perhaps most comprehensively explored in the work of Chaucer, whose mastery of a broad spectrum of short narrative forms is evident in *The Canterbury Tales*. The genre continued to develop as a popular and lively art until the 17th and 18th centuries, when the novel began to eclipse its popularity and currency.

PROLIFERATION OF FORMS

The Middle Ages was a time of the proliferation, though not necessarily the refinement, of short narratives. The short tale became an important means of diversion and amusement. From the Dark Ages to the Renaissance, various cultures adopted short fiction for their own purposes. Even the aggressive, grim spirit of the invading Germanic barbarians was amenable to expression in short prose. The myths and sagas extant in Scandinavia and Iceland indicate the kinds of bleak and violent tales the invaders took with them into southern Europe.

In contrast, the romantic imagination and high spirits of the Celts remained manifest in their tales. Wherever they appeared—in Ireland, Wales, or Brittany—stories steeped in magic and splendour also appeared. This spirit, easily recognized in such Irish mythological tales as *Longes mac n-Uislenn* (probably 9th-century), infused the chivalric romances that developed somewhat later on the Continent. The romances usually addressed one of three "Matters": the "Matter of Britain" (stories of King Arthur and his knights), the "Matter of France" (the Charlemagne cycle), or the "Matter of Rome" (stories out of antiquity, such as "Pyramus and Thisbe," "Paris and Helen"). Many, but not all, of the romances are too long to be considered short stories. Two of the most influential contributors of short material to the "Matter of Britain" in the 12th century were Chrétien de Troyes and Marie de France. The latter was gifted as a creator of the short narrative poems known as the Breton lays. Only occasionally did a popular short romance like *Aucassin and Nicolette* (13th century) fail to address any of the three Matters.

Also widely respected was the exemplum, a short didactic tale usually intended to dramatize or otherwise inspire model behaviour. Of all the exempla, the best known in the 11th and 12th centuries were the lives of the saints, some 200 of which are extant. The *Gesta Romanorum* ("Deeds of the Romans") offered skeletal plots of exempla that preachers could expand into moralistic stories for use in their sermons.

Among the common people of the late Middle Ages there appeared a literary movement counter to that of the romance and exemplum. Displaying a preference for common sense, secular humour, and sensuality, this movement accounted in a large way for the practical-minded animals in beast fables, the coarse and "merry" jestbooks, and the ribald fabliaux. All were important as short narratives, but perhaps the most intriguing of the three are the fabliaux. First appearing around the middle of the 12th century, fabliaux remained popular for 200 years, attracting the attention of Boccaccio and Chaucer. Some 160 fabliaux are extant, all in verse.

Often, the medieval storyteller—regardless of the kind of tale he preferred—relied on a framing circumstance that made possible the juxtaposition of several stories, each of them relatively autonomous. Because there was little emphasis on organic unity, most storytellers preferred a flexible format, one that allowed tales to be added or removed at random with little change in effect. Such a format is found in *The Seven Sages of Rome*, a collection of stories so popular that nearly every European country had its own translation. The framing circumstance in *The Seven Sages* involves a prince condemned to death. His advocates (the seven sages) relate a new story each day, thereby delaying the execution until his innocence is made known. This technique is clearly similar to that of *The Arabian Nights*, another collection to come out of the Middle Ages. Most stories in *The Arabian Nights* are framed by the story of Scheherazade (Shahrazad) in "Alf laylah wa laylah" ("A Thousand and One Nights"). Records indicate that the basis of this framing story was a medieval Persian collection, *Hezar Efsan* ("Thousand Romances," no longer extant). In both the Persian and Arabian versions of the frame, the clever Scheherazade avoids death by telling her king-husband a thousand stories. Though the framing device is identical in both versions, the original Persian stories within the frame were replaced or drastically altered as the collection was adapted by the Arabs during the Muslim Mamluk period (1250–1517 CE).

REFINEMENT

Short narrative received its most refined treatment in the Middle Ages from Chaucer and Boccaccio. Chaucer's versatility reflects the versatility of the age. In "The Miller's Tale" he artistically combines two fabliaux. In "The Nun's Priest's Tale" he draws upon material common to beast fables. He creates a brilliantly revealing sermon, complete with a narrative exemplum in "The Pardoner's Tale." This short list hardly exhausts the catalogue of forms Chaucer experimented with. By relating tale to teller and by exploiting relationships among the various tellers, Chaucer endowed *The Canterbury Tales* with a unique, dramatic vitality.

Boccaccio's genius, geared more toward *narrative* than *drama*, is of a different sort. Where Chaucer reveals a character through actions and assertions,

Boccaccio seems more interested in stories as pieces of action. With Boccaccio, the characters telling the stories, and usually the characters within, are of subordinate interest. Like Chaucer, Boccaccio frames his well-wrought tales in a metaphoric context. The trip to the shrine at Canterbury provides a meaningful backdrop against which Chaucer juxtaposes his earthy and pious characters. The frame of the *Decameron* (from the Greek *deka*, 10, and *hēmera*, day) has relevance as well: during the height of the Black Plague in Florence, Italy, 10 people meet and agree to amuse and divert each other by telling 10 stories each. Behind every story, in effect, is the inescapable presence of the Black Death. The *Decameron* is fashioned out of a variety of sources, including fabliaux, exempla, and short romances.

SPREADING POPULARITY

Immediately popular, the *Decameron* produced imitations nearly everywhere. In Italy alone, there appeared at least 50 writers of *novelle* (as short narratives were called) after Boccaccio.

Learning from the success and artistry of Boccaccio and, to a lesser degree, his contemporary Franco Sacchetti, Italian writers for three centuries kept the Western world supplied with short narratives. Sacchetti was no mere imitator of Boccaccio. More of a frank and unadorned realist, he wrote—or planned to write—300 stories (200 of the *Trecentonovelle* ["300 Short Stories"]

are extant) dealing in a rather anecdotal way with ordinary Florentine life. Two other well-known narrative writers of the 14th century, Giovanni Fiorentino and Giovanni Sercambi, freely acknowledged their imitation of Boccaccio. In the 15th century Masuccio Salernitano's collection of 50 stories, *Il novellino* (1475), attracted much attention. Though verbosity often substitutes for eloquence in Masuccio's stories, they are witty and lively tales of lovers and clerics.

With Masuccio the popularity of short stories was just beginning to spread. Almost every Italian in the 16th century, it has been suggested, tried his hand at *novelle*. Matteo Bandello, the most influential and prolific writer, attempted nearly everything from brief histories and anecdotes to short romances, but he was most interested in tales of deception. Various other kinds of stories appeared. Agnolo Firenzuolo's popular *Ragionamenti diamore* ("The Reasoning of Love") is characterized by a graceful style unique in tales of ribaldry. Anton Francesco Doni included several tales of surprise and irony in his miscellany, *I marmi* ("The Marbles"). And Gianfrancesco Straparola experimented with common folktales and with dialects in his collection, *Le piacevoli notti* ("The Pleasant Nights"). In the early 17th century, Giambattista Basile attempted to infuse stock situations (often of the fairy-tale type, such as "Puss and Boots") with realistic details. The result was often remarkable—a tale of hags or princes with very real motives and feelings.

Perhaps it is the amusing and diverting nature of Basile's collection of 50 stories that has reminded readers of Boccaccio. Or, it may be his use of a frame similar to that in the *Decameron*. Whatever the reason, Basile's *Cunto de li cunti* (1634; *The Story of Stories*) is traditionally linked with Boccaccio and referred to as *The Pentamerone* ("The Five Days"). Basile's similarities to Boccaccio suggest that in the 300 years between them the short story may have gained repute and circulation, but its basic shape and effect hardly changed.

This pattern was repeated in France, though the impetus provided by Boccaccio was not felt until the 15th century. A collection of 100 racy anecdotes, *Les Cent Nouvelles Nouvelles*, "The Hundred New Short Stories" (*c.* 1460), outwardly resembles the *Decameron*. Margaret of Angoulême's *Heptaméron* (1558–59; "The Seven Days"), an unfinished collection of 72 amorous tales, admits a similar indebtedness.

In the early 17th century Béroalde de Verville placed his own Rabelaisian tales within a banquet frame in a collection called *Le Moyen de parvenir*, "The Way of Succeeding" (*c.* 1610). Showing great narrative skill, Béroalde's stories are still very much in the tradition of Boccaccio. As a collection of framed stories, their main intent is to amuse and divert the reader.

As the most influential nation in Europe in the 15th and 16th centuries, Spain contributed to the proliferation of short prose fiction. Especially noteworthy are Don Juan Manuel's collection of lively exempla *Libro de los enxiemplos del conde Lucanor et de Patronio* (1328–35), which antedates the *Decameron*; the anonymous story "The Abencerraje," which was interpolated into a pastoral novel of 1559; and, most importantly, Miguel de Cervantes's experimental *Novelas ejemplares* (1613; "Exemplary Novels"). Cervantes's short fictions vary in style and seriousness, but their single concern is clear: to explore the nature of secular existence. This focus was somewhat new for short fiction, heretofore either didactic or escapist.

Despite the presence of these and other popular collections, short narrative in Spain was eventually overshadowed by a new form that began to emerge in the 16th century—the novel. Like the earlier Romans, the Spanish writers of the early Renaissance often incorporated short story material as episodes in a larger whole.

DECLINE OF SHORT FICTION

The 17th and 18th centuries mark the temporary decline of short fiction. The causes of this phenomenon are many: the emergence of the novel; the failure of the Boccaccio tradition to produce in three centuries much more than variations or imitations of older, well-worn material; and a renaissant fascination with drama and poetry, the superior forms of classical antiquity. Another cause for the disappearance of major works of short fiction is suggested by the growing preference for journalistic sketches. The increasing awareness of other lands and the growing interest in social conditions (accommodated by a publication boom) produced a plethora of descriptive and biographical sketches. Although these journalistic elements later were incorporated in the fictional short story, for the time being fact held sway over the imagination. Travel books, criminal biographies, social description, sermons, and essays occupied the market. Only occasionally did a serious story find its way into print, and then it was usually a production of an established writer like Voltaire or Addison.

Perhaps the decline is clearest in England, where the short story had its least secure foothold. It took little to obscure the faint tradition established in the 16th and 17th centuries by the popular jestbooks, by the *Palace of Pleasure* (an anthology of stories, mostly European), and by the few rough stories written by Englishmen (e.g., Barnabe Rich's *Farewell to Military Profession*, 1581).

During the Middle Ages short fiction had become primarily an amusing and diverting medium. The Renaissance and Enlightenment, however, made different demands of the form. The awakening concern with secular issues called for a new attention to actual conditions. Simply, the diverting stories were no longer relevant or viable. At first only the journalists and pamphleteers responded to the new demand. Short fiction disappeared, in effect, because it did not respond. When it did shake off its escapist trappings in the 19th century, it reappeared as the "modern short story." This was a new stage in the evolution of short fiction, one in which the short form undertook a new seriousness and gained a new vitality and respect.

EMERGENCE OF THE MODERN SHORT STORY

Though it was initially known by such names as *sketch*, *tale*, or *entertainment*, the short story as we know it in the 21st century was a product of the 19th century. Like many inventions, it did not spring from a solitary source.

THE 19TH CENTURY

The modern short story emerged almost simultaneously in Germany, the United States, France, and Russia. In Germany there had been relatively little difference between the stories of the late 18th century and those in the older tradition of Boccaccio. In 1795 Goethe contributed a set of stories to Schiller's journal, *Die Horen*, that were obviously created with the *Decameron* in mind. Significantly, Goethe did not call them "short stories" (*Novellen*) although the term was available to him. Rather, he thought of them as "entertainments" for German travelers (*Unterhaltungen deutscher Ausgewanderten*). Friedrich Schlegel's early discussion of the short narrative form, appearing soon after Goethe's "entertainments," also focused on Boccaccio (*Nachrichten von den poetischen Werken des G. Boccaccio*, 1801).

But a new type of short fiction was near at hand—a type that accepted some of the realistic properties of popular journalism. In 1827, 32 years after publishing his own "entertainments," Goethe commented on the difference between the newly emergent story and the older kind. "What is a short story," he asked, "but an event which, though unheard of, has occurred? Many a work which passes in Germany under the title *short story* is not a short story at all, but merely a tale or what else you would like to call it." Two influential critics, Christoph Wieland and Friedrich Schleiermacher, also argued that a short story properly concerned itself with events that actually happened or could happen. A short story, for them, had to be realistic.

Perhaps sensitive to this qualification, Heinrich von Kleist and E.T.A. Hoffmann called their short works on fabulous themes "tales" (*Erzählungen*). Somewhat like Poe, Kleist created an expression of human problems, partly metaphysical and partly psychological, by dramatizing the individual's confrontations with a fantastic, chaotic world. Hoffmann's intriguing tales of exotic places and of supernatural phenomena were likely his most influential. Another important writer, Ludwig Tieck, explicitly rejected realism as the definitive element in a short story. As he noted in his preface to the 1829 collection of his works and as he demonstrated in his stories, Tieck envisioned the short story as primarily a matter of intensity and ironic inversion. A story did not have to be realistic in any

outward sense, he claimed, so long as the chain of consequences was "entirely in keeping with character and circumstances." By allowing the writer to pursue an inner, and perhaps bizarre, reality and order, Tieck and the others kept the modern story open to nonjournalistic techniques.

In the United States, the short story, as in Germany, evolved in two strains. On the one hand there appeared the realistic story that sought objectively to deal with seemingly real places, events, or persons. The regionalist stories of the second half of the 19th century (including those by G.W. Cable, Bret Harte, Sarah Orne Jewett) are of this kind. On the other hand, there developed the impressionist story, a tale shaped and given meaning by the consciousness and psychological attitudes of the narrator. Predicated upon this element of subjectivity, these stories seem less objective and are less realistic in the outward sense. Of this sort are Poe's tales in which the hallucinations of a central character or narrator provide the details and facts of the story. Like the narrators in "The Tell-Tale Heart" (1843) and "The Imp of the Perverse" (1845), the narrator of "The Fall of the House of Usher" (1839) so distorts and transforms what he sees that the reader cannot hope to look objectively at the scene. Looking through an intermediary's eyes, the reader can see only the narrator's impressions of the scene.

Some writers contributed to the development of both types of story. Washington Irving wrote several realistic

E.H. Wehnert's scene from The Raven. *In poems such as* The Raven *by Edgar Allan Poe, the reader's only source of information on the events related in the poem is the poem's (quite unreliable) narrator.* Time & Life Pictures/Getty Images

sketches (*The Sketch-Book*, 1819–20; *The Alhambra*, 1832) in which he carefully recorded appearances and actions. Irving also wrote stories in which the details were taken not from ostensible reality but from within a character's mind. Much of the substance of "The Stout Gentleman" (1821), for example, is reshaped and recharged by the narrator's fertile imagination. "Rip Van Winkle" (1819) draws upon the symbolic surreality of Rip's dreams.

The short prose of Nathaniel Hawthorne illustrates that neither type of modern story, however, has exclusive rights to the use of symbol. On a few occasions, as in "My Kinsman, Major Molineux" (1832), Hawthorne's stories are about symbolic events as they are viewed subjectively by the central character. Hawthorne's greater gift, however, was for creating scenes, persons, and events that strike the reader as being actual historical facts and also as being rich in symbolic import. "Endicott and the Red Cross" (1837) may seem little more than a photographic sketch of a tableau out of history (the 17th-century Puritan leader cuts the red cross of St. George out of the colonial flag, the first act of rebellion against England), but the details are symbols of an underground of conflicting values and ideologies.

THE "IMPRESSIONIST" STORY

Several American writers, from Poe to James, were interested in the "impressionist" story that focusses on the impressions registered by events on the characters' minds, rather than the objective reality of the events themselves. In Herman Melville's "Bartleby the Scrivener" (1856) the narrator is a man who unintentionally reveals his own moral weaknesses through his telling of the story of Bartleby. Mark Twain's tales of animals ("The Celebrated Jumping Frog," 1865; "The Story of Old Ram," 1872; "Baker's Blue Jay Yarn," 1879), all impressionist stories, distort ostensible reality in a way that reflects on the men who are speaking. Ambrose Bierce's famous "An Occurrence at Owl Creek Bridge" (1891) is another example of this type of story in which the reader sees a mind at work—distorting, fabricating, and fantasizing—rather than an objective picture of actuality. In contrast, William Dean Howells usually sought an objectifying aesthetic distance. Though Howells was as interested in human psychology and behaviour as any of the impressionist writers, he did not want his details filtered through a biased, and thus distorting, narrator. Impressionism, he felt, gave license for falsifications. In the hands of many writers of his day, it did in fact result in sentimental romanticizing.

But in other hands the impressionist technique could subtly delineate human responses. Henry James was such a writer. Throughout his prefaces to the New York edition of his works, the use of an interpreting "central intelligence" is constantly emphasized. "Again and again, on review," James observes, "the shorter things in especial that I have gathered into [the Edition] have ranged themselves not as my own impersonal account of the affair in hand, but as my account of somebody's impression of it." This use of a central intelligence, who is the "impersonal author's concrete deputy or delegate" in the story, allows James all the advantages of impressionism and, simultaneously, the freedom and mobility common to stories narrated by a disembodied voice.

Respect for the Story

In at least one way, 19th-century America resembled 16th-century Italy: there was an abundance of second- and third-rate short stories. And, yet, respect for the form grew substantially, and most of the great artists of the century were actively participating in its development. The seriousness with which many writers and readers regarded the short story is perhaps most clearly evident in the amount and kind of critical attention it received. James, Howells, Harte, Twain, Melville, and Hawthorne all discussed it as an art form, usually offering valuable insights, though sometimes shedding more light on their own work than on the art as a whole.

But the foremost American critic of the short story was Edgar Allan Poe. Himself a creator of influential impressionist techniques, Poe believed that the definitive characteristic of the short story was its unity of effect. "A skillful literary artist has constructed a tale," Poe wrote in his review of Hawthorne's *Twice-Told Tales* in 1842.

If wise, he has not fashioned his thoughts to accommodate his incidents; but having conceived, with deliberate care, a certain unique or single effect to be wrought out, he then invents such incidents—he then combines such events as may best aid him in establishing this preconceived effect. If his very initial sentence tend not to the out-bringing of this effect, then he has failed in his first step. In the whole composition there should be no word written of which the tendency, direct or indirect, is not to the one pre-established design.

Poe's polemic primarily concerns craftsmanship and artistic integrity. It hardly prescribes limits on subject matter or dictates technique. As such, Poe's thesis leaves the story form open to experimentation and to growth while it demands that the form show evidence of artistic diligence and seriousness.

French Writers

The new respect for the short story was also evident in France, as Henry James observed, "[when in 1844 Prosper] Mérimée with his handful of little stories was appointed to the French Academy." As illustrated by "Columbia" (1841) or "Carmen" (1845), which gained additional fame as an opera, Mérimée's stories are masterpieces of detached and dry observation, though the subject matter itself is often emotionally charged. Nineteenth-century France produced short stories as various as 19th-century America—although the impressionist tale was generally less common in France. (It is as if, not having an outstanding impressionist storyteller themselves, the French adopted Poe, who was being ignored by the critics in his own country.) The two major French impressionist writers were Charles Nodier, who experimented with symbolic fantasies, and Gérard de Nerval, whose collection *Les Filles du feu* (1854; "Daughters of Fire") grew out of recollections of his childhood. Artists primarily known for their work in other forms also attempted the short story—novelists like Honoré de Balzac and Gustave Flaubert and poets like Alfred de Vigny and Théophile Gautier.

One of the most interesting writers of 19th-century France is Alphonse Daudet, whose stories reflect the spectrum of interest and techniques of the entire century. His earliest and most popular stories (*Lettres de mon moulin*, 1866; "Letters from My Mill") create a romantic, picturesque fantasy. His stories of the Franco-Prussian War (*Contes du Lundi*, 1873; "Monday's Tales") are more objectively realistic, and the sociological concern of his last works betrays his increasing interest in naturalistic determinism.

The greatest French storywriter, by far, is Guy de Maupassant, a master of the objective short story. Basically, Maupassant's stories are anecdotes that capture a revealing moment in the lives of middle class citizens. This crucial moment is typically recounted in a well-plotted design, though perhaps in some stories like "Boule de suif" (1880; "Ball of Tallow") and "The Necklace" (1881) the plot is too contrived, the reversing irony too neat, and the artifice too apparent. In other stories, like "The House of Madame Tellier" (1881), Maupassant's easy and fluid prose captures the innocence and the corruption of human behaviour.

RUSSIAN WRITERS

During the first two decades of the 19th century in Russia, fable writing became a fad. By all accounts the most widely read fabulist was Ivan Krylov whose stories borrowed heavily from Aesop, La Fontaine, and various Germanic sources. If Krylov's tales made short prose popular in Russia, the stories of the revered poet Aleksandr Pushkin gained serious attention for the form. Somewhat like Mérimée in France (who was one of the first to translate Pushkin, Gogol, and Turgenev into French), Pushkin cultivated a detached, rather classical style for his stories of emotional conflicts (*The Queen of Spades*, 1834). Also rather popular and respected was Mikhail Lermontov's "novel," *A Hero of Our Time* (1840), which actually consists of five stories that are more or less related.

But it is Nikolay Gogol who stands at the headwaters of the Russian short story. Dostoyevsky noted that all Russian short story writers "emerged from Gogol's overcoat," a punning allusion to the master's best known story. In a manner all his own, Gogol was developing impressionist techniques in Russia simultaneously with Poe in America. Gogol published his *Arabesques* (1835) five years before Poe collected some of his tales under a similar title. Like those of Poe, Gogol's tales of hallucination, confusing reality, and dream, are among his best stories ("Nevsky Prospect" and "Diary of a Madman," both 1835). The single most influential story in the first half of the 19th century in Russia was undoubtedly Gogol's "The Overcoat" (1842).

Ivan Turgenev appears, at first glance, antithetical to Gogol. In *A Sportsman's Notebook* (1852) Turgenev's simple use of language, his calm pace, and his restraint clearly differentiate him from Gogol. But like Gogol, Turgenev was more interested in capturing qualities of people and places than in building elaborate plots. A remaining difference between the two Russians, however, tends to make Turgenev more acceptable to 20th-century readers: Turgenev studiously avoided anything artificial. Though he may have brought into his realistic scenes a tale of a ghost ("Bezhin Meadow," 1852), he did not attempt to bring in a ghost (as Gogol had done in "The Overcoat"). In effect, Turgenev's allegiance was wholly to detached observation.

Developing some of the interests of Gogol, Fyodor Dostoyevsky experimented with the impressionist story. The early story "White Nights" (1848),

for example, is a "Tale of Love from the Reminiscence of a Dreamer" as the subtitle states. The title of one of his last stories, "The Dream of the Ridiculous Man" (1877), also echoes Poe and Gogol. Though sharing Dostoyevsky's interest in human motives, Leo Tolstoy used vastly different techniques. He usually sought psychological veracity through a more detached and, presumably, objective narrator ("The Death of Ivan Ilich," 1886; "The Kreutzer Sonata," 1891). Perhaps somewhat perplexed by Tolstoy's nonimpressionist means of capturing and delineating psychological impressions, Henry James pronounced Tolstoy the masterhand of the disconnection of method from matter.

The Russian master of the objective story was Anton Chekhov. No other storywriter so consistently as Chekhov turned out first-rate works. Though often compared to Maupassant, Chekhov is much less interested in constructing a well-plotted story. Nothing much actually happens in Chekhov's stories, though much is revealed about his characters and the quality of their lives. While Maupassant focuses on event, Chekhov keeps his eye on character. Stories like "The Grasshopper" (1892), "The Darling" (1898), and "In the Ravine" (1900)—to name only three—all reveal Chekhov's perception, his compassion, and his subtle humour and irony. One critic says of Chekhov that he is no moralist—he simply says "you live badly, ladies and gentlemen," but his smile has the indulgence of a very wise man.

Nikolay Gogol

(b. March 19, 1809, Sorochintsy, near Poltava, Ukraine, Russian Empire—d. Feb. 21, 1852, Moscow, Russia)

The Ukrainian-born Russian writer Nikolay Gogol laid the foundations for the great 19th-century tradition of Russian realism. Gogol tried acting and worked at minor government jobs in St. Petersburg before achieving literary success with Evenings on a Farm near Dikanka *(1831–32). His pessimism emerged in such stories as* Taras Bulba *(1835) and* Diary of a Madman *(1835). His farcical drama* The Government Inspector *(1836) lampooned a corrupt government bureaucracy. From 1836 to 1846 he lived in Italy. During this time he wrote his masterpiece, the novel* Dead Souls *(1842), a satire about serfdom and bureaucratic inequities in which he hoped to castigate abuses and guide his countrymen through laughter, and his story "The Overcoat" (1842). Blending elements of realism (natural details from the characters' daily lives) with elements of fantasy (the central character returns as a ghost), Gogol's story seems to anticipate both the impressionism of Dostoyevsky's* Notes from the Underground *and the realism of Tolstoy's* The Death of Ivan Ilich. *His collected stories (1842) received great acclaim. Soon afterward he came under the influence of a fanatical priest who prompted him to burn the manuscript of the second volume of* Dead Souls. *He died a few days later at age 42, perhaps of intentional starvation, on the verge of madness.*

THE 20TH CENTURY AND AFTER

In the first half of the 20th century the appeal of the short story continued to grow. Literally hundreds of writers—including, as it seems, nearly every major dramatist, poet, and novelist—published thousands of excellent stories. William Faulkner suggested that writers often try their hand at poetry, find it too difficult, go on to the next most demanding form, the short story, fail at that, and only then settle for the novel. In the 20th century Germany, France, Russia, and the U.S. lost what had once appeared to be their exclusive domination of the form. Innovative and commanding writers emerged in countries that had previously exerted little influence on the genre: Sicily, for example, produced Luigi Pirandello; Czechoslovakia, Franz Kafka; Japan, Akutagawa Ryūnosuke and, later, Murakami Haruki; Argentina, Jorge Luis Borges and Julio Cortázar. Literary journals with international circulation, such as Ford Madox Ford's *Transatlantic Review,* *Scribner's Magazine,* and Harriet Weaver's *Egoist,* provided a steady and prime exposure for young writers.

As the familiarity with it increased, the short story form itself became more varied and complex. The fundamental means of structuring a story underwent a significant change. The overwhelming or unique event that usually informed the 19th-century story fell out of favour with the storywriters of the early 20th century. They grew more interested in subtle actions and unspectacular events. Sherwood Anderson, one of the most influential U.S. writers of the early 20th century, observed that the common belief in his day was that stories had to be built around a plot, a notion that, in Anderson's opinion, appeared to poison all storytelling. His own aim was to achieve form, not plot, although form was more elusive and difficult. The record of the short story in the 20th century was dominated by this increased sensitivity to—and experimentation with—form. Although the popular writers of the century (such as O. Henry in the U.S. and Paul Morand in France) may have continued to structure stories according to plot, the greater artists turned elsewhere for structure, frequently eliciting the response from cursory readers that "nothing *happens* in these stories." Narratives such as Ernest Hemingway's "A Clean Well-Lighted Place" may seem to have no structure at all, so little physical action develops; but stories of this kind are actually structured around a psychological, rather than physical, conflict. In several of Hemingway's stories (as in many by D.H. Lawrence, Katherine Mansfield, and others), physical action and event are unimportant except insofar as the actions reveal the psychological underpinnings of the story. Stories came to be structured, also, in accordance with an underlying archetypal model: the specific plot and characters are important insofar as they allude to a traditional plot or figure, or to patterns that have recurred with wide implications in the history of humankind. Katherine Anne Porter's "Flowering Judas," for example, echoes and ironically inverts the traditional Christian legend. Still other stories are formed by means of motif, usually a thematic repetition of an image or detail that represents the dominant idea of the story. "The Dead," the final story in James Joyce's *Dubliners*, builds from a casual mention of death and snow early in the story to a culminating paragraph that links them in a profound vision. Seldom, of course, is the specific structure of one story appropriate for a different story. Faulkner, for example, used the traditional pattern of the knightly quest (in an ironic way) for his story "Was," but for "Barn Burning" he relied on a psychologically organic form to reveal the story of young Sarty Snopes.

No single form provided an answer to structural problems. As the primary structuring agent, spectacular and suspenseful action was rather universally rejected around midcentury perhaps because motion pictures and television could present it much more vividly. As the periodicals that had supplied escapist stories to mass audiences declined, the short story became the favoured form of a smaller but intellectually more demanding readership. The Argentine Borges, for example, attracted an international following with his *Ficciones*, stories that involved the reader in dazzling displays of erudition and imagination, unlike anything previously encountered in the genre. Similarly, the American Donald Barthelme's composition consisted of bits and pieces of, for example, television

Katherine Anne Porter. Hulton Archive/Getty Images

commercials, political speeches, literary allusions, overheard conversations, graphic symbols, and dialogue from Hollywood movies—all interspersed with his own original prose in a manner that defied easy comprehension and yet compelled the full attention of the reader. The short story also lent itself to the rhetoric of student protest in the 1960s and was found in a bewildering variety of mixed-media forms in the "underground" press that publicized this life-style throughout the world. A continuing interest in the short story was apparent in the early 21st century, which produced both solid classics by writers such as William Trevor and experimental tales available in many anthologies and literary magazines. Only a secure and valued (not to mention flexible) genre could withstand and, moreover, encourage such experimentation.

SHORT STORY: TERMS AND CONCEPTS

Short stories share many features and devices with novels and other long stories. Both genres, for example, can be centred on detectives or mysteries, and both can be written using a frame story or irony, all of which are covered here. In terms of length, the conte and the novella fall somewhere in between the short story and the novel. The dilemma tale and the literary sketch are unique to the short narrative, and the Arabic *maqāmah* is a specific subgenre.

CONTE

A conte is a short tale, often recounting an adventure. The term may also refer to a narrative that is somewhat shorter than the average novel but longer than a short story. The word is derived from the French word *conter,* "to relate." Better known examples include Jean de La Fontaine's *Contes et nouvelles en vers* (*Tales and Novels in Verse*), published over the course of many years; Charles Perrault's *Contes de ma mère l'oye* (1697; *Tales of Mother Goose*); and Auguste, comte de Villiers de L'Isle-Adam's *Contes cruels* (1883; *Cruel Tales*).

DETECTIVE STORY

The type of popular literature in which a crime is introduced and investigated and the culprit is revealed is called a detective story. Its traditional elements are: a seemingly perfect crime; a wrongly accused suspect at whom circumstantial evidence points; the bungling of dim-witted or cynical police; the greater powers of observation and superior mind of the detective; and the startling and unexpected denouement, in which the detective reveals how the identity of the culprit was ascertained. Detective stories frequently operate on the principle that superficially convincing evidence is ultimately irrelevant. Usually, it is also axiomatic that the clues from which a logical solution to the problem can be reached be fairly presented to the reader at exactly the same time that the sleuth receives them and that the sleuth deduce the solution to the puzzle from a logical interpretation of these clues.

The first detective story was "The Murders in the Rue Morgue" by Edgar Allan Poe, published in April 1841. The profession of detective had come into being only a few decades earlier, and Poe is generally thought to have been influenced by the *Mémoires* (1828–29) of François-Eugène Vidocq, who in 1817 founded the world's first detective bureau, in Paris. Poe's fictional French detective, C. Auguste Dupin, appeared in two other stories, "The Mystery of Marie Roget" (1845) and "The Purloined Letter" (1845).

Sherlock Holmes (right) *explaining to Dr. Watson what he has deduced from a pipe left behind by a visitor; illustration by Sidney Paget for Sir Arthur Conan Doyle's* The Adventure of the Yellow Face, The Strand Magazine, *1893.* Photos.com/Jupiterimages

The detective story soon expanded to novel length.

The French author Émile Gaboriau's *L'Affaire Lerouge* (1866) was an enormously successful novel that had several sequels. Wilkie Collins's *The Moonstone* (1868) remains one of the finest English detective novels. Anna Katharine Green became one of the first American detective novelists with *The Leavenworth Case* (1878). *The Mystery of a Hansom Cab* (1886) by the Australian Fergus Hume was a phenomenal commercial success.

The greatest of all fictional detectives, Sherlock Holmes, along with his loyal, somewhat obtuse companion Dr. Watson, made his first appearance in Arthur (later Sir Arthur) Conan Doyle's novel *A Study in Scarlet* (1887) and continued into the 20th century in such collections of stories as *The Memoirs of Sherlock Holmes* (1894) and the longer *Hound of the Baskervilles* (1902). So great was the appeal of Sherlock Holmes's detecting style that the death of Conan Doyle did little to end Holmes's career. Several writers, often expanding upon circumstances mentioned in the original works, have attempted to carry on the Holmesian tradition.

The early years of the 20th century produced a number of distinguished detective novels, among them Mary Roberts Rinehart's *The Circular Staircase* (1908) and G.K. Chesterton's *The Innocence of Father Brown* (1911) and other novels with the clerical detective. From 1920 on, the names of many fictional detectives became household words: Inspector French, introduced in Freeman Wills Crofts's *The Cask* (1920); Hercule Poirot, in Agatha Christie's *The Mysterious Affair at Styles* (1920), and Miss Marple, in *Murder at the Vicarage* (1930); Lord Peter Wimsey, in Dorothy L. Sayers's *Whose Body?* (1923); Philo Vance, in S.S. Van Dine's *The Benson Murder Case* (1926); Albert Campion, in Margery Allingham's *The Crime at Black Dudley* (1929; also published as *The Black Dudley Murder*); and Ellery Queen, conceived by Frederic Dannay and Manfred B. Lee, in *The Roman Hat Mystery* (1929).

In a sense, the 1930s was the golden age of the detective story, with the aforementioned detectives continuing in new novels. The decade was also marked by the books of Dashiell Hammett, who drew upon his own experience as a private detective to produce both stories and novels, notably *The Maltese Falcon* (1930) featuring Sam Spade. In Hammett's work, the character of the detective became as important as the "whodunit" aspect of ratiocination was earlier. *The Thin Man* (1934), with Nick and Nora Charles, was more in the conventional vein, with the added fillip of detection by a witty married couple. Successors to Hammett included Raymond Chandler and Ross Macdonald, who also emphasized the characters of their tough but humane detectives Philip Marlowe and Lew Archer, respectively. At the end of the 1940s, Mickey Spillane preserved the hard-boiled crime fiction approach of Hammett and others, but his emphasis on sex and sadism became a formula that brought him amazing commercial success beginning with *I, the Jury* (1947).

The introduction of the mass-produced paperback book in the late 1930s made detective-story writers wealthy, among them the Americans Erle Stanley Gardner, whose criminal lawyer Perry Mason unraveled crimes in court; Rex Stout, with his fat, orchid-raising detective Nero Wolfe and his urbane assistant Archie Goodwin; and Frances and Richard Lockridge, with another bright married couple, Mr. and Mrs. North. In France, Georges Simenon produced novel after novel at a rapid-fire pace, making his hero, Inspector Maigret, one of the best-known detectives since Sherlock Holmes. Other writers who carried out the tradition of Holmes or broke new ground included Nicholas Blake (pseudonym of the poet C. Day-Lewis), Michael Innes, Dame

Ngaio Marsh, Josephine Tey, Carter Dickson (John Dickson Carr), and P.D. James. After 1945, writers such as John le Carré adapted the detective-story format to the spy novel, in which he addressed the mysteries and character of the Cold War. At the turn of the 21st century, a number of female detectives had joined the ranks, including Anna Southwood (a character developed by Australian novelist Jean Bedford), Thóra Gudmundsdóttir (by Icelandic writer Yrsa Sigurðardóttir), and Precious Ramotswe (by Rhodesian-born British writer Alexander McCall Smith).

The Mystery Writers of America, a professional organization founded in 1945 to elevate the standards of mystery writing, including the detective story, has exerted an important influence through its annual Edgar Awards for excellence.

DILEMMA TALE

The dilemma tale, also called a judgment tale, is an African form of short story whose ending is either open to conjecture or is morally ambiguous, thus allowing the audience to comment or speculate upon the correct solution to the problem posed in the tale. Typical issues raised involve conflicts of loyalty, the necessity to choose a just response to a difficult situation, and the question of where to lay the blame when several parties seem equally guilty. An example is the story of a young boy who in a time of crisis must choose between loyalty to his own father, who is a cruel and unjust man, and loyalty to the kindly foster-father who brought him up.

Another tale deals with a man who died while hunting an ox to feed his three wives. The first wife learns through a dream what has happened to him, the second leads her fellow wives to the place where he died, and the third restores him to life. Which of the three most deserves his praise?

A third tale has a tortoise as central character. Tortoise wishes to be thought of as equal in power and authority to Hippopotamus and Elephant. When his boastings reach their ears, however, they snub him by saying he is only a small being of no account. So Tortoise challenges both of them to a tug of war and through a trick pits them against each other, thus winning from each the grudging consent that he is their equal. The audience must decide exactly how equal the three of them are.

A final example is the tale of three brothers, all married to the same girl, who journey together to a strange land. One night the girl is murdered by a robber, and the eldest brother, with whom she is sleeping, is condemned to death on suspicion. He begs leave to visit his father before he dies. When he is late in returning, the second brother offers to die in his place, but, as he is about to be executed, the third brother steps forward and "confesses" that he is the murderer. At that moment the eldest brother rides in, just in time to embrace his fate. Which of the brothers, the listeners are asked, is the most noble? As these four examples show, dilemma tales function both as instruction and entertainment, and they help to establish social norms for the audience.

FRAME STORY

An overall unifying story within which one or more tales are related is called a frame story, or a frame tale. In the single story, the opening and closing constitutes a frame. In the cyclical frame story—that is, a story in which several tales are related—some frames are externally imposed and only loosely bind the diversified stories. For example, in *The Thousand and One Nights,* the frame consists of the story of Scheherazade, who avoids death by telling her king-husband a story every night and leaving it incomplete. Another example is the *Jatakatthavannana,* a collection of some 550 widely popular and often illustrated stories of former lives of the Buddha (known as *Jataka*s). It is cast within a framework of Buddhist ethical teaching.

Other frames are an integral part of the tales. Giovanni Boccaccio's *Decameron,* for example, presents a frame story centred on 10 people fleeing the Black Death who gather in the countryside and as an amusement relate 10 stories each. The stories are woven together by a common theme, the way of life of the refined bourgeoisie, who combined respect for conventions with an open-minded attitude toward personal behaviour. In Geoffrey Chaucer's

Canterbury Tales (1387–1400) too, the pilgrimage frame brings together varied tellers of tales, who emerge as vivid personalities and develop dramatic relationships among themselves and with their tales.

IN MEDIAS RES

Fiction that begins with the narrative technique of plunging immediately into a crucial situation that is part of a related chain of events is said to begin in medias res, a Latin phrase meaning "in the midst of things." The opening circumstance is an extension of previous events that will be developed (or reconstructed) in later action. The narrative then goes directly forward, and exposition of earlier events is supplied by flashbacks or other techniques. The principle is based on the practice of Homer in the *Iliad* and the *Odyssey.* The *Iliad,* for example, begins dramatically with the quarrel between Achilles and Agamemnon during the Trojan War. The Latin poet and critic Horace has pointed out the immediate interest created by this opening in contrast to beginning the story ab ovo ("from the egg")—that is, from the birth of Achilles.

INTERIOR MONOLOGUE

The interior monologue is a narrative technique that exhibits the thoughts passing through the minds of the protagonists. These ideas may be either loosely related impressions approaching free association or more rationally structured sequences of thought and emotion.

Interior monologues encompass several forms, including dramatized inner conflicts, self-analysis, imagined dialogue (as in T.S. Eliot's "The Love Song of J. Alfred Prufrock" [1915]), and rationalization. It may be a direct first-person expression apparently devoid of the author's selection and control, as in Molly Bloom's monologue concluding James Joyce's *Ulysses* (1922), or a third-person treatment that begins with a phrase such as "he thought" or "his thoughts turned to."

The term *interior monologue* is often used interchangeably with *stream of consciousness*. But while an interior monologue may mirror all the half thoughts, impressions, and associations that impinge upon the character's consciousness, it may also be restricted to an organized presentation of that character's rational thoughts. Closely related to the soliloquy and dramatic monologue, the interior monologue was first used extensively by Édouard Dujardin in *Les Lauriers sont coupés* (1887; *We'll to the Woods No More*) and later became a characteristic device of 20th-century psychological novels.

VIRGINIA WOOLF

(b. Jan. 25, 1882, London, Eng.—d. March 28, 1941, near Rodmell, Sussex)

The novels of British novelist, essayist, and critic Virginia Woolf exerted a major influence on fiction through her nonlinear approach to narrative. Daughters of the eminent man of letters Leslie Stephen, Virginia and her sister Vanessa became the early nucleus of the Bloomsbury group. Virginia Stephen married Leonard Woolf in 1912, and in 1917 they founded the Hogarth Press. Her best novels—including Mrs. Dalloway *(1925) and* To the Lighthouse *(1927)—are experimental. In them she examines the human experience of time, the indefinability of character, and external circumstances as they impinge on consciousness.* Orlando *(1928) is a historical fantasy about a single character who experiences England from the Elizabethan era to the early 20th century, and* The Waves *(1931), perhaps her most radically experimental work, uses interior monologue and recurring images to trace the inner lives of six characters. Such works confirmed her place among the major figures of literary modernism. Her best critical studies are collected in* The Common Reader *(1925, 1932). Her long essay* A Room of One's Own *(1929) addressed the status of women, and women artists in particular. Her other novels include* Jacob's Room *(1922),* The Years *(1937), and* Between the Acts *(1941). She also wrote a biography of Roger Fry. Her health and mental stability were delicate throughout her life; and in a recurrence of mental illness, she drowned herself. Her diaries and correspondence have been published in several editions.*

IRONY

In the language device known as irony the real meaning of the spoken or written communication is concealed or contradicted by the literal meanings of the words (verbal irony) or in a situation in which there is an incongruity between what is expected and what occurs (dramatic irony).

Verbal irony arises from a sophisticated or resigned awareness of contrast between what is and what ought to be and expresses a controlled pathos without sentimentality. It is a form of indirection that avoids overt praise or censure, as in the casual irony of the statement "That was a smart thing to do!" (meaning "very foolish").

Dramatic irony depends on the structure of a work rather than its use of words. In plays it is often created by the audience's awareness of a fate in store for the characters that they themselves are unaware of, as when Agamemnon accepts the flattering invitation to walk upon the purple carpet that is to become his shroud. The surprise ending of an O. Henry short story is also an example of dramatic irony, as is the more subtly achieved effect of Anton Chekhov's story "Lady with the Dog," in which an accomplished Don Juan engages in a routine flirtation only to find himself seduced into a passionate lifelong commitment to a woman who is no different from all the others.

In the 20th and 21st centuries irony was often used to emphasize the multilayered, contradictory nature of modern (and postmodern) experience. For instance, in Toni Morrison's *Sula* (1973) the black community lives in a neighbourhood called the Bottom, located in the hills above a largely white town. American ethnic writers in particular employed irony in works ranging from memoirs (e.g., Maxine Hong Kingston's *The Woman Warrior* [1976]) to novels (e.g., Gerald Vizenor's *The Heirs of Columbus* [1991]) to disrupt racial stereotypes.

The term *irony* has its roots in the Greek comic character Eiron, a clever underdog who by his wit repeatedly triumphs over the boastful character Alazon. The Socratic irony of the Platonic dialogues derives from this comic origin. Feigning ignorance and humility, Socrates goes about asking silly and obvious questions of all sorts of people on all sorts of subjects, only to expose their ignorance as more profound than his own. The nonliterary use of irony is usually considered sarcasm.

LITERARY SKETCH

The genre of the literary sketch is characterized by a short prose narrative, often an entertaining account of some aspect of a culture written by someone within that culture for readers outside of it— for example, anecdotes of a traveler in India published in an English magazine. Informal in style, the sketch is less dramatic but more analytic and descriptive than the tale and the short story. A writer of a sketch maintains a chatty and familiar tone, understating his major points and suggesting, rather than stating, conclusions.

One common variation of the sketch is the character sketch, a form of casual biography usually consisting of a series of anecdotes about a real or imaginary person.

The sketch was introduced after the 16th century in response to growing middle-class interest in social realism and exotic and foreign lands. The form reached its height of popularity in the 18th and 19th centuries and is represented by such famous sketches as those of Joseph Addison and Richard Steele in *The Spectator* (1711–12). They created characters such as Mr. Spectator, Sir Roger de Coverley, Captain Sentry, and Sir Andrew Freeport, representatives of various levels of English society, who comment on London manners and morals. *The Sketch Book of Geoffrey Crayon, Gent.* (1819–20) is Washington Irving's account of the English landscape and customs for readers in the United States.

MAQĀMAH

The *maqāmah* (an Arabic word meaning "assembly") is an Arabic literary genre in which entertaining anecdotes, often about rogues, mountebanks, and beggars, written in an elegant, rhymed prose (*saj'*), are presented in a dramatic or narrative context most suitable for the display of the author's eloquence, wit, and erudition.

Discussion near a village, from the 43rd maqāmah *of the* Maqāmāt *("Assemblies") of al-Ḥarīrī, miniature painted by Yaḥyā ibn Maḥmūd al-Wāsiṭī, 1237; in the Bibliothèque Nationale, Paris.* Courtesy of the Bibliothèque Nationale, Paris

The first collection of such writings, which make no pretense of being factual, was the *Maqāmāt* of al-Hamadhānī (d. 1008). It consists mainly of picaresque stories in alternating prose and verse woven round two imaginary characters. The genre was revived and finally established in the 11th century by al-Ḥarīrī of Basra (Iraq), whose *Maqāmāt*, closely imitating al-Hamadhānī's, is regarded as a masterpiece of literary style and learning.

AL-HAMADHĀNĪ

(b. 969, Hamadan, Iran—d. 1008, Herāt, Ghaznavid Afghanistan)

The Arabic-language author al-Hamadhānī is famed for introducing the maqāmah *("assembly") form in literature.*

Badīʿ al-Zamān Abū al-Faḍl Aḥmad ibn al-Ḥusayn al-Hamadhānī was often called Badīʿ al-Zamān ("Wonder of the Age"). He achieved an early success through a public debate with Abū Bakr al-Khwarizmī, a leading savant, in Nīshāpūr. He subsequently traveled throughout the area occupied today by Iran and Afghanistan before settling in Herāt and marrying. Al-Hamadhānī is credited with the composition of 400 maqāmahs, of which some 52 are extant (Eng. trans. by W.J. Prendergast, The Maqámát of Badíʿ al-Zamān al-Hamadhānī, *1915). These maqāmahs are written in a combination of prose, rhymed prose, and poetry and recount typically the encounters of the narrator ʿĪsā ibn Hishām with Abū al-Fatḥ al-Iskandarī, a witty orator and talented poet who roams in search of fortune unencumbered by Islamic conventions of honour.*

MYSTERY STORY

The mystery story is an ages-old popular genre of tales dealing with the unknown as revealed through human or worldly dilemmas. It may be a narrative of horror and terror, a pseudoscientific fantasy, a crime-solving story, an account of diplomatic intrigue, an affair of codes and ciphers and secret societies, or any situation involving an enigma. By and large, mystery stories may be divided into two sorts: tales of the supernatural and riddle stories.

Supernatural tales are of ancient origin and form a substantial part of the body of folk literature. But the literary cultivation of fear and curiosity for its own sake began to emerge in the 18th-century pre-Romantic era with the Gothic novel. This genre was invented by a worldly Englishman, Horace Walpole, whose *Castle of Otranto* (1765) may be said to have founded the horror story as a permanent form. Mary Wollstonecraft Shelley introduced the pseudoscientific note in her famous novel *Frankenstein* (1818), about the creation of a monster that ultimately destroys its creator, Dr. Frankenstein.

In the Romantic era the German storyteller E.T.A. Hoffmann and the American writer Edgar Allan Poe raised the mystery story to a level far above mere entertainment through their skillful intermingling of reason and madness, eerie atmosphere and everyday reality. They invested their spectres, doubles, and haunted houses with a psychological symbolism that gave their tales a haunting credibility.

The Gothic influence persisted throughout the 19th century in such works as Joseph Sheridan Le Fanu's *House by the Churchyard* and "Green Tea," Wilkie Collins's *Moonstone,* and Bram Stoker's vampire tale *Dracula.* Later masters of the mystery tale were Ambrose Bierce, Arthur Machen, Algernon Blackwood, Lord Dunsany, and H.P. Lovecraft. However, isolated masterpieces have been produced by writers not usually associated with the genre, for example, Guy de Maupassant's "Horla," A.E. Coppard's "Adam and Eve and Pinch Me," Saki's "Sredni Vashtar" and "The Open Window," and W.F. Harvey's "August Heat." Some of the best-known mystery stories owe their power to their development of full-bodied characters in a realistic social environment and the very absence of mysterious atmosphere. In this category are Aleksandr Pushkin's "Queen of Spades" and W.W. Jacobs's "Monkey's Paw."

Riddle stories, too, have an ancient heritage. The riddle of Samson, propounded in the Bible (Judges 14:12–18), is the most famous early example, but puzzles were also popular among the ancient Egyptians and the Greeks. The distinguishing feature of the riddling mystery story is that the reader be confronted with a number of mysterious facts and situations, explanation of which is reserved until the end of the story.

Poe's short story "The Gold Bug" is a classic example of one perennially popular type of mystery, the story of a search for lost treasure. In the more sinister field of murder are innumerable tales of roguery involving mystery and crime but without the familiar detective interludes. Two notable riddle stories of modern times offered no solution to the riddle posed and gained wide attention by their novelty: "The Lady, or the Tiger?" by Frank R. Stockton and "The Mysterious Card" by Cleveland Moffett.

More nearly akin to the detective story than any of these are the spy stories, tales of international intrigue and adventure, entertainingly written by John Buchan, Valentine Williams, Cyril McNeile, William Le Queux, and many others. Two directions taken by the modern spy story were typified by Ian Fleming's enormously popular James Bond thrillers, using technical marvels that approached science-fiction fantasy, and John le Carré's austerely realistic Cold War-based stories (e.g., *The Spy Who Came in from the Cold,* 1963).

SATIRE

Satire is a chiefly literary and dramatic artistic form, in which human or individual vices, follies, abuses, or short-comings are held up to censure by means of ridicule, derision, burlesque, irony, parody, caricature, or other methods, sometimes with an intent to inspire social reform.

Satire is a protean term. Together with its derivatives, it is one of the most heavily worked literary designations and one of the most imprecise. The great English lexicographer Samuel Johnson defined satire as "a poem in which wickedness or folly is censured," and more elaborate definitions are rarely more satisfactory. No strict definition can encompass the complexity of a word that signifies, on one hand, a kind of literature—as when one speaks of the satires of the Roman poet Horace or calls the American novelist Nathanael West's *A Cool Million* a satire—and, on the other, a mocking spirit or tone that manifests itself in many literary genres but can also enter into almost any kind of human communication. Wherever wit is employed to expose something foolish or vicious to criticism, there satire exists, whether it be in song or sermon, in painting or political debate, on television or in the movies. In this sense satire is everywhere. In literary works, satire can be direct or indirect. With direct satire, the narrator speaks directly to the reader. With indirect satire, the author's intent is realized within the narrative and its story. Although this chapter deals primarily with satire as a literary phenomenon, it records its manifestations in a number of other areas of human activity as well.

HISTORICAL DEFINITIONS

The terminological difficulty is pointed up by a phrase of the Roman rhetorician Quintilian: "satire is wholly our own" ("satura tota nostra est"). Quintilian seems to be claiming satire as a Roman phenomenon, although he had read the Greek dramatist Aristophanes and was familiar with a number of Greek forms that one would call satiric. However, the Greeks had no specific word for satire; and by *satura* (which meant originally something like "medley" or "miscellany" and from which comes the English *satire*) Quintilian intended to specify that kind of poem "invented" by Lucilius, written in hexameters on certain appropriate themes, and characterized by a Lucilian-Horatian tone. *Satura* referred, in short, to a poetic form, established and fixed by Roman practice. (Quintilian mentions also an even older kind of satire written in prose by Marcus Terentius Varro and, one might add, by Menippus and his followers Lucian and Petronius.) After Quintilian's day, *satura* began to be used metaphorically to designate works that were satirical in tone but not in form. As soon as a noun enters the domain of metaphor, as one modern scholar has pointed out, it clamours for extension; and *satura* (which had no verbal, adverbial, or adjectival forms) was immediately broadened

by appropriation from the Greek *satyros* and its derivatives. The odd result is that the English *satire* comes from the Latin *satura*; but *satirize, satiric,* etc., are of Greek origin. By about the 4th century CE the writer of satires came to be known as *satyricus*. St. Jerome, for example, was called by one of his enemies "a satirist in prose" ("satyricus scriptor in prosa"). Subsequent orthographic modifications obscured the Latin origin of the word *satire: satura* becomes *satyra*, and in England by the 16th century it was written *satyre*.

Elizabethan writers, anxious to follow Classical models but misled by a false etymology, believed that *satyre* derived from the Greek satyr play: satyrs being notoriously rude, unmannerly creatures, it seemed to follow that the word *satyre* should indicate something harsh, coarse, rough. The English author Joseph Hall wrote:

> *The Satyre should be like the Porcupine,*
> *That shoots sharpe quils out in each angry line,*
> *And wounds the blushing cheeke, and fiery eye,*
> *Of him that heares, and readeth guiltily.*
> (Virgidemiarum, V,3, 1–4)

The false etymology that derives satire from satyrs was finally exposed in the 17th century by the Classical scholar Isaac Casaubon. But the old tradition has aesthetic if not etymological appropriateness and has remained strong.

In the prologue to his book, Hall makes a claim that has caused confusion like that following from Quintilian's remark on Roman satire. Hall boasts:

I first adventure: follow me who list,
And be the second English Satyrist.

But Hall knew the satirical poems of Geoffrey Chaucer and John Skelton, among other predecessors, and probably meant that he was the first to imitate systematically the formal satirists of Rome.

INFLUENCE OF HORACE AND JUVENAL

By their practice, the great Roman poets Horace and Juvenal set indelibly the lineaments of the genre known as the formal verse satire and, in so doing, exerted pervasive, if often indirect, influence on all subsequent literary satire. They gave laws to the form they established, but it must be said that the laws were quite loose indeed. Consider, for example, style. In three of his Satires (I, iv; I, x; II, i) Horace discusses the tone appropriate to the satirist who out of a moral concern attacks the vice and folly he sees around him. As opposed to the harshness of Lucilius, Horace opts for mild mockery and playful wit as the means most effective for his ends. Although I portray examples of folly, he says, I am not a prosecutor and I do not like to give pain; if I laugh at the nonsense I see about me, I am not motivated by malice. The satirist's verse, he implies, should reflect this attitude: it should be easy and unpretentious, sharp when necessary, but flexible enough to vary from grave to gay. In short, the character of the satirist as projected by Horace is that of an urbane man of the world, concerned about folly, which he sees everywhere, but moved to laughter rather than rage.

Juvenal, more than a century later, conceives the satirist's role differently. His most characteristic posture is that of the upright person who looks with horror on the corruptions of his time, his heart consumed with anger and frustration. Why does he write satire? Because tragedy and epic are irrelevant to his age. Viciousness and corruption so dominate Roman life that, for an honest person, it is difficult not to write satire. He looks about him, and his heart burns dry with rage; never has vice been more triumphant. How can he be silent (*Satires*, I)? Juvenal's declamatory manner, the amplification and luxuriousness of his invective, are wholly out of keeping with the stylistic prescriptions set by Horace. At the end of the scabrous sixth satire, a long, perfervid invective against women, Juvenal flaunts his innovation: in this poem, he says, satire has gone beyond the limits established by his predecessors; it has taken to itself the lofty tone of tragedy.

The results of Juvenal's innovation have been highly confusing for literary history. What is satire if the two poets universally acknowledged to be supreme masters of the form differ so completely in their work as to be almost incommensurable? The formulation of the English poet John Dryden has been widely accepted. Roman satire has two kinds, he says: comical satire and tragical satire, each with its own kind of legitimacy. These denominations have come to mark the boundaries of the satiric spectrum, whether reference is to poetry or prose or to some form of satiric expression in another medium. At the Horatian end of the spectrum, satire merges imperceptibly into comedy, which has an abiding interest in human follies but has not satire's reforming intent. The distinction between the two modes, rarely clear, is marked by the intensity with which folly is pursued: fops and fools and pedants appear in both, but only satire has a moral purpose. And, although the great engine of both comedy and satire is irony, in satire, as the 20th-century critic Northrop Frye has said, irony is militant.

Nicolas Boileau, Dryden, and Alexander Pope, writing in the 17th and 18th centuries—the modern age of satire—catch beautifully, when they like, the deft Horatian tone; however, satire's wit can also be sombre, deeply probing, and prophetic, as it explores the ranges of the Juvenalian end of the satiric spectrum, where satire merges with tragedy, melodrama, and nightmare. Pope's *Dunciad* ends with these lines:

John Dryden. Hulton Archive/Getty Images

Lo! thy dread Empire, CHAOS! is restor'd;
Light dies before thy uncreating word:
Thy hand, great Anarch! lets the curtain fall;
And Universal Darkness buries All.

It is the same darkness that falls on Book IV of Jonathan Swift's *Gulliver's Travels*, on some of Mark Twain's satire—*The Mysterious Stranger, To The Person Sitting in Darkness*—and on George Orwell's *1984.*

JONATHAN SWIFT

(b. Nov. 30, 1667, Dublin, Ire.—d. Oct. 19, 1745, Dublin)

The Irish author Jonathan Swift is the foremost prose satirist in English. He was a student at Dublin's Trinity College during the anti-Catholic Revolution of 1688 in England. Irish Catholic reaction in Dublin led Swift, a Protestant, to seek security in England, where he spent various intervals before 1714. He was ordained an Anglican priest in 1695. His first major work, A Tale of a Tub (1704), comprises three satiric sketches on religion and learning. Swift also became known for religious and political essays and impish pamphlets written under the name "Isaac Bickerstaff." Reluctantly setting aside his loyalty to the Whigs, in 1710 he became the leading writer for the Tories because of their support for the established church. Journal to Stella (written 1710–13) consists of letters recording his reactions to the changing world. As a reward for writing and editing Tory publications, in 1713 he was awarded the deanery of St. Patrick's Cathedral, Dublin. He spent nearly all the rest of his life in Ireland, where he devoted himself to exposing English wrongheadedness and their unfair treatment of the Irish. His ironic tract "A Modest Proposal" (1729) proposes ameliorating Irish poverty by butchering children and selling them as food to wealthy English landlords. His famously brilliant and bitter satire Gulliver's Travels (1726), ostensibly the story of its hero's encounters with various races and societies in remote regions, reflects Swift's vision of humanity's ambiguous position between bestiality and rationality.

STRUCTURE OF VERSE SATIRE

Roman satire is hardly more determinate in its structure than in its style. The poems are so haphazardly organized, so randomly individual, that there seems little justification for speaking of them as a literary kind at all. Beneath the surface complexity of the poems, however, there exists, as one modern scholar has pointed out, a structural principle common to the satires of the Roman poets and their French and English followers. These poems have a bipartite structure: a thesis part, in which some vice or folly is examined critically from many different angles and points of view, and an antithesis part, in which an opposing virtue is recommended. The two parts are disproportionate in length and in importance, for satirists have always been more disposed to castigate wickedness than exhort to virtue.

Most verse satires are enclosed by a "frame." Just as a novel by the early-20th-century writer Joseph Conrad may be framed by a situation in which his narrator sits on a veranda in the tropics, telling his tale, stimulated into elaboration by the queries of his listeners, so the satire will be framed by a conflict of sorts between the satirist (or, more reasonably, his persona, a fictive counterpart, the "I" of the poem) and an adversary. Usually, the adversary has a minor role, serving only to prod the speaker into extended comment on the issue (vice or folly) at hand. He may be sketchily defined, or he may be as effectively projected as Horace's Trebatius (*Satires*, II, i) or his awful bore (I, vi) or his slave Davus, who turns the tables on his master (II, vii). Similarly, the background against which the two talk may be barely suggested, or it may form an integral part of the poem, as in Horace's "Journey to Brundisium" (I, v) or in Juvenal's description of the valley of Egeria, where Umbricius unforgettably pictures the turbulence and decadence of Rome (*Satires*, III). In any event, the frame is usually there, providing a semidramatic situation in which vice and folly may reasonably be dissected.

The satirist has at his disposal an immense variety of literary and rhetorical devices: he may use beast fables, dramatic incidents, fictional experiences, imaginary voyages, character sketches, anecdotes, proverbs, homilies; he may employ invective, sarcasm, burlesque, irony, mockery, raillery, parody, exaggeration, understatement—wit in any of its forms—anything to make the object of attack abhorrent or ridiculous. Amid all this confusing variety, however, there is pressure toward order—internally, from the arraignment of vice and appeal to virtue, and externally, from the often shadowy dramatic situation that frames the poem.

THE SATIRIC SPIRIT

Thus, although the formal verse satire of Rome is quantitatively a small body of work, it contains most of the elements later literary satirists employ. When satire is spoken of today, however, there is usually no sense of formal specification whatever. One has in mind a work imbued with the satiric spirit—a spirit that appears (whether as mockery, raillery, ridicule, or formalized invective) in the literature or folklore of all peoples, early and late, preliterate and civilized. According to Aristotle (*Poetics*, IV, 1448b–1449a), Greek Old Comedy developed out of ritualistic ridicule and invective—out of satiric utterances, that is, improvised and hurled at individuals by the leaders of the phallic songs. The function of these "iambic" utterances, it has been shown, was magical. They were thought to drive away evil influences so that the positive fertility magic of the phallus might be operative. This early connection of primitive "satire" with magic has a remarkably widespread history.

In the 7th century BCE, the poet Archilochus, said to be the "first" Greek literary satirist, composed verses of such potency against his prospective father-in-law, Lycambes, that Lycambes and his daughter hanged themselves. In the next century the sculptors Bupalus and Athenis "knit their necks in halters," it is said, as a result of the "bitter rimes and biting libels" issued by the satirical poet Hipponax. Similar tales exist in other cultures. The chief function of the ancient

Arabic poet was to compose satire (*hijāʾ*) against the tribal enemy. The satires were thought always to be fatal, and the poet led his people into battle, hurling his verses as he would hurl a spear. Old Irish literature is laced with accounts of the extraordinary power of the poets, whose satires brought disgrace and death to their victims:

> . . . saith [King] Lugh to his poet, "what power can you wield in battle?"
> "Not hard to say," quoth Carpre. . . . "I will satirize them, so that through the spell of my art they will not resist warriors."
> ("*The Second Battle of Moytura*," trans. by W. Stokes, Revue Celtique, XII [1891], 52–130.)

According to saga, when the Irish poet uttered a satire against his victim, three blisters would appear on the victim's cheek, and he would die of shame. One story will serve as illustration: after Deirdriu of the Sorrows came to her unhappy end, King Conchobar fell in love again—this time with the lovely Luaine. They were to be married. When the great poet Aithirne the Importunate and his two sons (also poets) saw Luaine, however, they were overcome with desire for her. They went to Luaine and asked her to sleep with them. She refused. The poets threatened to satirize her. And the story says:

> The damsel refused to lie with them. So then they made three

satires on her, which left three blotches on her cheeks, to wit, Shame and Blemish and Disgrace. . . . Thereafter the damsel died of shame. . . .
("*The Wooing of Luaine...*" trans. by W. Stokes, Revue Celtique, XXIV [1903], 273–285.)

SATIRICAL LITERATURE

When the satiric utterance breaks loose from its background in ritual and magic, as in ancient Greece (when it is free, that is, to develop in response to literary stimuli rather than the "practical" impulsions of magic), it is found embodied in an indefinite number of literary forms that profess to convey moral instruction by means of laughter, ridicule, mockery. The satiric spirit proliferates everywhere, adapting itself to whatever mode (verse or prose) seems congenial. Its targets range from one of Pope's dunces to the entire human race, as in *Satyr Against Mankind* (1675), by John Wilmot, the earl of Rochester, from Erasmus's attack on corruptions in the church to Swift's excoriation of all civilized institutions in *Gulliver's Travels*. Its forms are as varied as its victims: from an anonymous medieval invective against social injustice to the superb wit of Chaucer and the laughter of Rabelais; from the burlesque of Luigi Pulci to the scurrilities of Pietro Aretino and the "black humour" of Lenny Bruce; from the flailings of John Marston and the mordancies of Francisco Gómez de Quevedo y Villegas to the bite of Jean de La Fontaine and the great dramatic structures of Ben Jonson and Molière; from an epigram of Martial to the fictions of Nikolay Gogol and of Günter Grass and the satirical utopias of Yevgeny Zamyatin, Aldous Huxley, and Orwell.

It is easy to see how the satiric spirit would combine readily with those forms of prose fiction that deal with the ugly realities of the world but that satire should find congenial a genre such as the fictional utopia seems odd. From the publication of Thomas More's eponymous *Utopia* (1516), however, satire has been an important ingredient of utopian fiction. More drew heavily on the satire of Horace, Juvenal, and Lucian in composing his great work. For example, like a poem by Horace, *Utopia* is framed by a dialogue between "Thomas More" (the historical man a character in his own fiction) and a seafaring philosopher named Raphael Hythloday. The two talk throughout a long and memorable day in a garden in Antwerp. "More's" function is to draw Hythloday out and to oppose him on certain issues, notably his defense of the communism he found in the land of Utopia. "More" is the adversary. Hythloday's role is to expound on the institutions of Utopia but also to expose the corruption of contemporary society. Thus he functions as a satirist. Here Hythloday explains why Englishmen, forced off their land to make way for sheep, become thieves:

> *Forsooth . . . your sheep that were wont to be so meek and tame and so small eaters, now as I hear say,*

> *be become so great devourers and so wild, that they eat up and swallow down the very men themselves. They consume, destroy, and devour whole fields, houses, and cities. For look in what parts of the realm doth grow the finest and therefore dearest wool, there noblemen and gentlemen, yea and certain abbots, holy men no doubt, not contenting themselves with the yearly revenues and profits that were wont to grow to their fore-fathers and predecessors of their lands, nor being content that they live in rest and pleasure nothing profiting, yea, much annoying the weal-public, leave no ground for tillage. They enclose all into pastures; they throw down houses; they pluck down towns and leave nothing standing but only the church to be made a sheep-house.*
> (*More's* Utopia, *Everyman edition, 1951.*)

Here are characteristic devices of the satirist, dazzlingly exploited: the beast fable compressed into the grotesque metaphor of the voracious sheep; the reality-destroying language that metamorphoses gentlemen and abbots into earthquakes and a church into a sheep barn; the irony coldly encompassing the passion of the scene. Few satirists of any time could improve on this.

Just as satire is a necessary element of the work that gave the literary form utopia its name, so the utopias of Lilliput, Brobdingnag, and Houyhnhnmland are essential to the satire of More's great follower Jonathan Swift. He sent Gulliver to different lands from those Hythloday discovered, but Gulliver found the same follies and the same vices, and he employed a good many of the same rhetorical techniques his predecessor had used to expose them. *Gulliver's Travels*, as one scholar points out, is a salute across the centuries to Thomas More. With this kind of precedent, it is not surprising that in the 20th century, when utopia turned against itself, as in Aldous Huxley's *Brave New World* (1932), the result was satire unrelieved.

THE SATIRIST, THE LAW, AND SOCIETY

Indeed, the relations of satirists to the law have always been delicate and complex. Both Horace and Juvenal took extraordinary pains to avoid entanglements with authority—Juvenal ends his first satire with the self-protective announcement that he will write only of the dead. In England in 1599 the Archbishop of Canterbury and the Bishop of London

In Jonathon Swift's satirical Gulliver's Travels, *Gulliver journeys to many places, including Lilliput, where he encounters many of the same vices as those found by the character Raphael Hythloday in Thomas More's* Utopia. Hulton Archive/Getty Images

issued an order prohibiting the printing of any satires whatever and requiring that the published satires of Hall, John Marston, Thomas Nashe, and others be burned.

Today the satirist attacks individuals only at the risk of severe financial loss to himself and his publisher. In totalitarian countries he even risks imprisonment or death. Under extreme conditions satire against the reigning order is out of the question. Such was the case in the Soviet Union and most other communist countries. For example, the poet Osip Mandelshtam was sent to a concentration camp and his death for composing a satirical poem on Stalin.

One creative response the satirist makes to social and legal pressures is to try by rhetorical means to approach his target indirectly. That is, a prohibition of direct attack fosters the manoeuvres of indirection that will make the attack palatable: e.g., irony, burlesque, and parody. It is a nice complication that the devices that render satire acceptable to society at the same time sharpen its point. "Abuse is not so dangerous," said Dr. Johnson, "when there is no vehicle of wit or delicacy, no subtle conveyance." The conveyances are born out of prohibition.

Anthony Cooper, 3rd earl of Shaftesbury, writing in the 18th century, recognized the "creative" significance of legal and other repressions on the writing of satire. "The greater the weight [of constraint] is, the bitterer will be the satire. The higher the slavery, the more exquisite the buffoonery." Shaftesbury's insight requires the aforementioned qualification. Under a massively efficient tyranny, satire of the forms, institutions, or personalities of that tyranny is impossible. But, under the more relaxed authoritarianism of an easier going day, remarkable things could be done. Max Radin, a Polish-born American author, noted how satirical journals in Germany before World War I, even in the face of a severe law, vied with each other to see how close they could come to caricatures of the Kaiser without actually producing them. "Satire which the censor understands," said the Austrian satirist Karl Kraus, "deserves to be banned."

The 20th-century American critic Kenneth Burke summed up this paradoxical aspect of satire's relation with the law by suggesting that the most inventive satire is produced when the satirist knowingly takes serious risks and is not sure whether he will be acclaimed or punished. The whole career of Voltaire is an excellent case in point. Although bigots and tyrants may have turned pale at his name, as a famous hyperbole has it, Voltaire's satire was sharpened and his life rendered painfully complicated as he sought to avoid the penalties of the law and the wrath of those he had angered. Men such as Voltaire and Kraus and the Russian Ye.I. Zamyatin attack evil in high places, pitting their wit and moral authority against cruder forms of power. In this engagement there is frequently something of the heroic.

Readers have an excellent opportunity to examine the satirist's claim to social approval by reason of the literary convention that decrees that he must justify his problematic art. Nearly all satirists write apologies, and nearly all the apologies project an image of the satirist as a plain, honest man, wishing harm to no worthy person but appalled at the evil he sees around him and forced by his conscience to write satire. Pope's claim is the most extravagant:

> Yes, I am proud; I must be proud
> to see
> Men not afraid of God, afraid of me:
> Safe from the Bar, the Pulpit, and
> the Throne,
> Yet touch'd and sham'd by
> Ridicule alone.
> O sacred Weapon! left for Truth's
> defence,
> Sole Dread of Folly, Vice, and
> Insolence!
> (Epilogue to the Satires, II, 208–13)

After the great age of satire, which Pope brought to a close, such pretensions would have been wholly anachronistic. Ridicule depends on shared assumptions against which the deviant stands in naked relief. The satirist must have an audience that shares with him commitment to certain intellectual and moral standards that validate his attacks on aberration. The greatest satire has been written in periods when ethical and rational norms were sufficiently powerful to attract widespread assent yet not so powerful as to compel absolute conformity—those periods when the satirist could be of his society and yet apart, could exercise a double vision.

Neoclassic writers had available to them as an implicit metaphor the towering standard of the classical past. For the 19th and 20th centuries no such metaphors have been available. It is odd, however, that, whereas the 19th century in general disliked and distrusted satire (there are of course obvious exceptions), our own age, bereft of unifying symbols, scorning traditional rituals, searching for beliefs, still finds satire a congenial mode in almost any medium. Although much 20th-century satire was dismissed as self-serving and trivial, there were notable achievements. Joseph Heller's novel *Catch-22* (1961) once again made use of farce as the agent of the most probing criticism: Who is sane, the book asks, in a world whose major energies are devoted to blowing itself up? Beneath a surface of hilariously grotesque fantasy, in which characters from Marx Brothers' comedy carry out lethal assignments, there is exposed a dehumanized world of hypocrisy, greed, and cant. Heller was a satirist in the great tradition. If he could no longer, like Pope, tell men with confidence what they should be for, he was splendid at showing them what they must be against. The reader laughs at the mad logic of *Catch-22*, and, as he laughs, he learns. This is precisely the way satire has worked from the beginning.

SATIRE: TERMS AND CONCEPTS

Parody, burlesque, pasquinade, and travesty are among specialized types of satire.

Readers may also come across a subgenre of satire known as fool's literature.

ANATOMY

In literature, the term *anatomy* refers to the separation or division of a topic into parts for detailed examination or analysis. Among the better-known examples are John Lyly's *Euphues: The Anatomy of Wit* and Robert Burton's *Anatomy of Melancholy.* The literary critic Northrop Frye, in his book *Anatomy of Criticism,* narrowed the definition of the word to mean a work resembling a Menippean satire, or one in which a mass of information is brought to bear on the subject being satirized, usually a particular attitude or type of behaviour. The word is from a Greek word meaning "dissection."

BURLESQUE

A comic imitation of a serious literary or artistic form that relies on an extravagant incongruity between a subject and its treatment is called burlesque. In this genre, the serious is treated lightly and the frivolous seriously. Genuine emotion is sentimentalized, and trivial emotions are elevated to a dignified plane. Burlesque is closely related to parody, in which the language and style of a particular author, poem, or other work is mimicked, although burlesque is generally broader and coarser.

The long history of burlesque includes such early examples in Greece as *Batrachomyomachia (The Battle of the Frogs and Mice),* an anonymous burlesque of Homer, and the comedies of Aristophanes (5th–4th century BCE). The long-winded medieval romance is satirized in Geoffrey Chaucer's 14th-century "Tale of Sir Thopas." The Charlemagne story and the whole theme of chivalry is mocked in the epic-style *Morgante* by Luigi Pulci. Italian burlesque of the 15th century attacked the concept of chivalry as a dying aristocratic notion lacking in common sense, and it thus anticipates Miguel de Cervantes's novel *Don Quixote,* which is, however, of a size and seriousness that makes it somewhat more than simple burlesque. In the France of Louis XIV, burlesque was used by the "Moderns" in their quarrel with the "Ancients" and vice versa. The *Virgile Travesty* (1648–53) of Paul Scarron is one of the best known of many burlesque or antiheroic epics on classical themes.

English burlesque is chiefly dramatic, notable exceptions being Samuel Butler's satiric poem *Hudibras* (1663–78), an indictment of Puritan hypocrisy; the mock heroic couplets of John Dryden and Alexander Pope; and the prose burlesques of Jonathan Swift and Henry Fielding. George Villiers's play *The Rehearsal* (1671), which mocks the Restoration drama of Dryden and Thomas Otway; John Gay's *Beggar's Opera* (1728); Henry Fielding's *Tom Thumb* (1730); Richard Brinsley Sheridan's *The Critic* (1779); and Henry Carey's "most tragical tragedy" *Chrononhotonthologos* (1734) are the outstanding survivals from an age when burlesque was cruelly satirical and often defamatory. The heroic Bombardinion's lines in the following fragment from Carey's play resemble the more kindly, punning Victorian burlesque, however:

> Go call a coach, and let a coach
> be called;
> And let the man who calls it be the
> caller;
> And in his calling, let him noth-
> ing call,
> But coach! coach! coach! Oh! for
> a coach,
> ye gods!

Authors of Victorian burlesque—light entertainment with music, the plots of which were frivolously modeled on those of history, literature, or classical mythology—included H.J. Byron, J.R. Planché, and W.S. Gilbert (before his partnership with Arthur Sullivan). Before the end of the 19th century, burlesque yielded in popular favour to musical comedy in Britain and had become almost exclusively identified with vaudeville humour in the United States.

FOOL'S LITERATURE

A type of allegorical satire popular throughout Europe from the 15th to the 17th century featured the fool, or jester, who represented the weaknesses, vices, and grotesqueries of contemporary society. The first outstanding example of this so-called fool's literature was *Das Narrenschiff* (1494; *The Ship of Fools*), a long poem by the German satirist Sebastian Brant.

SEBASTIAN BRANT

(b. 1457, Strassburg, Ger.—d. May 10, 1521, Strassburg)

The German poet Sebastian Brant wrote the most popular German literary work of the 15th century. He taught law and later was appointed imperial councillor and court palatine by Maximilian I. His varied writings include works on law, religion, politics, and especially morals. The Ship of Fools (1494), the work for which he is remembered, is an allegory. It tells the tale of more than 100 fools gathered on a ship bound for Narragonia, the fools' paradise. An unsparing, bitter, and sweeping satire, especially of the corruption in the Roman Catholic Church, Das Narrenschiff was translated into Latin, Low German, Dutch, and French and adapted in English by Alexander Barclay (The Shyp of Folys of the Worlde, 1509). It stimulated the development of biting moral satires such as Thomas Murner's poem Narrenbeschwörung (1512; "Exorcism of Fools") and Erasmus's Encomium moriae (1509; In Praise of Folly). The American writer Katherine Anne Porter used Brant's title for her Ship of Fools (1962), an allegorical novel in which the German ship Vera is a microcosm of life.

LAMPOON

The word *lampoon* is from the French word *lampon*, probably from *lampons!* meaning "let us gulp down!" (a frequent refrain in 17th-century French satirical poems). A virulent satire in prose or verse that is a gratuitous and sometimes unjust and malicious attack on an individual. Although the term came into use in the 17th century from the French, examples of the lampoon are found as early as the 3rd century BCE in the plays of Aristophanes, who lampooned Euripides in *Frogs* and Socrates in *Clouds*. In English literature the form was particularly popular during the Restoration and the 18th century, as exemplified in the lampoons of John Dryden, Thomas Brown, and John Wilkes, as well as dozens of anonymous satires.

PARODY

Parody, from the Greek *parōidía*, meaning "a song sung alongside another," is a form of satirical criticism or comic mockery that imitates the style and manner of a particular writer or school of writers so as to emphasize the weakness of the writer or the overused conventions of the school. Differing from burlesque by the depth of its technical penetration and from travesty, which treats dignified subjects in a trivial manner, true parody mercilessly exposes the tricks of manner and thought of its victim yet cannot be written without a thorough appreciation of the work that it ridicules.

An anonymous poet of ancient Greece imitated the epic style of Homer in *Batrachomyomachia* (*The Battle of the Frogs and Mice*), one of the earliest examples of parody. Aristophanes parodied the dramatic styles of Aeschylus and Euripides in *The Frogs*. Chaucer parodied the chivalric romance in "The Tale of Sir Thopas" (c. 1375), as did Cervantes in *Don Quixote* (1605). Rabelais parodied the Scholastics in *Gargantua and Pantagruel* (1532–34). Shakespeare mimicked Christopher Marlowe's high dramatic style in the players' scene in *Hamlet* and was himself parodied by John Marston, who wrote a travesty of *Venus and Adonis* entitled *The Metamorphosis of Pigmalions Image* (1598). The 2nd duke of Buckingham in *The Rehearsal* (1671) and Sheridan in *The Critic* (1779) both parodied the heroic drama, especially Dryden's *Conquest of Granada* (1670). In *The Splendid Shilling* (1705) John Phillips caught all the superficial epic mannerisms of Milton's *Paradise Lost* (1667). Racine parodied Corneille's lofty dramatic style in *Les Plaideurs* (1668, "The Litigants"). Fielding parodied Richardson's sentimental novel *Pamela* (1740) in *Shamela* (1741) and *Joseph Andrews* (1742) and mimicked the heroic play in *Tom Thumb* (1730).

In England the first collection of parodies to score a wide success was *Rejected Addresses* (1812) by Horace and James Smith, a series of dedicatory odes on the reopening of the Drury Lane Theatre in the manner of such contemporary poets as Scott, Byron, Southey, Wordsworth, and Coleridge. Unique among the Victorians is Lewis Carroll, whose parodies preserve verses that would otherwise not have survived—for example, Robert Southey's "Old Man's Comforts" (the basis for "You Are Old, Father William") and the verses of Isaac Watts that gave rise to "How Doth the Little Crocodile" and "The Voice of the Lobster."

In the United States the 19th-century poems of Poe, Whitman, Whittier, and Bret Harte were mimicked by their contemporaries, particularly by the poet and translator Bayard Taylor. Because of the variety of accents of 19th-century immigrants, U.S. parody often played on dialect (e.g., Charles G. Leland's *Hans Breitmann's Ballads* first published under that title in 1884, a parody of the German poets Heine and Uhland in macaronic German American). Among later parodists, Samuel Hoffenstein is outstanding for his carefully damaging versions of A.E. Housman and the Georgian poets.

The art of parody was encouraged in the 20th century and after by such periodicals as *Punch* and *The New Yorker*. The scope of parody has been widened to take in the far more difficult task of parodying prose. One of the most successful examples is Sir Max Beerbohm's *Christmas Garland* (1912), a series of Christmas stories in the style and spirit of various contemporary writers, most notably Henry James. Another innovation is double parody, invented by Sir John Squire in the period between World Wars I and II. Double parody is the rendering of the sense of one poet in the style of another—for example, Squire's version of Thomas Gray's "Elegy Written in a Country Churchyard" written in the style of Edgar Lee Masters's *Spoon River*

Anthology resulted in "If Gray Had Had to Write His Elegy in the Cemetery of Spoon River Instead of in That of Stoke Poges." Also outstanding among modern parodists have been Sir Arthur Quiller-Couch, Stephen Leacock, and E.B. White.

PASQUINADE

A pasquinade is a brief and generally anonymous satirical comment in prose or verse that ridicules a contemporary leader or national event. *Pasquinade* is derived from "Pasquino," the popular name for the remains of an ancient Roman statue unearthed in Rome in 1501. "Pasquino," supposedly named after a local shopkeeper near whose house or shop the statue was discovered, was the focus for bitingly critical political squibs attached to its torso by anonymous satirists. These pasquinades and their imitations, some ascribed to important 16th-century writers such as Aretino, were collected and published. After the 16th century the vogue of posting pasquinades died out, and the term acquired its more general meaning.

TRAVESTY

In literature, the treatment of a noble and dignified subject in an inappropriately trivial manner is called a travesty. It is a crude form of burlesque in which the original subject matter is changed little but is transformed into something ridiculous through incongruous language and style. An early example of travesty is the humorous treatment of the Pyramus and Thisbe legend in Shakespeare's *A Midsummer Night's Dream* (1595-96). After 1660, travesty became a popular literary device in England as seen in John Phillips's *Don Quixote* (1687), a vulgar mockery of the original work, and Charles Cotton's travesty of Virgil, *Scarronides: or, Virgile Travestie. Being the First Book of Virgil's Aeneis in English, Burlesque* (1664), an imitation of the French *Virgile travesty* (1648-53) by Paul Scarron. (The use of the word *travesty*—literally, "dressed in disguise"—in the title of Scarron's work gave rise to the English word, first as an adjective.) Later the French developed the *féeries folies,* a musical burlesque that travestied fairy tales.

CHAPTER 8

BIOGRAPHY

A biography is commonly a work of nonfiction, the usual subject of which is the life of an individual. Starting in the 20th century, the term also was used to describe other types of portrait, for example, that of a region or continent (*Night Comes to the Cumberlands: A Biography of a Depressed Area*, 1963; *Africa: A Biography of a Continent*, 1997), an object (*America's Constitution: A Biography*, 2005), and an ethnic group (*Latinos: A Biography of the People*, 1992). One of the oldest forms of literary expression, the biography still typically seeks to re-create in words the life of a human being—as understood from the historical or personal perspective of the author—by drawing upon all available evidence, including that retained in memory as well as written, oral, and pictorial material. These portraits may be of several types.

HISTORICAL ASPECTS

Biography is sometimes regarded as a branch of history, and earlier biographical writings—such as the 15th-century *Mémoires* of the French counselor of state, Philippe de Commynes, or George Cavendish's 16th-century life of Thomas Cardinal Wolsey—have often been treated as historical material rather than as literary works in their own right. Some entries in ancient Chinese chronicles included biographical sketches. Embedded in the Roman historian Tacitus's *Annals* is the most famous biography of the emperor Tiberius. Conversely, Sir Winston Churchill's magnificent life of his ancestor John Churchill, first duke of Marlborough, can be read as a history (written from a special point of view) of Britain and much of Europe during the War of the Spanish Succession (1701–14). Yet there is general recognition today that history and biography are quite distinct forms of literature. History usually deals in generalizations about a period of time (for example, the Renaissance), about a group of people in time (the English colonies in North America), about an institution (monasticism during the Middle Ages). Biography more typically focuses upon a single human being and deals in the particulars of that person's life.

Both biography and history, however, are often concerned with the past, and it is in the hunting down, evaluating, and selection of sources that they are akin. In this sense biography can be regarded as a craft rather than an art: techniques of research and general rules for testing evidence can be learned by anyone and thus need involve comparatively little of that personal commitment associated with art.

A biographer in pursuit of an individual long dead is usually hampered by a lack of sources: it is often impossible to check or verify what written evidence there is; no witnesses are available to cross-examine. No method has yet been developed by which to overcome such problems. Each life, however, presents its own opportunities as well as specific difficulties to the biographer: the ingenuity with which the biographer handles gaps in the record—by providing information, for example, about the age that casts light upon the subject—has much to do with the quality of the resulting work. James Boswell knew comparatively little about Samuel Johnson's earlier years. It is one of the greatnesses of his *Life of Samuel Johnson LL.D.* (1791) that he succeeded, without inventing matter or deceiving the reader, in giving the sense of a life progressively unfolding. Other masterpieces of reconstruction in the face of little evidence are A.J.A. Symons's biography of the English author and eccentric Frederick William Rolfe, *The Quest for Corvo* (1934), and Stephen Greenblatt's masterful *Will in the World: How Shakespeare Became Shakespeare* (2004), which susses out Shakespeare's life from his works and milieu. A further difficulty is the unreliability of most collections of papers, letters, and other memorabilia edited before the 20th century. Not only did editors feel free to omit and transpose materials, but sometimes the authors of documents revised their personal writings for the benefit of posterity, often falsifying the record and presenting their biographers with a difficult situation when the originals were no longer extant.

The biographer writing the life of a person recently dead is often faced with the opposite problem: an abundance of living witnesses and a plethora of materials, which include the subject's papers and letters, sometimes transcriptions

William Shakespeare. Oli Scarff/Getty Images

of telephone conversations and conferences, as well as the record of interviews granted to the biographer by the subject's friends and associates. Frank Friedel, for example, in creating a biography of the U.S. president Franklin D. Roosevelt, had to wrestle with something like 40 tons of paper. But finally, when writing the life of any person, whether long or recently dead, the biographer's chief responsibility is vigorously to test the authenticity of the collected materials by whatever rules and techniques are available. When the subject of a biography is still alive and a contributor to the work, the biographer's task is to examine the subject's perspective against multiple, even contradictory sources.

PSYCHOLOGICAL ASPECTS

Assembling a string of facts in chronological order does not constitute the life of a person. It only gives an outline of events. The biographer therefore seeks to elicit from his materials the motives for his subject's actions and to discover the shape of his personality. The biographer who has known the subject in life enjoys the advantage of his or her own direct impressions, often fortified by what the subject has revealed in conversations, and of having lived in the same era (thus avoiding the pitfalls in depicting distant centuries). But on the debit side, such a biographer's view is coloured by the emotional factor almost inevitably present in a living association. Conversely, the biographer who knows the subject only from written evidence, and perhaps from the report of witnesses, lacks the insight generated by a personal relationship but can generally command a greater objectivity in his effort to probe his or her subject's inner life.

Biographers of the 20th and 21st centuries had at their disposal the psychological theories and practice of Sigmund Freud and of his followers and rivals. The extent to which these relatively recent biographical tools for the unlocking of personality were employed and the results of their use varied greatly. Some biographers deployed upon their pages the apparatus of psychological revelation—analysis of behaviour symbols, interpretation based on the Oedipus complex, detection of Jungian archetypal patterns of behaviour, and the like. Other biographers, usually the authors of scholarly large-scale lives, continued to ignore the psychological method. Still others, though avoiding explicit psychological analysis and terminology, nonetheless presented aspects of their subjects' behaviours in such a way as to suggest psychological interpretations. In general, the movement, since World War I, was toward a discreet use of the psychological method, from Katherine Anthony's *Margaret Fuller* (1920) and Joseph Wood Krutch's study of Edgar Allan Poe (1926), which enthusiastically embraced such techniques, through Erik Erikson's *Young Man Luther* (1958) and *Gandhi's Truth on the Origins of Militant Nonviolence* (1969), where they were adroitly and sagaciously used by a biographer who was himself a psychiatrist, to Leon Edel's vast biography of Henry James (5 vol., 1953–72), where they were used with sophistication by a man of letters. The science of psychology also began to affect the biographer's very approach to his subject: a number of 20th-century authors sought to explore their own involvement with the person they wrote about before embarking upon the life itself. This type of psychological approach was still in evidence at the turn of the 21st century, which saw publication of such volumes as *Granite and Rainbow: The Hidden Life of Virginia Woolf* (1998), an examination of the material below the surface of the renowned writer's life.

ETHICAL ASPECTS

The biographer, particularly the biographer of a contemporary, is often confronted with an ethical problem: how much of the truth, as he has been able to ascertain it, should be printed? Since the inception of biographical criticism in the later 18th century, this somewhat arid—because unanswerable—question has dominated both literary and popular discussion of biographical literature. Upon the publication of the *Life of Samuel Johnson*, James Boswell was bitterly accused of slandering his celebrated subject. More than a century and a half later, Lord Moran's *Winston Churchill: The Struggle for Survival, 1940–1965* (1966), in which Lord Moran used the Boswellian techniques of reproducing conversations from his immediate notes and jottings, was attacked in much the same terms (though the question was complicated by Lord Moran's confidential position as Churchill's physician). In the United States, William Manchester's *Death of a President* (1967), on John F. Kennedy, created an even greater stir in the popular press. There the issue is usually presented as "the public's right to know." For the biographer it is a problem of his obligation to preserve historical truth as measured against the personal anguish he may inflict on others in doing so. Since no standard of "biographical morality" has ever been agreed upon—Boswell, Lord Moran, and Manchester have all, for example, had eloquent defenders—the individual biographer must steer his own course. Beginning in the 20th century, that course was sometimes complicated by the refusal of the custodians of the papers of important persons, particularly national political figures, to provide access to all the documents.

AESTHETIC ASPECTS

Biography, while related to history in its search for facts and its responsibility to truth, is truly a branch of literature because it seeks to elicit from facts, by selection and design, the illusion of a life actually being lived. Within the bounds of given data, biographers seek to transform plain information into illumination. If they invent or suppress material to create an effect, they fail truth. If they are content to recount facts, they fail art. This tension, between the requirements of authenticity and the necessity for an imaginative ordering of materials to achieve lifelikeness, is perhaps best exemplified in the biographical problem of time. Biographers seek to portray the unfolding of a life with all its crosscurrents of interests, changing emotional states, and events. Yet to avoid reproducing the confusion and clutter of actual daily existence, they must interrupt the flow of diurnal time and group materials so as to reveal traits of personality, grand themes of experience, and the actions and attitudes leading to moments of high decision. Their achievements as biographers will be measured, in great part, by their ability to suggest the sweep of chronology and yet to highlight the major patterns of behaviour that give a life its shape and meaning.

KINDS OF BIOGRAPHY

Biographies are difficult to classify. It is easily recognizable that there are many kinds of lifewriting, but one kind can easily shade into another. No standard basis for classification has yet been developed. A fundamental division offers, however, a useful preliminary view: biographies written from personal knowledge of the subject and those written from research.

FIRSTHAND KNOWLEDGE

The biography that results from what might be called a vital relationship between the biographer and the subject often represents a conjunction of two main biographical forces: a desire on the part of the writer to preserve "the earthly pilgrimage of a man," as the 19th-century historian Thomas Carlyle calls it (*Critical and Miscellaneous Essays*, 1838), and an awareness that he has the special qualifications, because of direct observation and access to personal papers, to undertake such a task. This kind of biography is, in one form or another, to be found in most of the cultures that preserve any kind of written biographical tradition, and it is commonly to be found in all ages from the earliest literatures to the present. In its first manifestations, it was often produced by, or based upon the recollections of, the disciples of a religious figure—such as the biographical fragments concerning Buddha, portions of the Hebrew Bible, and the Christian gospels. It is sometimes called "source biography" because it preserves original materials, the testimony of the biographer, and often intimate papers of the subject (which have proved invaluable for later biographers and historians—as exemplified by Einhard's 9th-century *Vita Karoli imperatoris* ["Life of Charlemagne"] or Thomas Moore's *Letters and Journals of Lord Byron* [1830]). Biography based on a living relationship has produced a wealth of masterpieces: Tacitus's life of his father-in-law in the *Agricola*, William Roper's life of his father-in-law Sir Thomas More (1626), John Gibson Lockhart's biography (1837–38) of his father-in-law Sir Walter Scott, Johann Peter Eckermann's *Conversations with Goethe* (1836; trans. 1839), Virginia Woolf's biography of her fellow Bloomsbury member Roger Fry (1940), and Ernest Jones's *Life and Work of Sigmund Freud* (1953–57). Indeed, what is generally acknowledged as the greatest biography ever written belongs to this class: James Boswell's *Life of Samuel Johnson*.

JAMES BOSWELL

(b. Oct. 29, 1740, Edinburgh, Scot.—d. May 19, 1795, London, Eng.)

The Scottish writer James Boswell is renowned as the friend and biographer of Samuel Johnson. Boswell, a lawyer, met Johnson in 1763 and visited him often (1772–84), making a superlatively detailed record in his journals of Johnson's conversations. His Journal of a Tour to the Hebrides *(1785) is mainly an account of Johnson's responses to their 1773 trip to Scotland. Boswell's two-volume* Life of Samuel Johnson, LL.D. *(1791) is regarded as one of the greatest English biographies. Despite their acclaim for his work, contemporary critics derided the author. Boswell took intense pleasure in his literary fame but felt himself to be a failure. His later years were prevailingly unhappy. His eccentricities of manner seemed merely self-indulgent in a man of 50 or more: people were afraid to talk freely in his presence, fearing that their talk would be reported, and his habit of getting drunk and noisy at other people's tables (he was never a solitary drinker) made him a difficult guest. Clearly a skillful biographer, Boswell also proved to be an extraordinary diarist when several of his journals were published in the 20th century.*

RESEARCH

Biographies that are the result of research rather than firsthand knowledge present a rather bewildering array of forms. First, however, there should be mentioned two special kinds of biographical activity.

REFERENCE COLLECTIONS

Since the late 18th century, the Western world—and, in the 20th century, the rest of the world as well—has produced increasing numbers of compilations of biographical facts concerning both the living and the dead. These collections stand apart from literature. Many nations have multivolume biographical dictionaries such as the *Dictionary of National Biography* in Britain and the *American National Biography* in the United States. General encyclopaedias contain extensive information about figures of world importance. Classified collections such as *Lives of the Lord Chancellors* (Britain) and biographical manuals devoted to scholars, scientists, and other groups are available in growing numbers. Information about living persons is gathered into such national collections as *Who's Who?* (Britain), *Chi è?* (Italy), and *Who's Who in America?*

CHARACTER SKETCHES

The short life, however, is a genuine current in the mainstream of biographical literature and is represented in many ages and cultures. Excluding early quasi-biographical materials about religious or political figures, the short biography first appeared in China at about the end of the 2nd century BCE, and two centuries later it was a fully developed literary form in the Roman Empire. The *Shiji* ("Historical Records"), by Sima Qian (145?–*c.* 85 BCE), include lively biographical sketches, extremely short and anecdotal with plentiful dialogue, grouped by character-occupation types such as "maligned statesmen," "rash generals," "assassins," a method that became established tradition with the *Hanshu* (*History of the Former Han Dynasty*), by Sima Qian's successor and imitator, Pan Gu (32–92 CE). Toward the end of the 1st century CE, in the Mediterranean world, Plutarch's *Lives of the Noble Grecians and Romans*, which are contrasting pairs of biographies, one Greek and one Roman, appeared. There followed within a brief span of years the *Lives of the Caesars*, by the Roman emperor Hadrian's librarian Suetonius. These works established a quite subtle mingling of character sketch with chronological narrative that has ever since been the dominant mark of this genre. Plutarch, from an ethical standpoint emphasizing the political virtues of man as governor, and Suetonius, from the promptings of sheer biographical curiosity, develop their subjects with telling details of speech and action. Although Plutarch, generally considered to be the superior artist, has greatly influenced other arts than biographical literature—witness Shakespeare's Roman plays, which are based on his *Lives*—Suetonius

created in the *Life of Nero* one of the supreme examples of the form. Islamic literature, from the 10th century, produced short "typed" biographies based on occupation—saints, scholars, and the like—or on arbitrarily chosen personal characteristics. The series of brief biographies has continued to the present day with such representative collections as, in the Renaissance, Giorgio Vasari's *Lives of the Most Eminent Italian Painters, Sculptors, and Architects*; Thomas Fuller's *History of the Worthies of England* in the 17th century; Samuel Johnson's *Lives of the English Poets* in the 18th; and, in more recent times, the "psychographs" of the American Gamaliel Bradford (*Damaged Souls*, 1923), Lytton Strachey's *Eminent Victorians* (1918) and the "profiles" that have become a hallmark of the weekly magazine *The New Yorker*.

Further classification of biographies compiled by research can be achieved by regarding the comparative objectivity of approach. For convenience, six categories, blending one into the other in infinite gradations and stretching from the most objective to the most subjective, can be employed.

INFORMATIVE BIOGRAPHY

This, the first category, is the most objective and is sometimes called "accumulative" biography. The author of such a work, avoiding all forms of interpretation except selection—for selection, even in the most comprehensive accumulation, is inevitable—seeks to unfold a life by presenting, usually in chronological order, the paper remains, the evidences, relating to that life. This biographer takes no risks but, in turn, seldom wins much critical acclaim: this work is likely to become a prime source for biographers who follow. During the 19th century, the *Life of Milton: Narrated in Connection with the Political, Ecclesiastical, and Literary History of his Time* (7 vol., 1859-94), by David Masson, and *Abraham Lincoln: A History* (10 vol., 1890), by John G. Nicolay and John Hay, offer representative samples. In the 20th century such works as Edward Nehls's, *D.H. Lawrence: A Composite Biography* (1957-59) and David Alec Wilson's collection of the life records of Thomas Carlyle (1923-29), in six volumes, continued the traditions of this kind of life writing.

CRITICAL BIOGRAPHY

This second category, scholarly and critical, unlike the first, does offer a genuine presentation of a life. These works are very carefully researched; sources and "justifications" (as the French call them) are scrupulously set forth in notes, appendixes, bibliographies; inference and conjecture, when used, are duly labeled as such; no fictional devices or manipulations of material are permitted, and the life is generally developed in straight chronological order. Yet such biography, though not taking great risks, does employ the arts of selection and arrangement. The densest of these works, completely dominated by fact, have small appeal except to the specialist. Those written with the greatest skill and insight are in the first rank of modern life writing. In these scholarly biographies—the "life and times" or the minutely detailed life—the author is able to deploy an enormous weight of matter and yet convey the sense of a personality in action, as exemplified in Leslie Marchand's *Byron* (1957), with some 1,200 pages of text and 300 pages of notes, Dumas Malone's *Jefferson and His Time* (4 vol., 1948-70), Churchill's *Marlborough* (1933-38), Douglas S. Freeman's *George Washington* (1948-57). The critical biography aims at evaluating the works as well as unfolding the life of its subject, either by interweaving the life in its consideration of the works or else by devoting separate chapters to the works. Critical biography has had its share of failures: except in skillful hands, criticism clumsily intrudes upon the continuity of a life, or the works of the subject are made to yield doubtful interpretations of character, particularly in the case of literary figures. It has to its credit, however, such fine biographies as Arthur S. Link, *Wilson* (5 vol., 1947-65); Richard Ellmann, *James Joyce* (1959); Ernest Jones, *The Life and Works of Sigmund Freud*; Douglas S. Freeman, *Lee* (1934-35); and Edgar Johnson, *Charles Dickens* (1952).

STANDARD BIOGRAPHY

This third, and central, category of biography, balanced between the objective and the subjective, represents the mainstream of biographical literature, the practice of biography as an art. From antiquity until the present—within the limits of the psychological awareness of the particular age and the availability of materials—this kind of biographical literature has had as its objective what Sir Edmund Gosse called "the faithful portrait of a soul in its adventures through life." It seeks to transform, by literary methods that do not distort or falsify, the truthful record of fact into the truthful effect of a life being lived. Such biography ranges in style and method from George Cavendish's 16th-century life of Cardinal Wolsey, Roger North's late-17th-century lives of his three brothers, and Boswell's life of Johnson to modern works like Lord David Cecil's *Melbourne*, Garrett Mattingly's *Catherine of Aragon*, Andrew Turnbull's *Scott Fitzgerald*, Leon Edel's *Henry James*, and Judith Thurman's *Secrets of the Flesh: A Life of Colette*.

INTERPRETATIVE BIOGRAPHY

This fourth category of life writing is subjective and has no standard identity. At its best it is represented by the earlier works of Catherine Drinker Bowen, particularly her lives of Tchaikovsky, *"Beloved Friend"* (1937), and Oliver Wendell Holmes, *Yankee from Olympus* (1944). She molds her sources into a vivid narrative, worked up into dramatic scenes that always have some warranty of documentation—the dialogue, for example, is sometimes devised from the indirect discourse of letter or diary. She does not invent materials; but she quite freely manipulates

them—that is to say, interprets them—according to the promptings of insight, derived from arduous research, and with the aim of unfolding her subject's life as vividly as possible. (Bowen, much more conservative in her later works, clearly demonstrates the essential distance between the third and fourth categories: her distinguished life of Sir Edward Coke, *The Lion and the Throne* [1957], foregoes manipulation and the "re-creation" of dialogue and limits interpretation to the artful deployment of biographical resources.) Many interpretative biographies stop just short of fictionalizing in the freedom with which they exploit materials. The works of Frank Harris (*Oscar Wilde*, 1916) and Hesketh Pearson (*Tom Paine, Friend of Mankind*, 1937; *Beerbohm Tree*, 1956) demonstrate this kind of biographical latitude.

FICTIONALIZED BIOGRAPHY

The books in this fifth category belong to biographical literature only by courtesy. Materials are freely invented, scenes and conversations are imagined. Unlike the interpretive variety, fictionalized biography often depends almost entirely upon secondary sources and cursory research. Its authors, well represented on the paperback shelves, have created a hybrid form designed to mate the appeal of the novel with a vague claim to authenticity. This form is exemplified by writers such as Irving Stone, in his *Lust for Life* (on van Gogh) and *The Agony and the Ecstasy* (on Michelangelo). Whereas the compiler of biographical information (the first category) risks no involvement, the writer of fictionalized biography admits no limit to it.

Fiction Presented as Biography

The sixth and final category is outright fiction, the novel written as biography or autobiography. It has enjoyed brilliant successes. Such works do not masquerade as lives. Rather, they imaginatively take the place of biography where perhaps there can be no genuine life writing for lack of materials. Among the most highly regarded examples of this genre are, in the guise of autobiography, Robert Graves's books on the Roman emperor Claudius, *I, Claudius* and *Claudius the God and His Wife Messalina*; Mary Renault's *The King Must Die* on the legendary hero Theseus; and Marguerite Yourcenar's *Memoirs of Hadrian*. The diary form of autobiography was amusingly used by George and Weedon Grossmith to tell the trials and tribulations of their fictional character Charles Pooter in *The Diary of a Nobody* (1892). In the form of biography this category includes Graves's *Count Belisarius* and Hope Muntz's *Golden Warrior* (on Harold II, vanquished at the Battle of Hastings, 1066). Some novels-as-biography, using fictional names, are designed to evoke rather than re-create an actual life, such as W. Somerset Maugham's *The Moon and Sixpence* (Gauguin) and *Cakes and Ale* (Thomas Hardy) and Robert Penn Warren's *All the King's Men* (Huey Long). The novel *The*

More I Owe You (2010) by Michael Sledge imagines the Brazilian segment of U.S. poet Elizabeth Bishop's life.

Special-Purpose Biography

In addition to these six main categories, there exists a large class of works that might be denominated "special-purpose" biography. In these works the art of biography has become the servant of other interests. They include potboilers (written as propaganda or as a scandalous exposé) and "as-told-to" narratives (often popular in newspapers) designed to publicize a celebrity. This category includes also "campaign biographies" aimed at forwarding the cause of a political candidate (Nathaniel Hawthorne's *Life of Franklin Pierce* [1852] being an early example); the weighty commemorative volume, frequently commissioned by the widow (which, particularly in Victorian times, usually enshrouded the subject in monotonous eulogy); and pious works that are properly called hagiography, or lives of holy men, written to edify the reader.

Informal Autobiography

Autobiography, like biography, manifests a wide variety of forms, beginning with the intimate writings made during a life that were not intended (or apparently not intended) for publication. Whatever its form or time, however, autobiography has helped define a nation's citizens and political ambitions. The form is crucial to not only how an individual meets the challenge of stating "I am" but how a nation and a historical period do so.

LETTERS, DIARIES, AND JOURNALS

Broadly speaking, the order of this category represents a scale of increasingly self-conscious revelation. Collected letters, especially in carefully edited modern editions such as W.S. Lewis's of the correspondences of the 18th-century man of letters Horace Walpole (34 vol., 1937–65), can offer a rewarding though not always predictable experience: some eminent people commit little of themselves to paper, while other lesser figures pungently re-create themselves and their world. The 15th-century *Paston Letters* constitute an invaluable chronicle of the web of daily life woven by a tough and vigorous English family among the East Anglian gentry during the Wars of the Roses. The composer Mozart and the poet Byron, in quite different ways, are among the most revealing of letter writers. Diarists have made great names for themselves out of what seems a humble branch of literature. For example, in the 20th century the young Jewish girl Anne Frank created such an impact by her recording of narrow but intense experience that her words were translated to

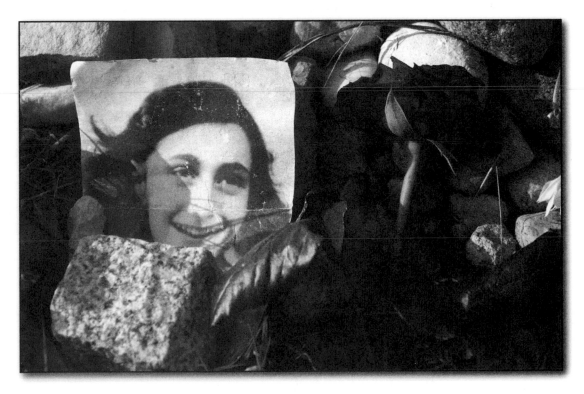

Anne Frank. Nigel Treblin/AFP/Getty Images

stage and screen. And a comparatively minor figure of 17th-century England, Samuel Pepys—he was secretary to the navy—has immortalized himself in a diary that exemplifies the chief qualifications for this kind of writing: candour, zest, and an unselfconscious enjoyment of self. The somewhat more formal journal is likewise represented by a variety of masterpieces, from the notebooks, which reveal the teeming, ardent brain of Leonardo da Vinci, and William Wordsworth's sister Dorothy's sensitive recording of experience in her *Journals* (1897), to French foreign minister Armand de Caulaincourt's recounting of his flight from Russia with Napoleon (translated as *With Napoleon in Russia*, 1935) and the *Journals* of the brothers Goncourt, which present a confidential history of the literary life of mid-19th-century Paris.

MEMOIRS AND REMINISCENCES

Autobiographies that usually emphasize *what* is remembered rather than *who* is remembering are known as memoirs and reminiscences. The author, instead of recounting his life, deals with those experiences of his life, people, and events that he considers most significant. (The extreme contrast to memoirs is the spiritual autobiography, so concentrated on the life of the soul that the author's outward life and its events remains a blur. The artless *res gestae*, a chronology of events, occupies the middle ground.)

In the 15th century, Philippe de Commynes, modestly effacing himself except to authenticate a scene by his presence, presents in his *Mémoires* a life of Louis XI, master of statecraft, as witnessed by one of the most sagacious counsellors

ANNE FRANK

(b. June 12, 1929, Frankfurt am Main, Ger.—d. March 1945, Bergen-Belsen concentration camp, near Hannover)

Anne Frank was a young Jewish girl who kept a record of the two years her family spent in hiding in Amsterdam to escape Nazi persecution. After the family was betrayed by informers in 1944, they were arrested by the Gestapo and transported to concentration camps. Anne and her sister Margot died of typhus at Bergen-Belsen, and their mother died at Auschwitz. Only their father Otto survived the Holocaust. Friends searching the hiding place found her diary, which her father published as The Diary of a Young Girl *(1947). Precocious in style and insight, it traces her emotional growth amid adversity and is a classic of war literature. The diary has been translated into more than 65 languages and is the most widely read diary of the Holocaust, and Anne is probably the best-known of Holocaust victims. A new English translation, published in 1995, contained material edited out of the original version, making the new work nearly one-third longer. The Frank family's hiding place on the Prinsengracht—a canal in Amsterdam—has become a museum.*

of the age. The memoirs of Giacomo Casanova boast of an 18th-century rake's adventures. The portraitist Elisabeth Vigée-Lebrun's memoirs, *Souvenirs de ma vie* (1835–37; "Reminiscences of My Life"; Eng. trans. *Memoirs of Madame Vigée Lebrun*), provide a lively account of her life and times, including her friendship with Marie-Antoinette. Those of Hector Berlioz explore with great brilliance the trials of a great composer, the reaches of an extraordinary personality, and the musical life of Europe in the first part of the 19th century. The memoir form is eminently represented in modern times by Sir Osbert Sitwell's polished volumes, presenting a tapestry of recollections that, as has been observed, "tells us little about what it feels like to be in Sir Osbert's skin"—a phrase perfectly illustrating the difference between memoirs and formal autobiography. The American composer John Adams also produced a thoughtful volume entitled *Hallelujah Junction* (2008) that reflects on his early life, the trajectory of his career, and his musical influences.

FORMAL AUTOBIOGRAPHY

This category offers a special kind of biographical truth: a life, reshaped by recollection, with all of recollection's conscious and unconscious omissions and distortions. The novelist Graham Greene says that, for this reason, an autobiography is only "a sort of life" and uses the phrase as the title for his own autobiography (1971). Any such work is a true picture of what, at one moment in a life, the subject wished—or is impelled—to reveal of that life. An event recorded in the autobiographer's youthful journal is likely to be somewhat different from that same event recollected in later years. Memory being plastic, the autobiographer regenerates materials as they are being used. The advantage of possessing unique and private information, accessible to no researching biographer, is counterbalanced by the difficulty of establishing a stance that is neither overmodest nor aggressively self-assertive. The historian Edward Gibbon declares, "I must be conscious that no one is so well qualified as myself to describe the service of my thoughts and actions." The 17th-century English poet Abraham Cowley provides a rejoinder: "It is a hard and nice subject for a man to write of himself; it grates his own heart to say anything of disparagement and the reader's ears to hear anything of praise from him."

There are but few and scattered examples of autobiographical literature in antiquity and the Middle Ages. In the 2nd century BCE the Chinese classical historian Sima Qian included a brief account of himself in the *Shiji* ("Historical Records"). It is stretching a point to include, from the 1st century BCE, the letters of Cicero (or, in the early Christian era, the letters of St. Paul). And Julius Caesar's *Commentaries* tell little about Caesar, though they present a masterly picture of the conquest of Gaul and the operations of the Roman military machine at its most efficient. The *Confessions* of St. Augustine, of the 5th century CE, belong to a special category of autobiography, and the 14th-century *Letter to Posterity* of the Italian poet Petrarch is but a brief excursion in the field.

Speaking generally, then, it can be said that autobiography begins with the Renaissance in the 15th century. The first example was written not in Italy but in England by a woman entirely untouched by the "new learning" or literature. In her old age the mystic Margery Kempe of Lynn in Norfolk dictated an account of her bustling, far-faring life, which, however concerned with religious experience, racily reveals her somewhat abrasive personality and the impact she made upon her fellows. This is done in a series of scenes, mainly developed by dialogue. Though calling herself, in abject humility, "the creature," Kempe knew, and has effectively transmitted the proof, that she was a remarkable person.

The first full-scale formal autobiography was written a generation later by a celebrated humanist publicist of the age, Enea Silvio Piccolomini, after he was elevated to the papacy, in 1458, as Pius II—the result of an election that he recounts with astonishing frankness spiced with malice. In the first book of his autobiography—misleadingly named *Commentarii*, in evident imitation of Caesar—Pius II traces his career up to becoming pope. The succeeding 11 books (and a fragment of a 12th, which breaks off a few months before his death in 1464) present a panorama of the age, with its cruel and cultivated Italian tyrants, cynical *condottieri* (professional soldiers),

recalcitrant kings, the politics and personalities behind the doors of the Vatican, and the urbane but exuberant character of the Pope himself. Pius II exploits the plasticity of biographical art by creating opportunities—especially when writing of himself as the connoisseur of natural beauties and antiquities—for effective autobiographical narration. His "Commentaries" show the art of formal autobiography in full bloom in its beginnings. They rank as one of its half dozen greatest exemplars.

The neglected autobiography of the Italian physician and astrologer Gironimo Cardano, a work of great charm; the celebrated adventures of the goldsmith and sculptor Benvenuto Cellini in Italy of the 16th century; the uninhibited autobiography of the English historian and diplomat Lord Herbert of Cherbury, in the early 17th; and Colley Cibber's *Apology for the Life of Colley Cibber, Comedian* in the early 18th—these are representative examples of biographical literature from the Renaissance to the Age of Enlightenment. The latter period itself produced three works that are especially notable for their very different reflections of the spirit of the times as well as of the personalities of their authors: the urbane autobiography of Edward Gibbon, the great historian; the plainspoken, vigorous success story of an American who possessed all the talents, Benjamin Franklin; and the somewhat morbid introspection of a revolutionary Swiss-French political and social theorist, the *Confessions* of J.-J. Rousseau. The latter led to two autobiographical explorations in poetry during the Romantic Movement in England, Wordsworth's *Prelude* and Byron's *Childe Harold*, cantos III and IV. Significantly, it is at the end of the 18th century that the word *autobiography* apparently first appears in print, in *The Monthly Review*, 1797.

SPECIALIZED FORMS OF AUTOBIOGRAPHY

These might roughly be grouped under four heads: thematic, religious, intellectual, and fictionalized. The first grouping includes books with such diverse purposes as Adolf Hitler's *Mein Kampf* (1924), *The Americanization of Edward Bok* (1920), and Richard Wright's *Native Son* (1940). Religious autobiography claims a number of great works, ranging from the *Confessions* of St. Augustine and Peter Abelard's *Historia Calamitatum* (*The Story of My Misfortunes*) in the Middle Ages to the autobiographical chapters of Thomas Carlyle's *Sartor Resartus* ("The Everlasting No," "Centre of Indifference," "The Everlasting Yea") and John Henry Cardinal Newman's beautifully wrought *Apologia* in the 19th century. That century and the early 20th saw the creation of several intellectual autobiographies. The *Autobiography* of the philosopher John S. Mill, severely analytical, concentrates upon "an education which was unusual and remarkable." It is paralleled, across the Atlantic, in the bleak but astringent quest of *The Education of Henry Adams* (printed privately 1906; published 1918).

Edmund Gosse's sensitive study of the difficult relationship between himself and his Victorian father, *Father and Son* (1907), and George Moore's quasi-novelized crusade in favour of Irish art, *Hail and Farewell* (1911–14), illustrate the variations of intellectual autobiography. Finally, somewhat analogous to the novel as biography (for example, Graves's *I, Claudius*) is the autobiography thinly disguised as, or transformed into, the novel. This group includes such works as Samuel Butler's *Way of All Flesh* (1903), James Joyce's *Portrait of the Artist as a Young Man* (1916), George Santayana's *Last Puritan* (1935), and the gargantuan novels of Thomas Wolfe (*Look Homeward, Angel* [1929], *Of Time and the River* [1935]).

HISTORY OF BIOGRAPHY IN THE WEST

As we have seen from several preceding examples, the history of biography in the West is an ancient one. Greeks and Romans provide the earliest instances.

ANTIQUITY

In the Western world, biographical literature can be said to begin in the 5th century BCE with the poet Ion of Chios, who wrote brief sketches of such famous contemporaries as Pericles and Sophocles. It continued throughout the classical period for a thousand years, until the dissolution of the Roman Empire in the 5th century CE. Broadly speaking, the first half of this period exhibits a considerable amount of biographical activity, of which much has been lost. Such fragments as remain of the rest—largely funeral elegies and rhetorical exercises depicting ideal types of character or behaviour—suggest that from a literary point of view the loss is not grievous. (An exception is the life of the Roman art patron Pomponius Atticus, written in the 1st century BCE by Cornelius Nepos.) Biographical works of the last centuries in the classical period, characterized by numerous sycophantic accounts of emperors, share the declining energies of the other literary arts. But although there are few genuine examples of life writing, in the modern sense of the term, those few are masterpieces. The two greatest teachers of the classical Mediterranean world, Socrates and Jesus Christ, both prompted the creation of magnificent biographies written by their followers. To what extent Plato's life of Socrates keeps to strict biographical truth cannot now be ascertained (though the account of Socrates given by Plato's contemporary the soldier Xenophon, in his *Memorabilia*, suggests a reasonable faithfulness) and he does not offer a full-scale biography. Yet in his two consummate biographical dialogues—*The Apology* (recounting the trial and condemnation of Socrates) and the *Phaedo* (a portrayal of Socrates' last hours and death)—he brilliantly re-creates the response of an extraordinary character to the crisis of existence. Some 400 years later there came into being four lives of Jesus, the profound religious

significance of which has inevitably obscured their originality—their homely detail, anecdotes, and dialogue that, though didactic in purpose, also evoke a time and a personality. The same century, the first of the Christian era, gave birth to the three first truly "professional" biographers—Plutarch and Suetonius (discussed earlier) and the historian Tacitus, whose finely wrought biography of his father-in-law, *Agricola*, concentrating on the administration rather than the man, has something of the monumental quality of Roman architecture. The revolution in thought and attitude brought about by the growth of Christianity is signaled in a specialized autobiography, the *Confessions* of St. Augustine. But the biographical opportunity suggested by Christian emphasis on the individual soul was, oddly, not to be realized. If the blood of the martyrs fertilized the seed of the new faith, it did not promote the art of biography. The demands of the church and the spiritual needs of men, in a twilight world of superstition and violence, transformed biography into hagiography. There followed a thousand years of saints' lives: the art of biography forced to serve ends other than its own.

THE MIDDLE AGES

This was a period of biographical darkness, an age dominated by the priest and the knight. The priest shaped biography into an exemplum of other-worldliness, while the knight found escape from daily brutishness in allegory, chivalric romances, and broad satire (the fabliaux). Nevertheless, glimmerings can be seen. A few of the saints' lives, like Eadmer's *Life of Anselm*, contain anecdotal materials that give some human flavour to their subjects. The 13th-century French nobleman Jean, sire de Joinville's life of St. Louis (Louis IX of France), *Mémoires*, offers some lively scenes. The three most interesting biographical manifestations came early. Bishop Gregory of Tours's *History of the Franks* depicts artlessly but vividly, from firsthand observation, the lives and personalities of the four grandsons of Clovis and their fierce queens in Merovingian Gaul of the 6th century. Bede's *Ecclesiastical History of the English People*, of the 8th century, though lacking the immediacy and exuberance—and the violent protagonists—of Gregory, presents some valuable portraits, like those of "the little dark man," Paulinus, who converted the King of Northumbria to Christianity.

Most remarkable, however, a self-consciously wrought work of biography came into being in the 9th century: this was *The Life of Charlemagne*, written by a cleric at his court named Einhard. He is aware of his biographical obligations and sets forth his point of view and his motives:

> I have been careful not to omit any facts that could come to my knowledge, but at the same time not to offend by a prolix style those minds that despise everything modern. . . . No man can write with more accuracy than I of events that took place about me, and of facts concerning which I had personal knowledge.

He composes the work to ensure that Charlemagne's life is not "wrapped in the darkness of oblivion" and out of gratitude for "the care that King Charles bestowed upon me in my childhood, and my constant friendship with himself and his children." Though Einhard's biography, by modern standards, lacks sustained development, it skillfully reveals the chief patterns of Charlemagne's character—his constancy of aims, powers of persuasion, passion for education. Einhard's work is far closer to modern biography than the rudimentary poetry and drama of his age are to their modern counterparts.

THE RENAISSANCE

Like the other arts, biography stirs into fresh life with the Renaissance in the 15th century. Its most significant examples were autobiographical, as has already been mentioned. Biography was chiefly limited to uninspired panegyrics of Italian princes by their court humanists, such as Simonetta's life of the great *condottiere*, Francesco Sforza, duke of Milan.

During the first part of the 16th century in England, now stimulated by the "new learning" of Erasmus, John Colet, Thomas More, and others, there were written three works that can be regarded as the initiators of modern biography: More's *History of Richard III*, William

Roper's *Mirrour of Vertue in Worldly Greatness; or, The life of Syr Thomas More*, and George Cavendish's *Life of Cardinal Wolsey*. The *History of Richard III* (written about 1513 in both an English and a Latin version) unfortunately remains unfinished. It cannot meet the strict standards of biographical truth because, under the influence of classical historians, a third of the book consists of dialogue that is not recorded from life. However, it is a brilliant work, exuberant of wit and irony, that not only constitutes a biographical landmark but is also the first piece of modern English prose. With relish, More thus sketches Richard's character:

> He was close and secret, a deep dissembler, lowly of countenance, arrogant of heart, outwardly companionable where he inwardly hated, not hesitating to kiss whom he thought to kill.

Worked up into dramatic scenes, this biography, as reproduced in the *Chronicles* of Edward Hall and Raphael Holinshed, later provided both source and inspiration for Shakespeare's rousing melodramatic tragedy, *Richard III*. The lives written by Roper and Cavendish display interesting links, though the two men were not acquainted: they deal with successive first ministers destroyed by that brutal master of politics, Henry VIII; they are written from first hand observation of their subjects by, respectively, a son-in-law and a household officer; and

they exemplify, though never preach, a typically Renaissance theme: *Indignatio principis mors est*—"the Prince's anger is death." Roper's work is shorter, more intimate, and simpler. In a series of moving moments, it unfolds the struggle within Sir Thomas More between his duty to conscience and his duty to his king. Cavendish offers a more artful and richly developed narrative, beautifully balanced between splendid scenes of Wolsey's glory and vanity and ironically contrasting scenes of disgrace, abasement, and painfully achieved self-knowledge.

The remaining period of the Renaissance, however, is disappointingly barren. In Russia, where medieval saints' lives had also been produced, there appears a modest biographical manifestation in the *Stepennaya Kniga* ("Book of Degrees," 1563), a collection of brief lives of princes and prelates. Somewhat similarly, in France, which was torn by religious strife, Pierre Brantôme wrote his *Lives of Famous Ladies* and *Lives of Famous Men*. The Elizabethan Age in England, for all its magnificent flowering of the drama, poetry, and prose, did not give birth to a single biography worthy of the name. Sir Fulke Greville's account of Sir Philip Sidney (1652) is marred by tedious moralizing. Francis Bacon's accomplished life of the first Tudor monarch, *The Historie of the Raigne of King Henry the Seventh* (1622), turns out to be mainly a history of the reign. But Sir Walter Raleigh suggests an explanation for this lack of biographical expression in the introduction to his *History of the*

World (1614): "Whosoever, in writing a modern history, shall follow truth too near the heels, it may haply strike out his teeth"—as Sir John Hayward could testify, having been imprisoned in the Tower of London because his account (1599) of Richard II's deposition, two centuries earlier, had aroused Queen Elizabeth's anger.

THE 17TH AND 18TH CENTURIES

In the 17th century the word *biography* was first employed to create a separate identity for this type of writing. That century and the first half of the 18th presents a busy and sometimes bizarre biographical landscape. It was an era of experimentation and preparation rather than of successful achievement. In the New World, the American Colonies began to develop a scattered biographical activity, none of it of lasting importance. France offers the celebrated *Letters* of the Marquise de Sévigné to her daughter, an intimate history of the Age of Louis XIV; numerous memoirs, such as those of Louis de Rouvroy, duc de Saint-Simon, and the acerbic ones of the Cardinal de Retz (1717); and the philosopher and critic Pierre Bayle's *Dictionnaire historique et critique* (1697), which was followed by specialized biographical collections and reference works. England saw an outpouring, beginning in the earlier 17th century, of Theophrastan "characters" (imaginary types imitated from the work of Theophrastus, a follower of Aristotle), journals, diaries, the disorganized but vivid jottings of John Aubrey (later published in 1898 as *Brief Lives*); and in the earlier 18th century there were printed all manner of sensational exposés, biographical sketches of famous criminals, and the like. In this era women appear for the first time as biographers. Lady Fanshawe wrote a life of her ambassador-husband (1829); Lucy Hutchinson, one of her Puritan warrior-husbands (written after 1664, published 1806); and Margaret Cavendish, duchess of Newcastle, produced a warm, bustling life—still good reading today—of her duke, an amiable mediocrity (*The Life of the Thrice Noble Prince William Cavendishe, Duke Marquess, and Earl of Newcastle*, 1667). This age likewise witnessed the first approach to a professional biographer, the noted lover of angling, Izaak Walton, whose five lives (of the poets John Donne [1640] and George Herbert [1670], the diplomat Sir Henry Wotton [1651], and the ecclesiastics Richard Hooker [1665] and Robert Sanderson [1678]) tend to endow their diverse subjects with something of Walton's own genteel whimsicality but nonetheless create skillful biographical portraits. The masterpieces of the age are unquestionably Roger North's biographies (not published until 1742, 1744) of his three brothers: Francis, the lord chief justice, "my best brother"; the lively merchant-adventurer Sir Dudley, his favourite; and the neurotic scholar John. Also the author of an autobiography, Roger North likewise produced, as a preface to his life of Francis, the first extensive critical essay on biography, which anticipates some of the ideas of Samuel Johnson and James Boswell.

The last half of the 18th century witnessed the remarkable conjunction of these two remarkable men, from which sprang what is generally agreed to be the world's supreme biography, Boswell's *Life of Samuel Johnson LL.D.* (1791). Dr. Johnson, literary dictator of his age, critic and lexicographer who turned his hand to many kinds of literature, created the first English professional biographies in *The Lives of the English Poets*. In essays and in conversation, Johnson set forth principles for biographical composition: the writer must tell the truth—"the business of the biographer is often to...display the minute details of daily life," for it is these details that re-create a living character; and men need not be of exalted fame to provide worthy subjects.

For more than one reason the somewhat disreputable and incredibly diligent Scots lawyer James Boswell can be called the unique genius of biographical literature, bestriding both autobiography and biography. Early in his acquaintance with Johnson he was advised by the Doctor "to keep a journal of my [Boswell's] life, full and unreserved." Boswell followed this advice to the letter. His gigantic journals offer an unrivaled self-revelation of a fascinatingly checkered character and career—whether as a young rake in London or thrusting himself upon the aged Rousseau or making his way to Voltaire's seclusion at Ferney in Switzerland with the aim of converting that celebrated skeptic to Christianity. Boswell actively helped to stage the life of Johnson that he knew he was going to write—drawing out Johnson in conversation, setting up scenes he thought likely to yield rich returns—and thus, at moments, he achieved something like the novelist's power over his materials, being himself an active part of what he was to re-create. Finally, though he invented no new biographical techniques, in his *Life of Samuel Johnson* he interwove with consummate skill Johnson's letters and personal papers, Johnson's conversation as assiduously recorded by the biographer, material drawn from interviews with large numbers of people who knew Johnson, and his own observation of Johnson's behaviour, to elicit the living texture of a life and a personality. Boswell makes good his promise that Johnson "will be seen as he really was." The influence of Boswell's work penetrated throughout the world and, despite the development of new attitudes in biographical literature, has persisted to this day as a pervasive force. Perhaps equally important to life writers has been the inspiration provided by the recognition accorded Boswell's *Life* as a major work of literary art. Since World War II there have often been years, in the United States, when the annual bibliographies reveal that more books or articles were published about Johnson and Boswell than about all the rest of biographical literature together.

THE 19TH CENTURY

The *Life of Johnson* may be regarded as a representative psychological expression of the Age of Enlightenment, and it certainly epitomizes several typical characteristics of that age: devotion to urban life, confidence in common sense, emphasis on man as a social being. Yet in its extravagant pursuit of the life of one individual, in its laying bare the eccentricities and suggesting the inner turmoil of personality, it may be thought of as part of that revolution in self-awareness, ideas, aspirations, exemplified in Rousseau's *Confessions*, the French Revolution, the philosophical writings of the German philosopher Immanuel Kant, the political tracts of Thomas Paine, and the works of such early Romantic poets as Robert Burns, William Blake, Wordsworth—a revolution that in its concern with the individual psyche and human freedom seemed to augur well for biographical literature. This promise, however, was not fulfilled in the 19th century.

That new nation, the United States of America, despite the stimulus of a robust and optimistic society, flamboyant personalities on the frontier, a generous share of genius, and the writing of lives by eminent authors such as Washington Irving and Henry James, produced no biographies of real importance. One professional biographer, James Parton, published competent, well-researched narratives, such as his lives of Aaron Burr and Andrew Jackson, but they brought him thin rewards and are today outmoded. In France, biography was turned inward, to romantic introspection, a trend introduced by Étienne Pivert de Senancour's *Obermann* (1804). It was followed by

autobiographies thinly disguised as novels such as Benjamin Constant's *Adolphe* (1816), *La Vie de Henri Brulard* of Stendhal (Marie-Henri Beyle), and similar works by Alphonse de Lamartine and Alfred de Musset, in which the emotional malaise of the hero is subjected to painstaking analysis. In Great Britain the 19th century opened promisingly with an outburst of biographical–autobiographical production, much of which came from prominent figures of the Romantic Movement, including Samuel Taylor Coleridge, Robert Southey, William Hazlitt, and Thomas De Quincey. Thomas Moore's *Letters and Journals of Lord Byron* (1830), John Gibson Lockhart's elaborate life (1837–38) of his father-in-law, Sir Walter Scott, and, later, Elizabeth Cleghorn Gaskell's *Life of Charlotte Brontë* (1857), James Anthony Froude's study of Carlyle (2 vol. 1882; 2 vol. 1884), John Forster's *Life of Charles Dickens* (1872–74) all followed, to some degree, what may loosely be called the Boswell formula. Yet most of these major works are marred by evasions and omissions of truth—though Lockhart and Froude, for example, were attacked as conscienceless despoilers of the dead—and, before the middle of the century, biography was becoming stifled. As the 20th century biographer and critic Sir Harold Nicolson wrote in *The Development of English Biography* (1927), "Then came earnestness, and with earnestness hagiography descended on us with its sullen cloud." Insistence on respectability, at the expense of candour, had led Carlyle to observe acridly, "How delicate, how decent is English biography, bless its mealy mouth!" and to pillory its productions as "vacuum-biographies."

The 20th Century and After

The period of modern biography was ushered in, generally speaking, by World War I. All the arts were in ferment, and biographical literature shared in the movement, partly as a reaction against 19th-century conventions, partly as a response to advances in psychology, and partly as a search for new means of expression. This revolution, unlike that at the end of the 18th century, was eventually destined to enlarge and enhance the stature of biography. The chief developments of modern life writing may be conveniently classified under five heads: (1) an increase in the numbers and general competence of biographies throughout the Western world; (2) the influence on biographical literature of the counterforces of science and fictional writing; (3) the decline of formal autobiography and of biographies springing from a personal relationship; (4) the range and variety of biographical expression; and (5) the steady, though moderate, growth of a literature of biographical criticism. Only the first three of these developments need much elaboration.

Little has been said about biography since the Renaissance in Germany, Spain, Italy, Scandinavia, and the Slavic countries because, as in the case of Russia, there had been comparatively little biographical literature and because biographical trends, particularly since the end of the 18th century, generally followed those of Britain and France. Russian literary genius in prose is best exemplified during both the 19th and 20th centuries in the novel. In the 19th century, however, Leo Tolstoy's numerous autobiographical writings, such as *Childhood* and *Boyhood*, and Sergey Aksakov's *Years of Childhood* and *A Russian Schoolboy*, and in the 20th century, Maksim Gorky's autobiographical trilogy (*Childhood*; *In the World*; and *My Universities*, 1913–23) represented, in specialized form, a limited biographical activity. The close control of literature exercised by the 20th-century communist governments of eastern Europe has created a wintry climate for biography. The rest of Europe, outside the iron curtain, has manifested in varying degrees the fresh biographical energies and practices illustrated in British–American life writing: biography is now, as never before, an international art that shares a more or less common viewpoint.

The second characteristic of modern biography, its being subject to the opposing pressures of science and fictional writing, has a dark as well as a bright side. Twentieth-century fiction, boldly and restlessly experimental, has, on the one hand, influenced the biographer to aim at literary excellence, to employ devices of fiction suitable for biographical ends. On the other hand, however, fiction has also probably encouraged the production of popular pseudobiography,

Leo Tolstoy. Hulton Archive/Getty Images

hybrids of fact and fancy, as well as of more subtle distortions of the art form. Science has exerted two quite different kinds of pressure: the prestige of the traditional sciences, in their emphasis on exactitude and rigorous method, has undoubtedly contributed to a greater diligence in biographical research and an uncompromising scrutiny of evidences; but science's vast accumulating of facts—sometimes breeding the worship of fact for its own sake—has helped to create an atmosphere in which today's massive, note-ridden and fact-encumbered lives proliferate and has probably contributed indirectly to a reluctance in the scholarly community to take the risks inevitable in true biographical composition.

The particular science of psychology, as earlier pointed out, has conferred great benefits upon the responsible practitioners of biography. It has also accounted in large part, it would appear, for the third characteristic of modern biography: the decline of formal autobiography and of the grand tradition of biography resulting from a personal relationship. For psychology has rendered the self more exposed but also more elusive, more fascinatingly complex and, in the darker reaches, somewhat unpalatable. Because honesty would force the autobiographer into a self-examination both formidable to undertake and uncomfortable to publish, instead he or she generally turns his attention to outward experiences and writes memoirs and reminiscences—though France offers something of an exception in the journals of such writers as André Gide (1947–51),

Paul Valéry (1957), François Mauriac (1934–50), and Julien Green (1938–58). Similarly, psychology, in revealing the fallacies of memory, the distorting power of an emotional relationship, the deceits of observation, has probably discouraged biography written by a friend of its subject. Moreover, so many personal papers are today preserved that a lifelong friend of the subject scarcely has time to complete his biography.

After World War I, the work of Lytton Strachey played a somewhat similar role to that of Boswell in heading a "revolution" in biography. *Eminent Victorians* and *Queen Victoria* (1921), followed by *Elizabeth and Essex* (1928), with their artful selection, lacquered style, and pervasive irony, exerted an almost intoxicating influence in the 1920s and '30s. Writers seeking to capitalize on Strachey's popularity and ape Strachey's manner, without possessing Strachey's talents, produced a spate of "debunking" biographies zestfully exposing the clay feet of famous historical figures. By World War II, however, this kind of biography had been discredited. Strachey's adroit detachment and literary skill were recognized to be his true value, not his dangerously interpretative method. And, since that time, biography has steadied into an established, if highly varied, form of literature.

OTHER LITERATURES

Biography as an independent art form, with its concentration upon the individual life and its curiosity about the individual personality, is essentially a creation of the West. In Asia, for all its long literary heritage, and in Islam, too, biographical literature does not show the development, nor assume the importance, of Western life writing. In China, until comparatively recently, biography had been an appendage, or by-product, of historical writing and scholarly preoccupation with the art of government, in the continuing tradition of the "Historical Records" of Sima Qian and Pan Gu. In India it has been the enduring concern for spiritual values and for contemplation or mystical modes of existence that have exerted the deepest influence on literature from the 1st millennium BCE to the present, and this has not provided a milieu suitable to biographical composition. Generally speaking, the literary history of Japan, too, offers only fragmentary or limited examples of life writing.

It was not until the beginning of the 20th century in China that biography began to appear as an independent form (and this was evidently the result of Western influence), when Liang Qichao (1873–1929) wrote a number of lives, including one of Confucius, and was followed by Hu Shi (1891–1962), who, like his predecessor, worked to promote biographical composition as an art form. Except for China after the establishment of the communist state in 1949, biography in Asia—notably in India and Japan—has shared, to a limited extent, the developments in biographical literature demonstrated in the rest of the world.

BIOGRAPHY: TERMS AND CONCEPTS

A few of the myriad subsets of biography are included in the following text. Excluded is the clerihew, a type of humorous biographical verse form covered elsewhere, but included are the confession, the roman à clef, and table talk.

CONFESSION

Confessions are a subgenre of autobiography, either real or fictitious, in which intimate and hidden details of the subject's life are revealed. The first outstanding example of the genre was the *Confessions* of St. Augustine (c. 400 CE), a painstaking examination of Augustine's progress from juvenile sinfulness and youthful debauchery to conversion to Christianity and the triumph of the spirit over the flesh. Others include the *Confessions of an English Opium-Eater* (1822), by Thomas De Quincey, focusing on the writer's early life and his gradual addiction to drug taking, and *Confessions* (1782–89), the intimate autobiography of Jean-Jacques Rousseau. French novelist André Gide used the form to great effect in such works as *Si le grain ne meurt* (1920 and 1924; *If It Die...*), an account of his life from birth to marriage.

Such 20th-century poets as John Berryman, Robert Lowell, Sylvia Plath, and Anne Sexton wrote poetry in the confessional vein, revealing intensely personal, often painful perceptions and feelings.

Also in the tradition are the "confession magazines," collections of sensational and usually purely fictional autobiographical tales popular in the mid-20th century.

DIARY

The diary, also known as a journal, is a form of autobiographical writing, a regularly kept record of the diarist's activities and reflections. Written primarily for the writer's use alone, the diary has a frankness that is unlike writing done for publication. Its ancient lineage is indicated by the existence of the term in Latin, *diarium,* itself derived from *dies* ("day").

The diary form began to flower in the late Renaissance, when the importance of the individual began to be stressed. In addition to their revelation of the diarist's personality, diaries have been of immense importance for the recording of social and political history. *Journal d'un bourgeois de Paris,* kept by an anonymous French priest from 1409 to 1431 and continued by another hand to 1449, for example, is invaluable to the historian of the reigns of Charles VI and Charles VII. The same kind of attention to historical events characterizes *Memorials of the English Affairs* by the lawyer and parliamentarian Bulstrode Whitelocke (1605–75) and the diary of the French Marquis de Dangeau (1638–1720), which spans the years 1684 to his death. The English diarist John Evelyn is surpassed only by the greatest diarist of all, Samuel Pepys, whose diary from Jan. 1, 1660 to

Samuel Pepys. Hulton Archive/Getty Images

May 31, 1669, gives both an astonishingly frank picture of his foibles and frailties and a stunning picture of life in London, at the court and the theatre, in his own household, and in his Navy office.

In the 18th century, a diary of extraordinary emotional interest was kept by Jonathan Swift and sent to Ireland as *The Journal to Stella* (written 1710–13; published 1766–68). This work is a surprising amalgam of ambition, affection, wit, and freakishness. The most notable English diary of the late 18th century was that of the novelist Fanny Burney (Madame d'Arblay). It was published in 1842–46. James Boswell's *Journal of a Tour to the Hebrides* (1785), a genuine diary though somewhat expanded, was one of the first to be published in its author's lifetime.

Interest in the diary increased greatly in the first part of the 19th century, in which period many of the great diaries, including Pepys's, were first published. Those of unusual literary interest include the *Journal* of Sir Walter Scott (published in 1890); the *Journals* of Dorothy Wordsworth (published after her death in 1855), which show her influence on her brother William; and the diary of Henry Crabb Robinson (1775–1867), published in 1869, with much biographical material on his literary acquaintances, including Goethe, Schiller, Wordsworth, and Coleridge. The posthumous publication of the diaries of the Russian artist Marie Bashkirtseff (1860–84) produced a great sensation in 1887, as did the publication of the diary of the Goncourt brothers, beginning in 1888.

In the 20th century, the *Journal of Katherine Mansfield* (1927), the two-volume *Journal* of André Gide (1939, 1954), and the five-volume *Diary of Virginia Woolf* (1977–84) are among the most notable examples.

HAGIOGRAPHY

The body of literature describing the lives and veneration of the Christian saints is called hagiography. The literature of hagiography embraces acts of the martyrs (i.e., accounts of their trials and deaths); biographies of saintly monks, bishops, princes, or virgins; and accounts of miracles connected with saints' tombs, relics, icons, or statues.

Hagiographies have been written from the 2nd century CE to instruct and edify readers and glorify the saints. In the Middle Ages it was customary to read aloud at divine office and in the monastic refectory (dining hall) biographies of the principal saints on their feast days. Besides biographies of single saints, other works of hagiography told the stories of a class of saints, such as Eusebius of Caesarea's account of the martyrs of Palestine (4th century AD) and Pope Gregory I the Great's *Dialogues,* a collection of stories about Saint Benedict and other 6th-century Latin monks. Perhaps the most important hagiographic collection is the *Legenda aurea* (*Golden Legend*) of Jacobus de Voragine in the 13th century. Modern critical hagiography began in 17th-century Flanders with the Jesuit ecclesiastic Jean Bolland and his successors, who became known as Bollandists.

The importance of hagiography derives from the vital role that the veneration of the saints played throughout medieval civilization in both eastern and western Christendom. Second, this literature preserves much valuable information not only about religious beliefs and customs but also about daily life, institutions, and events in historical periods for which other evidence is either imprecise or nonexistent.

The hagiographer has a threefold task: to collect all the material relevant to each particular saint, to edit the documents according to the best methods of textual criticism, and to interpret the evidence by using literary, historical, and any other pertinent criteria.

MEMOIR

The memoir is a history or record composed from personal observation and experience. Closely related to, and often confused with, autobiography, a memoir usually differs chiefly in the degree of emphasis placed on external events. Whereas writers of autobiography are concerned primarily with themselves as subject matter, writers of memoir are usually persons who have played roles in, or have been close observers of, historical events and whose main purpose is to describe or interpret the events. The English Civil Wars of the 17th century, for example, produced many such reminiscences, most notable of which are the *Memoirs* of Edmund Ludlow and Sir John Reresby. The French have particularly excelled at this genre. One of the greatest memoirists of his time was the duc de Saint-Simon, whose *Mémoires* (covering the early 1690s through 1723), famous for their penetrating character sketches, provide an invaluable source of information about the court of Louis XIV. Another of the great French memoirists was François-René, vicomte de Chateaubriand, who devoted the last years of his life to his *Mémoires d'outre-tombe* (1849–50; "Memoirs from Beyond the Tomb"). In the 20th century, many distinguished statesmen and military men have described their experiences in memoirs. Notable reminiscences of World War II are the memoirs of England's Viscount Montgomery (1958) and Charles de Gaulle's *Mémoires de guerre* (1954–59; *War Memoirs,* 1955–60).

ROMAN À CLEF

A novel that has the extraliterary interest of portraying well-known real people more or less thinly disguised as fictional characters is called a roman à clef (a French phrase meaning "novel with a key"). The tradition goes back to 17th-century France, when fashionable members of the aristocratic literary coteries, such as Mlle de Scudéry, enlivened their historical romances by including in them fictional representations of well-known figures in the court of Louis XIV. In the 20th century, Somerset Maugham's *The Moon and Sixpence* (1919) is thought to be related to the life of the painter Paul Gauguin, and his *Cakes and Ale* (1930) is said to contain caricatures of the novelists Thomas Hardy and Hugh Walpole. A more common type of roman à clef are Aldous Huxley's *Point Counter Point* (1928) and Simone de Beauvoir's *Mandarins* (1954), in which the disguised characters are immediately recognizable only to a small circle of insiders. Jack Kerouac fictionalized his own experiences in *On the Road* (1957). *Primary Colors* (1996) drew widespread attention in the United States as much for its protagonist—based closely on U.S. Pres. Bill Clinton—as for its anonymous author, later revealed to be political journalist Joe Klein.

SIMONE DE BEAUVOIR

(b. Jan. 9, 1908, Paris, France—d. April 14, 1986, Paris)

The French writer and feminist Simone de Beauvoir was a member of the intellectual fellowship of philosopher-writers who have given a literary transcription to the themes of Existentialism. As a student at the Sorbonne, she met Jean-Paul Sartre, with whom she formed a lifelong intellectual and romantic, albeit unorthodox, bond. She is known primarily for her treatise The Second Sex *(1949), a scholarly and passionate plea for the abolition of what she called the myth of the "eternal feminine." The book became a classic of feminist literature. She also wrote four admired volumes of autobiography (1958–72)—notably* Memoirs of a Dutiful Daughter*— philosophical works that explore themes of Existentialism, and fiction, notably* The Mandarins *(1954, Prix Goncourt). She addressed the issue of aging in* A Very Easy Death *(1964), on her mother's death in a hospital, and in* The Coming of Age *(1970; also translated as* Old Age*) is a bitter reflection on society's indifference to the elderly.*

TABLE TALK

A type of literature that records informal conversation at or as if at a dining table; especially, the social talk of a celebrity recorded for publication. Collections of such conversations exist from as early as the 3rd century CE, and the term has been in use in English since about the 16th century. The practice of recording conversations and sayings of the famous became especially popular in the 17th century. This material is especially useful for biographers and can be a form of literary biography in itself. One of the best-known examples of this is James Boswell's biography of Samuel Johnson, which consists mostly of Johnson's own words reproduced by Boswell.

CHAPTER 9

LITERARY CRITICISM

The reasoned consideration of literary works and issues is called literary criticism. It applies, as a term, to any argumentation about literature, whether or not specific works are analyzed. Plato's cautions against the risky consequences of poetic inspiration in general in his *Republic* are thus often taken as the earliest important example of literary criticism.

More strictly construed, the term covers only what has been called "practical criticism," the interpretation of meaning and the judgment of quality. Criticism in this narrow sense can be distinguished not only from aesthetics (the philosophy of artistic value) but also from other matters that may concern the student of literature: biographical questions, bibliography, historical knowledge, sources and influences, and problems of method. Thus, especially in academic studies, "criticism" is often considered to be separate from "scholarship." In practice, however, this distinction often proves artificial, and even the most single-minded concentration on a text may be informed by outside knowledge, while many notable works of criticism combine discussion of texts with broad arguments about the nature of literature and the principles of assessing it.

Criticism will here be taken to cover all phases of literary understanding, though the emphasis will be on the evaluation of literary works and of their authors' places in literary history. For another particular aspect of literary criticism, see textual criticism.

FUNCTIONS

The functions of literary criticism vary widely, ranging from the reviewing of books as they are published to systematic theoretical discussion. Though reviews may sometimes determine whether a given book will be widely sold, many works succeed commercially despite negative reviews, and many classic works, including Herman Melville's *Moby Dick* (1851), have acquired appreciative publics long after being unfavourably reviewed and at first neglected. One of criticism's principal functions is to express the shifts in sensibility that make such revaluations possible. The minimal condition for such a new appraisal is, of course, that the original text survive. The literary critic is sometimes cast in the role of scholarly detective, unearthing, authenticating, and editing unknown manuscripts. Thus, even rarefied scholarly skills may be put to criticism's most elementary use, the bringing of literary works to a public's attention.

The variety of criticism's functions is reflected in the range of publications in which it appears. Criticism in the daily press rarely displays sustained acts of analysis and may sometimes do little more than summarize a publisher's claims for a book's interest. Weekly and biweekly magazines serve to introduce new books but are often more discriminating in their judgments, and some of these magazines, such as *The* (London) *Times Literary Supplement* and *The New York Review of Books*, are far from indulgent toward

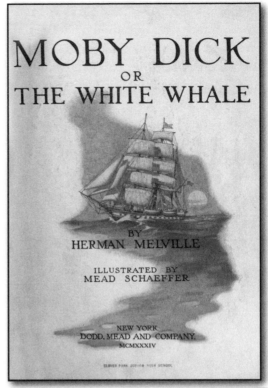

Although Herman Melville's Moby Dick *initially received poor reviews, it came to be seen as a literary classic and is still being taught more than 160 years after first publication.* Buyenlarge/Archive Photos/Getty Images

popular works. Sustained criticism can also be found in monthlies and quarterlies with a broad circulation, in "little magazines" for specialized audiences, and in scholarly journals and books.

Because critics often try to be lawgivers, declaring which works deserve respect and presuming to say what they are "really" about, criticism is a perennial target of resentment. Misguided or malicious critics can discourage an author who has been feeling his way toward a new mode that offends received taste.

Pedantic critics can obstruct a serious engagement with literature by deflecting attention toward inessential matters. As the French philosopher-critic Jean-Paul Sartre observed, the critic may announce that French thought is a perpetual discussion between Pascal and Montaigne not to make those thinkers more alive but to make thinkers of his own time more dead. Criticism can antagonize authors even when it performs its function well. Authors who regard literature as needing no advocates or investigators are less than grateful when told that their works possess unintended meaning or are imitative or incomplete.

What such authors may tend to forget is that their works, once published, belong to them only in a legal sense. The true owner of their works is the public, which will appropriate them for its own concerns regardless of the critic. The critic's responsibility is not to the author's self-esteem but to the public and to his own standards of judgment, which are usually more exacting than the public's. Justification for his role rests on the premise that literary works are not in fact self-explanatory. A critic is socially useful to the extent that society wants, and receives, a fuller understanding of literature than it could have achieved without him. In filling this appetite, the critic whets it further, helping to create a public that cares about artistic quality. Without sensing the presence of such a public, an author may either prostitute his talent or squander it in sterile acts of defiance. In this sense, the critic is not a parasite but, potentially, someone who is responsible in part for the existence of good writing in his own time and afterward.

Although some critics believe that literature should be discussed in isolation from other matters, criticism usually seems to be openly or covertly involved with social and political debate. Because literature itself is often partisan, is always rooted to some degree in local circumstances, and has a way of calling forth affirmations of ultimate values, it is not surprising that the finest critics have never paid much attention to the alleged boundaries between criticism and other types of discourse. Especially in modern Europe, literary criticism has occupied a central place in debate about cultural and political issues. Sartre's own *What Is Literature?* (1947) is typical in its wide-ranging attempt to prescribe the literary intellectual's ideal relation to the development of his society and to literature as a manifestation of human freedom. Similarly, some prominent American critics, including Alfred Kazin, Lionel Trilling, Kenneth Burke, Philip Rahv, and Irving Howe, began as political radicals in the 1930s and sharpened their concern for literature on the dilemmas and disillusionments of that era. Trilling's influential *The Liberal Imagination* (1950) is simultaneously a collection of literary essays and an attempt to reconcile the claims of politics and art.

Such a reconciliation is bound to be tentative and problematic if the critic believes, as Trilling does, that literature possesses an independent value and a deeper faithfulness to reality than is contained in any political formula. In Marxist states, however, literature has usually been considered a means to social ends and, therefore, criticism has been cast in forthrightly partisan terms. Dialectical materialism does not necessarily turn the critic into a mere guardian of party doctrine, but it does forbid him to treat literature as a cause in itself, apart from the working class's needs as interpreted by the party. Where this utilitarian view prevails, the function of criticism is taken to be continuous with that of the state itself, namely, furtherance of the social revolution. The critic's main obligation is not to his texts but rather to the masses of people whose consciousness must be advanced in the designated direction. In periods of severe orthodoxy, the practice of literary criticism has not always been distinguishable from that of censorship.

HISTORICAL DEVELOPMENT

Like the foundations of much Western literature, the history of literary criticism can be traced to the ancient Greeks. It rests on such philosophical matters as the disputation of literature's value to society and the significance of the performance of a tragedy to the individual viewer.

ANTIQUITY

Although almost all of the criticism ever written dates from the 20th century, questions first posed by Plato and Aristotle are still of prime concern, and every critic who has attempted to justify the social value of literature has had to come to terms with the opposing argument made by Plato in *The Republic*. The poet as a man and poetry as a form of statement both seemed untrustworthy to Plato, who depicted the physical world as an imperfect copy of transcendent ideas and poetry as a mere copy of the copy. Thus, literature could only mislead the seeker of truth. Plato credited the poet with divine inspiration, but this, too, was cause for worry. A man possessed by such madness would subvert the interests of a rational polity. Poets were therefore to be banished from the hypothetical republic.

In his *Poetics*—still the most respected of all discussions of literature—Aristotle countered Plato's indictment by stressing what is normal and useful about literary art. The tragic poet is not so much divinely inspired as he is motivated by a universal human need to imitate, and what he imitates is not something like a bed (Plato's example) but a noble action. Such imitation presumably has a civilizing value for those who empathize with it. Tragedy does arouse emotions of pity and terror in its audience, but these emotions are purged in the process (*katharsis*). In this fashion Aristotle succeeded in portraying literature as satisfying and regulating human passions instead of inflaming them.

Although Plato and Aristotle are regarded as antagonists, the narrowness of their disagreement is noteworthy. Both maintain that poetry is mimetic, treat the arousing of emotion in the perceiver, and feel that poetry takes its justification, if any, from its service to the state. It was obvious to both men that poets wielded great power over others. Unlike many modern critics who have tried to show that poetry is more than a pastime, Aristotle had to offer reassurance that it was not socially explosive.

Aristotle's practical contribution to criticism, as opposed to his ethical defense of literature, lies in his inductive treatment of the elements and kinds of poetry. Poetic modes are identified according to their means of imitation, the actions they imitate, the manner of imitation, and its effects. These distinctions assist the critic in judging each mode according to its proper ends instead of regarding beauty as a fixed entity. The ends of tragedy, as Aristotle conceived them, are best served by the harmonious disposition of six elements: plot, character, diction, thought, spectacle, and song. Thanks to Aristotle's insight into universal aspects of audience psychology, many of his dicta have proved to be adaptable to genres developed long after his time.

Later Greek and Roman criticism offers no parallel to Aristotle's originality. Much ancient criticism, such as that of Cicero, Horace, and Quintilian in Rome, was absorbed in technical rules of exegesis and advice to aspiring rhetoricians. Horace's verse epistle *The Art of Poetry* is an urbane amplification of Aristotle's emphasis on the decorum or internal propriety of each genre, now including lyric, pastoral, satire, elegy, and epigram, as well as Aristotle's epic,

tragedy, and comedy. This work was later to be prized by Neoclassicists of the 17th century not only for its rules but also for its humour, common sense, and appeal to educated taste. *On the Sublime*, by the Roman-Greek known as "Longinus," was to become influential in the 18th century but for a contrary reason: when decorum began to lose its sway encouragement could be found in Longinus for arousing elevated and ecstatic feeling in the reader. Horace and Longinus developed, respectively, the rhetorical and the affective sides of Aristotle's thought, but Longinus effectively reversed the Aristotelian concern with regulation of the passions.

THE MEDIEVAL PERIOD

In the Christian Middle Ages criticism suffered from the loss of nearly all the ancient critical texts and from an antipagan distrust of the literary imagination. Such Church Fathers as Tertullian, Augustine, and Jerome renewed, in churchly guise, the Platonic argument against poetry. But both the ancient gods and the surviving classics reasserted their fascination, entering medieval culture in theologically allegorized form. Encyclopaedists and textual commentators explained the supposed Christian content of pre-Christian works and the Hebrew Bible. Although there was no lack of rhetoricians to dictate the correct use of literary figures, no attempt was made to derive critical principles from emergent genres such as the fabliau and the chivalric romance. Criticism was in fact inhibited by the very coherence of the theologically explained universe. When nature is conceived as endlessly and purposefully symbolic of revealed truth, specifically literary problems of form and meaning are bound to be neglected. Even such an original vernacular poet of the 14th century as Dante appears to have expected his *Divine Comedy* to be interpreted according to the rules of scriptural exegesis.

THE RENAISSANCE

Renaissance criticism grew directly from the recovery of classic texts and notably from Giorgio Valla's translation of Aristotle's *Poetics* into Latin in 1498. By 1549 the *Poetics* had been rendered into Italian as well. From this period until the later part of the 18th century Aristotle was once again the most imposing presence behind literary theory. Critics looked to ancient poems and plays for insight into the permanent laws of art. The most influential of Renaissance critics was probably Lodovico Castelvetro, whose 1570 commentary on Aristotle's *Poetics* encouraged the writing of tightly structured plays by extending and codifying Aristotle's idea of the dramatic unities. It is difficult today to appreciate that this deference to antique models had a liberating effect. One must recall that imitation of the ancients entailed rejecting scriptural allegory and asserting the individual author's ambition to create works that would be unashamedly great and beautiful. Classicism, individualism, and national pride joined forces against literary asceticism. Thus,

a group of 16th-century French writers known as the Pléiade—notably Pierre de Ronsard and Joachim du Bellay—were simultaneously classicists, poetic innovators, and advocates of a purified vernacular tongue.

The ideas of the Italian and French Renaissance were transmitted to England by Roger Ascham, George Gascoigne, Sir Philip Sidney, and others. Gascoigne's "Certayne notes of Instruction" (1575), the first English manual of versification, had a considerable effect on poetic practice in the Elizabethan Age. Sidney's *Defence of Poesie* (1595) vigorously argued the poet's superiority to the philosopher and the historian on the grounds that his imagination is chained neither to lifeless abstractions nor to dull actualities. The poet "doth not only show the way, but giveth so sweet a prospect into the way, as will entice any man to enter into it." While still honouring the traditional conception of poetry's role as bestowing pleasure and instruction, Sidney's essay presages the Romantic claim that the poetic mind is a law unto itself.

NEOCLASSICISM AND ITS DECLINE

The Renaissance in general could be regarded as a neoclassical period, in that ancient works were considered the surest models for modern greatness. Neoclassicism, however, usually connotes narrower attitudes that are at once literary and social: a worldly-wise tempering of enthusiasm, a fondness for proved ways, a gentlemanly sense of propriety and balance. Criticism of the 17th and 18th centuries, particularly in France, was dominated by these Horatian norms. French critics such as Pierre Corneille and Nicolas Boileau urged a strict orthodoxy regarding the dramatic unities and the requirements of each distinct genre, as if to disregard them were to lapse into barbarity. The poet was not to imagine that his genius exempted him from the established laws of craftsmanship.

Neoclassicism had a lesser effect in England, partly because English Puritanism had kept alive some of the original Christian hostility to secular art, partly because English authors were on the whole closer to plebeian taste than were the court-oriented French, and partly because of the difficult example of Shakespeare, who magnificently broke all the rules. Not even the relatively severe classicist Ben Jonson could bring himself to deny Shakespeare's greatness, and the theme of Shakespearean genius triumphing over formal imperfections is echoed by major British critics from John Dryden and Alexander Pope through Samuel Johnson. The science of Newton and the psychology of Locke also worked subtle changes on neoclassical themes. Pope's *Essay on Criticism* (1711) is a Horatian compendium of maxims, but Pope feels obliged to defend the poetic rules as "Nature methodiz'd"—a portent of quite different literary inferences from Nature. Dr. Johnson, too, though he respected precedent, was above all a champion of moral sentiment and "mediocrity," the

appeal to generally shared traits. His preference for forthright sincerity left him impatient with such intricate conventions as those of the pastoral elegy.

The decline of Neoclassicism is hardly surprising. Literary theory had developed precious little during two centuries of artistic, political, and scientific ferment. The 18th century's important new genre, the novel, drew most of its readers from a bourgeoisie that had little use for aristocratic dicta. A Longinian cult of "feeling" gradually made headway, in various European countries, against Neoclassical canons of proportion and moderation. Emphasis shifted from concern for meeting fixed criteria to the subjective state of the reader and then of the author himself. The spirit of nationalism entered criticism as a concern for the origins and growth of one's own native literature and as an esteem for such non-Aristotelian factors as "the spirit of the age." Historical consciousness produced by turns theories of literary progress and primitivistic theories affirming, as one critic put it, that "barbarous" times are the most favourable to the poetic spirit. The new recognition of strangeness and strong feeling as literary virtues yielded various fashions of taste for misty sublimity, graveyard sentiments, medievalism, Norse epics (and forgeries), Oriental tales, and the verse of plowboys. Perhaps the most eminent foes of Neoclassicism before the 19th century were Denis Diderot in France and, in Germany, Gotthold Lessing, Johann von Herder, Johann Wolfgang von Goethe, and Friedrich Schiller.

ANCIENTS AND MODERNS

The Ancients and Moderns refers to a celebrated literary dispute that raged in France and England in the 17th century. The "Ancients" maintained that Classical literature of Greece and Rome offered the only models for literary excellence. The "Moderns" challenged the supremacy of the Classical writers. The rise of modern science tempted some French intellectuals to assume that, if René Descartes had surpassed ancient science, it might be possible to surpass other ancient arts. The first attacks on the Ancients came from Cartesian circles in defense of some heroic poems by Jean Desmarets de Saint-Sorlin that were based on Christian figures rather than Classical mythology. The dispute broke into a storm with the publication of Nicolas Boileau's L'Art poétique *(1674), which defined the case for the Ancients and upheld the Classical traditions of poetry. From then on, the quarrel became personal and vehement. Among the chief supporters of the Moderns were Charles Perrault and Bernard de Fontenelle. Supporters of the Ancients were Jean de La Fontaine and Jean de La Bruyère.*

In England the quarrel continued until well into the first decade of the 18th century. In 1690 Sir William Temple, in his Essay upon Ancient and Modern Learning *attacking the members of the Royal Society, rejected the doctrine of progress and supported the virtuosity and excellence of ancient learning. William Wotton responded to Temple's charges in his* Reflections upon Ancient and Modern Learning *(1694). He praised the Moderns in most but not all branches of learning, conceding the superiority of the Ancients in poetry, art, and oratory. The primary points of contention were then quickly clouded and confused, but eventually two main issues emerged: whether literature progressed from antiquity to the present as science did, and whether, if there was progress, it was linear or cyclical. These matters were seriously and vehemently discussed. Jonathan Swift, defending his patron Temple, satirized the conflict in his* Tale of a Tub *(1704) and, more importantly, in* The Battle of the Books *(1704). At a later date Swift was to make an even more devastating attack on the Royal Society in* Gulliver's Travels, *Book III, "The Voyage to Laputa."*

ROMANTICISM

Romanticism, an amorphous movement that began in Germany and England at the turn of the 19th century, and somewhat later in France, Italy, and the United States, found spokesmen as diverse as Goethe and August and Friedrich von Schlegel in Germany, William Wordsworth and Samuel Taylor Coleridge in England, Madame de Staël and Victor Hugo in France, Alessandro Manzoni in Italy, and Ralph Waldo Emerson and Edgar Allan Poe in the United States. Romantics tended to regard the writing of poetry as a transcendentally important activity, closely related to the creative perception of meaning in the world. The poet was credited with the godlike power that Plato had feared in him. Transcendental philosophy was, indeed, a derivative of Plato's metaphysical Idealism. In the typical view of Percy Bysshe Shelley, poetry "strips the veil of familiarity from the world, and lays bare the naked and sleeping beauty, which is the spirit of its forms."

Wordsworth's preface to *Lyrical Ballads* (1800), with its definition of poetry as the spontaneous overflow of powerful feelings and its attack on Neoclassical diction, is regarded as the opening statement of English Romanticism. In England, however, only Coleridge in his *Biographia Literaria* (1817) embraced the whole complex of Romantic doctrines emanating from Germany. The British empiricist tradition was too firmly rooted to be totally washed aside by the new metaphysics. Most of those who were later called Romantics did share an emphasis on individual passion and inspiration, a taste for symbolism and historical awareness, and a conception of art works as internally whole structures in which feelings are dialectically merged with their contraries. Romantic criticism coincided with the emergence of aesthetics as a separate branch of philosophy, and both signalled a weakening in ethical demands upon literature. The lasting achievement of Romantic theory is its recognition that artistic creations are justified, not by their promotion of virtue, but by their own coherence and intensity.

THE LATE 19TH CENTURY

The Romantic movement had been spurred not only by German philosophy

Charles Baudelaire, photograph by Étienne Carjat, 1863. Courtesy of the Bibliothèque Nationale, Paris

but also by the universalistic and utopian hopes that accompanied the French Revolution. Some of those hopes were thwarted by political reaction, while others were blunted by industrial capitalism and the accession to power of the class that had demanded general liberty. Advocates of the literary imagination now began to think of themselves as enemies or gadflies of the newly entrenched bourgeoisie. In some hands the idea of creative freedom dwindled to a bohemianism pitting "art for its own sake" against commerce and respectability. Aestheticism characterized both the Symbolist criticism of Charles Baudelaire in France and the self-conscious decadence of Algernon Swinburne, Walter Pater, and Oscar Wilde in England. At an opposite extreme, realistic and naturalistic views of literature as an exact record of social truth were developed by Vissarion Belinsky in Russia, Gustave Flaubert and Émile Zola in France, and William Dean Howells in the United States. Zola's program, however, was no less anti-bourgeois than that of the Symbolists. He wanted novels to document conditions so as to expose their injustice. Post-Romantic disillusion was epitomized in Britain in the criticism of Matthew Arnold, who thought of critical taste as a substitute for religion and for the unsatisfactory values embodied in every social class.

Toward the end of the 19th century, especially in Germany, England, and the United States, literary study became an academic discipline "at the doctoral level." Philology, linguistics, folklore study, and the textual principles that had been devised for biblical criticism provided curricular guidelines, while academic taste mirrored the prevailing impressionistic concern for the quality of the author's spirit. Several intellectual currents joined to make possible the writing of systematic and ambitious literary histories. Primitivism and medievalism had awakened interest in neglected early texts; scientific Positivism encouraged a scrupulous regard for facts; and the German idea that each country's literature had sprung from a unique national consciousness provided a conceptual framework. The French critic Hippolyte Taine's *History of English Literature* (published in French, 1863–69) reflected the prevailing determinism of scientific thought. For him a work could be explained in terms of the race, milieu, and moment that produced it. For other critics of comparable stature, such as Charles Sainte-Beuve in France, Benedetto Croce in Italy, and George Saintsbury in England, historical learning only threw into relief the expressive uniqueness of each artistic temperament.

THE 20TH CENTURY AND AFTER

The ideal of objective research has continued to guide Anglo-American literary scholarship and criticism and has prompted work of unprecedented accuracy. Bibliographic procedures have been revolutionized. Historical scholars, biographers, and historians of theory have placed criticism on a sounder basis of factuality. Important contributions to literary understanding have meanwhile been drawn from anthropology, linguistics, philosophy, and psychoanalysis. Impressionistic method has given way to systematic inquiry from which gratuitous assumptions are, if possible, excluded. Yet demands for a more ethically committed criticism have repeatedly been made, from the New Humanism of Paul Elmer More and Irving Babbitt in the United States in the 1920s, through the moralizing criticism of the Cambridge don F.R. Leavis and of the American poet Yvor Winters, to the late 20th-century demands for "relevance."

No sharp line can be drawn between academic criticism and criticism produced by authors and men and women of letters. Many of the latter are now associated with universities, and the main shift of academic emphasis, from impressionism to formalism, originated outside the academy in the writings of Ezra Pound, T.S. Eliot, and T.E. Hulme, largely in London about 1910. Only subsequently did such academics as I.A. Richards and William Empson in England and John Crowe Ransom and Cleanth Brooks in the United States adapt the New Criticism to reform of the literary curriculum—in the 1940s. New Criticism was the methodological counterpart to the strain of modernist literature characterized by allusive difficulty, paradox, and indifference or outright hostility to the democratic ethos. In certain respects the hegemony of New Criticism was political as well as literary. And anti-Romantic insistence on irony, convention, and aesthetic distance was accompanied by scorn for all revolutionary hopes. In Hulme conservatism and classicism were explicitly linked. Romanticism struck him as "spilt religion," a dangerous exaggeration of human freedom. In reality, however, New Criticism owed much to Romantic theory, especially to Coleridge's idea of organic form, and some of its notable practitioners were left of centre in their social thought.

The totality of Western criticism in the 20th and 21st centuries defies summary except in terms of its restless multiplicity and factionalism. Schools of literary practice, such as Imagism, Futurism, Dadaism, Surrealism, structuralism, and deconstruction found no want of defenders and explicators. Ideological groupings, psychological dogmas, and philosophical trends have generated polemics and analysis, and literary materials have been taken as primary data by sociologists and historians. Literary creators themselves continued to write illuminating commentary on their own principles and aims. In poetry, Paul Valéry, Ezra Pound, Wallace Stevens; in the theatre, George Bernard Shaw, Antonin Artaud, Bertolt Brecht; and in fiction, Marcel Proust, D.H. Lawrence, and Thomas Mann contributed to criticism in the act of justifying their art.

Most of the issues debated in 20th-century criticism appeared to be strictly empirical, even technical, in nature. By what means can the most precise and complete knowledge of a literary work be arrived at? Should its social and biographical context be studied or only the words themselves as an aesthetic structure? Should the author's avowed intention be trusted, or merely taken into account, or disregarded as irrelevant? How is conscious irony to be distinguished from mere ambivalence, or allusiveness from allegory? Which among many approaches—linguistic, generic, formal, sociological, psychoanalytic, and so forth—is best adapted to making full sense of a text? Would a synthesis of all these methods yield a total theory of literature? Such questions presuppose that literature is valuable and that objective knowledge of its workings is a desirable end. These assumptions are, indeed, so deeply buried in most critical discourse that they customarily remain hidden from critics themselves, who imagine that they are merely solving problems of intrinsic interest.

THE INFLUENCE OF SCIENCE

What separates modern criticism from earlier work is its catholicity of scope and method, its borrowing of procedures from the social sciences, and its unprecedented attention to detail. As literature's place in society has become more problematic and peripheral, and as humanistic education has grown into a virtual industry with a large group of professionals serving as one another's judges, criticism has evolved into a complex discipline, increasingly refined in its procedures but often lacking a sense of contact with the general social will. Major modern critics, to be sure, have not allowed their "close reading" to distract them from certain perennial questions

about poetic truth, the nature of literary satisfaction, and literature's social utility, but even these matters have sometimes been cast in "value-free" empirical terms.

Recourse to scientific authority and method, then, became the outstanding trait of 20th-century criticism. The sociology of Marx, Max Weber, and Karl Mannheim, Edmund Husserl's phenomenology, Claude Levi-Strauss's anthropological structuralism, the thorough-going analysis of writing and meaning by Jacques Derrida, the psychological models proposed by Sigmund Freud and C.G. Jung, and the historicized philosophizing of Michel Foucault—among many other influences—all found their way into criticism. The result was not simply an abundance of technical terms and rules, but a widespread belief that literature's governing principles could be located outside literature. Jungian "archetypal" criticism, for example, regularly identifies literary power with the presence of certain themes that are alleged to inhabit the myths and beliefs of all cultures, while psychoanalytic exegetes interpret poems in exactly the manner that Freud interpreted dreams. Such procedures may encourage the critic, wisely or unwisely, to discount traditional boundaries between genres, national literatures, and levels of culture. The critical enterprise begins to seem continuous with a general study of humankind. The impetus toward universalism can be discerned even in those critics who are most skeptical of it, the so-called historical relativists who attempted to reconstruct each epoch's outlook and to understand works as they appeared to their first readers. Historical relativism does undermine cross-cultural notions of beauty, but it reduces the record of any given period to data from which inferences can be systematically drawn. Here, too, in other words, uniform methodology tends to replace the intuitive connoisseurship that formerly typified the critic's sense of his role.

CRITICISM AND KNOWLEDGE

The debate over poetic truth may illustrate how modern discussion is beholden to extraliterary knowledge. Critics have never ceased disputing whether literature depicts the world correctly, incorrectly, or not at all, and the dispute has often had more to do with the support or condemnation of specific authors than with ascertainable facts about mimesis. Today it may be almost impossible to take a stand regarding poetic truth without also coming to terms with positivism as a total epistemology. The spectacular achievements of physical science have (with logic questioned by some) downgraded intuition and placed a premium on concrete, testable statements very different from those found in poems. Some of the most influential modern critics, notably I.A. Richards in his early works, accepted this value order and confined themselves to behavioristic study of how literature stimulates the reader's feelings.

A work of literature, for them, is no longer something that captures an external or internal reality, but is merely a locus for psychological operations. It can only be judged as eliciting or failing to elicit a desired response.

Other critics, however, have renewed the Shelleyan and Coleridgean contention that literary experience involves a complex and profound form of knowing. To do so they have had to challenge Positivism in general. Such a challenge cannot be convincingly mounted within the province of criticism itself and must depend rather on the authority of antipositivist epistemologists such as Alfred North Whitehead, Ernst Cassirer, and Michael Polanyi. If it is now respectable to maintain, with Wallace Stevens and others, that the world is known through imaginative apprehensions of the sort that poetry celebrates and employs, this is attributable to developments far outside the normal competence of critics.

The pervasive influence of science was most apparent in the passion for total explanation of the texts it brings under its microscope. Even formalist schools, which took for granted an author's freedom to shape his work according to the demands of art, treated individual lines of verse with a dogged minuteness that was previously unknown, hoping thereby to demonstrate the "organic" coherence of the poem. The spirit of explanation is also apparent in those schools that argued from the circumstances surrounding a work's origin to the work itself, leaving an implication that the former caused the latter. The determinism is rarely as explicit or relentless as it was in Taine's scheme of race, milieu, and moment, but this may reflect the fact that the 20th century handled causality in general with more sophistication than that with which it was handled in Taine's day.

Whether criticism will continue to aim at empirical exactitude or will turn in some new direction cannot be readily predicted, for the empiricist ideal and its sanctuary, the university, are not themselves secure from attack. The history of criticism is one of oscillation between periods of relative advance, when the imaginative freedom of great writers prompts critics to extend their former conceptions, and periods when stringent moral and formal prescriptions are laid upon literature. In times of social upheaval criticism may more or less deliberately abandon the ideal of disinterested knowledge and be mobilized for a practical end. Revolutionary movements provide obvious instances of such redirection, whether or not they identify their pragmatic goals with the cause of science. It should be evident that the future of criticism depends on factors that lie outside criticism itself as a rationally evolving discipline. When a whole society shifts its attitudes toward pleasure, unorthodox behaviour, or the meaning of existence, criticism must follow along.

As Matthew Arnold foresaw, the waning of religious certainty encouraged critics to invest their faith in literature, taking it as the one remaining source of value and order. This development stimulated critical activity, yet, paradoxically, it may also be responsible in part for a growing impatience with criticism. What Arnold could not have anticipated is that the faith of some moderns would be apocalyptic and Dionysian rather than a sober and attenuated derivative of Victorian Christianity. Thought in the 20th century yielded a strong undercurrent of anarchism which celebrated libidinous energy and self-expression at the expense of all social constraint, including that of literary form. In the critical writings of D.H. Lawrence, for example, fiction is cherished as an instrument of unconscious revelation and liberation. A widespread insistence upon prophetic and ecstatic power in literature seemed to be undermining the complex, irony-minded formalism that dominated modern discourse. As literary scholarship acquired an ever-larger arsenal of weapons for attacking problems of meaning, it met with increasing resentment from people who wish to be nourished by whatever is elemental and mysterious in literary experience.

An awareness of critical history suggests that this development is not altogether new, for criticism stands now approximately where it did in the later 18th century, when the Longinian spirit of expressiveness contested the sway of Boileau and Pope. To the extent that modern textual analysis has become what Hulme predicted, "a classical revival," it may not be welcomed by those who want a direct and intense rapport with literature. What is resisted now is not Neoclassical decorum but impersonal methodology, which is thought to deaden commitment. Such resistance may prove beneficial if it reminds critics that rationalized procedures are indeed no substitute for engagement. Excellent work continues to be written, not because a definitive method or synthesis of methods has been found, but on the contrary because the best critics still understand that criticism is an exercise of private sympathy, discrimination, and moral and cultural reflection.

CRITICISM: TERMS AND CONCEPTS

The following sampling of critical terms, both historical and contemporary, represents a mere fraction of the body of terms and concepts of use to the reader of literary criticism. It includes a sampling of schools of literary criticism.

AFFECTIVE FALLACY

The affective fallacy, according to the followers of New Criticism, is the misconception that arises from judging a poem by the emotional effect that it produces in the reader. The concept of affective fallacy is a direct attack on impressionistic criticism, which argues that the reader's response to a poem is the ultimate indication of its value.

Those who support the affective criterion for judging poetry cite its long and respectable history, beginning with Aristotle's dictum that the purpose of tragedy is to evoke "terror and pity." Edgar Allan Poe stated that "a poem deserves its title only inasmuch as it excites, by elevating the soul." Emily Dickinson said, "If I feel physically as if the top of my head were taken off, I know that is poetry." Many modern critics continue to assert that emotional communication and response cannot be separated from the evaluation of a poem.

ARCHETYPE

A primordial image, character, or pattern of circumstances that recurs throughout literature and thought consistently enough to be considered a universal concept or situation is an archetype (from the Greek word *archetypos*, meaning "original pattern").

The term was adopted and popularized by literary critics from the writings of the psychologist Carl Jung, who formulated a theory of a "collective unconscious." For Jung, the varieties of human experience have somehow been genetically coded and transferred to successive generations. These primordial image patterns and situations evoke startlingly similar feelings in both reader and author. The Canadian literary critic and theorist Northrop Frye was influential in extending the use of the term *archetype* to specifically literary contexts. Archetypal criticism has been connected with another group of thinkers more closely allied to its Jungian roots, including Maud Bodkin and James Hillman.

CULTURAL STUDIES

The interdisciplinary field of cultural studies is concerned with the role of social institutions in the shaping of culture. Originally identified with the Center for Contemporary Cultural Studies at the University of Birmingham (founded 1964) and with such scholars as Richard Hoggart, Stuart Hall, and Raymond Williams, today cultural studies is recognized as a discipline or area of concentration in many academic institutions and has had broad influence in sociology, anthropology, historiography, literary criticism, philosophy, and art criticism. Among its central concerns are the place of race (or ethnicity), class, and gender in the production of cultural knowledge.

DECONSTRUCTION

Deconstruction is a form of philosophical and literary analysis, derived mainly from work begun in the 1960s by the French philosopher Jacques Derrida, that questions the fundamental conceptual distinctions, or "oppositions," in Western philosophy through a close examination of the language and logic of philosophical and literary texts. In the 1970s the term was applied to work by Derrida, Paul de Man, J. Hillis Miller, and Barbara Johnson, among other scholars. In the 1980s it designated more loosely a range of radical theoretical enterprises in diverse areas of the humanities and social sciences, including—in addition to philosophy and literature—law, psychoanalysis, architecture, anthropology, theology, feminism, gay and lesbian studies, political theory, historiography, and film theory. In polemical discussions about intellectual trends of the late 20th-century, *deconstruction* was sometimes used pejoratively to suggest nihilism and frivolous skepticism. In popular usage the term has come to mean a critical dismantling of tradition and traditional modes of thought.

DECONSTRUCTION IN LITERARY STUDIES

Deconstruction's reception was coloured by its intellectual predecessors, most notably structuralism and New Criticism. Beginning in France in the 1950s, the structuralist movement in anthropology analyzed various cultural phenomena as general systems of "signs" and attempted to develop "metalanguages" of terms and concepts in which the different sign systems could be described. Structuralist methods were soon applied to other areas of the social sciences and humanities, including literary studies. Deconstruction offered a powerful critique of the possibility of creating detached, scientific metalanguages and was thus categorized (along with kindred efforts) as "post-structuralist." Anglo-American New Criticism sought to understand verbal works of art (especially poetry) as complex constructions made up of different and contrasting levels of literal and non-literal meanings, and it emphasized the role of paradox and irony in these artifacts. Deconstructive readings, in contrast, treated works of art not as the harmonious fusion of literal and figurative meanings but as instances of the intractable conflicts between meanings of different types. They generally examined the individual work not as a self-contained artifact but as a product of relations with other texts or discourses, literary and nonliterary. Finally, these readings placed special emphasis on the ways in which the works themselves offered implicit critiques of the categories that critics used to analyze them. In the United States in the 1970s and '80s, deconstruction played a major role in the animation and transformation of literary studies by literary theory (often referred to simply as "theory"), which was concerned with questions about the nature of language, the production of meaning, and the relationship between literature and the numerous discourses that structure human experience and its histories.

THE FURTHER SPREAD OF DECONSTRUCTION

Deconstruction's influence widened to include a variety of other disciplines. In psychoanalysis, deconstructive readings of texts by Sigmund Freud and others drew attention to the role of language in the formation of the psyche; showed how psychoanalytic case studies are shaped by the kinds of psychic mechanisms that they purport to analyze (thus, Freud's writings are themselves organized by processes of repression, condensation, and displacement); and questioned the logocentric presuppositions of psychoanalytic theory. Some strands of feminist thinking engaged in a deconstruction of the opposition between "man" and "woman" and critiqued essentialist notions of gender and sexual identity. The work of Judith Butler, for example, challenged the claim that feminist politics requires a distinct identity for women. Arguing that identity is the product or result of action rather than the source of it, they embraced a performative concept of identity modeled on the way in which linguistic acts (such as promising) work to bring into being the entities (the promise) to which they refer. This perspective was influential in gay and lesbian studies, or "queer theory," as the academic avant-garde linked to movements of gay liberation styled itself.

INFLUENCE AND CRITICISM

In all the fields it influenced, deconstruction called attention to rhetorical and performative aspects of language use, and it encouraged scholars to consider not merely what a text says but rather on the relationship—and potential conflict—between what a text says and what it "does." In various disciplines, deconstruction also prompted an exploration of fundamental oppositions and critical terms and a reexamination of ultimate goals. Most generally, deconstruction joined with other strands of poststructural and postmodern thinking to inspire a suspicion of established intellectual categories and a skepticism about the possibility of objectivity. Consequently, its diffusion was met with a sizeable body of opposition. Some philosophers, especially those in the Anglo-American tradition, dismissed it as obscurantist wordplay whose major claims, when intelligible, were either trivial or false. Others accused it of being ahistorical and apolitical. Still others regarded it as a nihilistic endorsement of radical epistemic relativism. Despite such attacks, deconstruction has had an enormous impact on a variety of intellectual enterprises.

EXPLICATION DE TEXTE

The method of literary criticism known as *explication de texte*, a French phrase meaning "explanation of text," involves a detailed examination of each element of a work, such as structure, style, and imagery. It further entails an exposition of the relationship of these parts to each other and to the whole work. The method was originally used to teach literature in France and has since become a tool for use by literary critics in other countries, particularly by practitioners of New Criticism.

FREUDIAN CRITICISM

The Freudian form of literary criticism uses the psychoanalytic theory of Sigmund Freud to interpret a work in terms of the known psychological conflicts of its author or, conversely, to construct the author's psychic life from unconscious revelations in his work.

Freudian critics depart from the traditional scope of criticism in reconstructing an author's psychic life on the basis of his writings. Edmund Wilson's *Wound and the Bow* (1941) explored this realm, and Van Wyck Brooks used this approach to biography in works such as *The Ordeal of Mark Twain* (1920). Professional analysts have applied their techniques to literature, notably Ernest Jones in *Hamlet and Oedipus* (1910 and 1949), which traces the famous problem of Hamlet's irresolution back to William Shakespeare's own Oedipal guilt.

INTENTIONAL FALLACY

The problem inherent in trying to judge a work of art by assuming the intent or purpose of the artist who created it is called the intentional fallacy. Introduced by W.K. Wimsatt, Jr., and Monroe C. Beardsley in *The Verbal Icon* (1954), the approach was a reaction to the popular belief that to know what the author intended—what he had in mind at the time of writing—was to know the correct interpretation of the work. Although a seductive topic for conjecture and frequently a valid appraisal of a work of art, the intentional fallacy forces the literary critic to assume the role of cultural historian or that of a psychologist who must define the growth of a particular artist's vision in terms of his mental and physical state at the time of his creative act.

Narodnost

A Russian term, *narodnost* is a doctrine or national principle, the meaning of which has changed over the course of Russian literary criticism. Originally denoting simply literary fidelity to Russia's distinct cultural heritage, *narodnost*, in the hands of radical critics such as Nikolay Dobrolyubov, came to be the measure of an author's social responsibility, both in portraying the aspirations of the common people (however these were perceived) and in making literature accessible to the masses. These complementary values of *narodnost* became prescribed elements of Socialist Realism, the officially approved style of writing in the Soviet Union from the early 1930s to the mid-1980s.

Narratology

The study of narrative structure, narratology looks at what narratives have in common and what makes one different from another. Like structuralism and semiotics, from which it derived, narratology is based on the idea of a common literary language, or a universal pattern of codes that operates within the text of a work. Its theoretical starting point is the fact that narratives are found and communicated through a wide variety of media—such as oral and written language, gestures, and music—and that the "same" narrative can be seen in many different forms. The development of this body of theory, and its corresponding terminology, accelerated in the mid-20th century.

The foundations of narratology were laid in such books as Vladimir Propp's *Morphology of the Folk Tale* (1928), which created a model for folktales based on seven "spheres of action" and 31 "functions" of narrative; Claude Lévi-Strauss's *Structural Anthropology* (1958), which outlined a grammar of mythology; A.J. Greimas's *Structural Semantics* (1966), which proposed a system of six structural units called "actants"; and Tzvetan Todorov's *The Grammar of the Decameron* (1969), which introduced the term *narratologie*. In *Narrative Discourse*, a partial translation of *Figures III* (1972) and *Narrative Discourse Revisited* (1983), Gérard Genette codified a system of analysis that examined both the actual narration and the act of narrating as they existed apart from the story or the content. Other influential theorists in narratology were Roland Barthes, Claude Bremond, Gerald Prince, Seymour Chatman, and Mieke Bal.

ROLAND BARTHES

(b. Nov. 12, 1915, Cherbourg, France—d. March 25, 1980, Paris)

The writings of French social and literary critic Roland Barthes on semiotics, the formal study of symbols and signs pioneered by Ferdinand de Saussure, helped establish two leading intellectual movements in the late 20th century. His early books examined the arbitrariness of the constructs of language and applied similar analyses to popular-culture phenomena. He analyzed mass culture in Mythologies *(1957).* On Racine *(1963) set off a literary furor, pitting him against more traditional French literary scholars. Another of Barthes's contributions was the even more radical* S/Z *(1970), a line-by-line analysis of a short story by Honoré de Balzac in which Barthes stressed the active role of the reader in constructing a narrative based on "cues" in the text.* The Empire of Signs *(1970) was a study of Japan. These and other significant works brought his theories wide (if belated) attention in the 1970s and helped establish both structuralism and the New Criticism. In 1976 he became the first person to hold the chair of literary semiology at the Collège de France.*

NEW CRITICISM

The post–World War I school of Anglo-American literary critical theory known as New Criticism insisted on the intrinsic value of a work of art and focused attention on the individual work alone as an independent unit of meaning. It was opposed to the critical practice of bringing historical or biographical data to bear on the interpretation of a work.

The primary technique employed in the New Critical approach is close, analytic reading of the text, a technique as old as Aristotle's *Poetics*. The New Critics, however, introduced refinements into the method. Early seminal works in the tradition were those of the English critics I.A. Richards (*The Principles of Literary Criticism*, 1924) and William Empson (*Seven Types of Ambiguity*, 1930). The movement did not have a name, however, until the appearance of John Crowe Ransom's *The New Criticism* (1941), a work that loosely organized the principles of this basically linguistic approach to literature. Some figures associated with New Criticism include Cleanth Brooks, R.P. Blackmur, and W.K. Wimsatt, Jr., although their critical pronouncements, along with those of Ransom, Richards, and Empson, are somewhat diverse and do not readily constitute a uniform school of thought. New Criticism was eclipsed as the dominant mode of Anglo-American literary criticism by the 1970s.

To the New Critics, poetry was a special kind of discourse, a means of communicating feeling and thought that could not be expressed in any other kind of language. It differed qualitatively from the language of science or philosophy, but it conveyed equally valid meanings. Such critics set out to define and formalize the qualities of poetic thought and language, using the technique of close reading with special emphasis on the connotative and associative values of words and on the multiple functions of figurative language—symbol, metaphor, and image—in the work. Poetic form and content could not be separated, because the experience of reading the particular words of a poem, including its unresolved tensions, is the poem's "meaning."

NEW HUMANISM

A critical movement known as the New Humanism arose in the United States between 1910 and 1930. It was based on the literary and social theories of the English poet and critic Matthew Arnold, who sought to recapture the moral quality of past civilizations—the best that has been thought and said—in an age of industrialization, materialism, and relativism.

Reacting against the scientifically oriented philosophies of literary realism and naturalism, New Humanists refused to accept deterministic views of human nature. They had three arguments: (1) human beings are unique among nature's creatures; (2) the essence of experience is fundamentally moral and ethical; and (3) the human

will, although subject to genetic laws and shaped by the environment, is essentially free. With these points of contention, the New Humanists—Paul Elmer More, Irving Babbitt, Norman Foerster, and Robert Shafer, to name only a few—outlined an entire program and aesthetic to incorporate their beliefs. By the 1930s the New Humanists had come to be regarded as cultural elitists and advocates of social and aesthetic conservatism, and their influence became negligible.

PLATONIC CRITICISM

Platonic criticism is a type of literary criticism based on the philosophical writings of Plato, especially his views on art expressed in *Phaedrus, Ion,* and the *Republic.* In practice Platonic criticism is part of an extensive approach to literature, involving an examination of the moral, ethical, and historical effects of a work of art.

In modern criticism the term refers to discussions and investigations of the work of art not in terms of its intrinsic, formal qualities but rather in recognition of its value as shaping social attitudes and in its vision of universal truths. For Plato, the visual world was an imitation of the ideal forms, which alone were real. Art, therefore, was no more than an imitation of an imitation and of value only insofar as it directed the soul toward the real (i.e., Truth, Beauty, or the Good).

POSTSTRUCTURALISM

The poststructuralist movement in literary criticism and philosophy begun in France in the late 1960s. Drawing upon the linguistic theories of Ferdinand de Saussure, the anthropology of Claude Lévi-Strauss, and the deconstructionist theories of Jacques Derrida, it held that language is not a transparent medium that connects one directly with a "truth" or "reality" outside. Rather, it is a structure or code, whose parts derive their meaning from their contrast with one another and not from any connection with an outside world. Writers associated with the movement include Roland Barthes, Jacques Lacan, Julia Kristeva, and Michel Foucault.

THE SUBLIME

In literary criticism, grandeur of thought, emotion, and spirit that characterizes great literature is discussed as the sublime. It is the topic of an incomplete treatise, *On the Sublime,* that was long attributed to the 3rd-century Greek philosopher Cassius Longinus but now believed to have been written in the 1st century CE by an unknown writer frequently designated Pseudo-Longinus.

The author of the treatise defines sublimity as "excellence in language," the "expression of a great spirit," and the power to provoke "ecstasy." Departing from traditional classical criticism, which sought to attribute the success of literary

The familiar opening phrases to such classic tales as Red Riding Hood *can instantly transport the reader or listener to another world.* The Bridgeman Art Library/Getty Images

works to their balance of certain technical elements—diction, thought, metaphor, music, and the like—he saw the source of the sublime in the moral, emotional, and imaginative depth of the writer and its expression in the flare-up of genius that rules alone could not produce.

The concept had little influence on modern criticism until the late 17th and 18th centuries, when it had its greatest impact in England. Its vogue there coincided with renewed interest in the plays of William Shakespeare, and it served as an important critical basis for Romanticism.

CONCLUSION

"Once upon a time there lived . . . " is one of countless formulas a storyteller intones to let you know that it's time to settle back and get comfortable, time to focus your mind's eye on the inner screen of your imagination. The variety of story signaled by "Once upon a time. . ." is likely to be some type of narrative that is centuries old—the Grimm Brothers' Hansel and Gretel, for example, or a trickster or fairy tale. In this age of Facebook, YouTube, and the blog, this era when the seasonal work of farming no longer marks out the week's or month's activities, we don't as a society tell stories quite as often as we once did. There's no forced "down time," when the crops are planted and we more or less have to wait for them to grow. That's when the story last flourished. Still sometimes in an idle moment, at least family lore can creep in—the story of the time Grandpa painted his car by hand or the story of what Great Aunt Marta did when she could no longer face her sorrow.

Even if the oral tradition is now sadly neglected, the art of storytelling lives on. In this volume, we have examined the roots of a variety of Western traditions, from fables, parables, and Icelandic sagas through romance and satire to the novel and the short story. We have also explored the purposes and varieties of biography and literary criticism through the ages.

GLOSSARY

anagogic Having a spiritual or mystical meaning beyond the literal, allegorical, and moral.

Beat movement American social and literary movement originating in the 1950s and centred in several bohemian artist communities (also called Beat generation).

didactic Intended to teach.

dystopia An imaginary place that is depressingly wretched and whose people often have a fearful existence.

euphemism The substitution of an agreeable or inoffensive word or expression for one that is harsh, indelicate, or otherwise unpleasant or taboo.

Existentialism A philosophy that centres on analyzing individual existence in an unfathomable universe and stresses individual responsibility for behaviour without any certainty of what is right or wrong.

fabliaux Short metrical tales made popular by professional storytellers and characterized by vivid detail and realistic observation. They are usually comic, coarse, and often cynical, especially in their treatment of women.

fabulist A creator or writer of fables, especially those that carry a moral lesson.

hard-boiled fiction A tough, unsentimental style of American crime writing containing graphic sex and violence; vivid but often sordid urban backgrounds; and fast-paced, slangy dialogue.

hermeneutic Interpretive.

melodrama In Western theatre, sentimental drama with an improbable plot that concerns the vicissitudes suffered by the virtuous at the hands of the villainous but ends happily with virtue triumphant.

metaphor Figure of speech that implies comparison between two unlike entities, as distinguished from a simile, an explicit comparison signalled by the words *like* or *as*.

milieu Environment or setting.

minnesinger One of a class of aristocratic German lyric poets and musicians of the 12th to the 14th centuries inspired by the French troubadours and characterized by having love and beauty as subjects of songs.

monologue In literature and drama, a soliloquy or an extended speech by one person.

panegyric A tribute or eulogistic oration that originally was a speech delivered at an ancient Greek general assembly (*panegyris*), such as the Olympic and Panathenaic festivals.

polemic A controversial discussion or argument; an aggressive attack on or the refutation of the opinions or principles of another.

rhetoric The study of principles and rules of composition formulated by critics of ancient times. It can also involve the study of writing or speaking as a means of communication or persuasion.

ribald Characterized by or using coarse, indecent humour.

roman-fleuve Series of novels, each one complete in itself, that deals with one central character, an era of national life, or successive generations of a family. French: "novel stream" or "novel cycle."

semiotics A general theory of signs and symbols that deals especially with their function in both artificially constructed and natural languages and comprises the three branches of syntactics, semantics, and pragmatics.

soliloquy Passage in a drama in which a character expresses his or her thoughts or feelings aloud while either alone on stage or with the other actors keeping silent.

squib A short humorous, satiric, or lampooning writing or speech.

Surrealism The principles, ideals, or practice of producing fantastic or incongruous imagery in art or literature by means of unnatural or irrational juxtapositions and combinations.

sycophantic Fawning or flattering.

tour de force A feat of strength, skill, or artistic merit.

uchronic An alternate history, one in which an actual event in human history has a different outcome.

verisimilitude The semblance of reality in dramatic or nondramatic fiction.

BIBLIOGRAPHY

Works on fiction writing in general include John Fowles, *Wormholes: Essays and Occasional Writings* (1998); Zadie Smith, *Changing My Mind: Occasional Essays* (2009); Eudora Welty, *On Writing* (2002); David Lodge, *The Practice of Writing* (1996); and the classic work Edith Wharton, *The Writing of Fiction* (1997; originally published in 1925), all by well-known writers. Also informative are Michael J. Hoffman and Patrick D. Murphy (eds.), *Essentials of the Theory of Fiction*, 3rd ed. (2005); Robert Boswell, *The Half-Known World: On Writing Fiction* (2008); Ming Dong Gu, *Chinese Theories of Fiction: A Non-Western Narrative System* (2006).

Short narratives are the subject of Dana Gioia and R.S. Gwynn, *The Art of the Short Story* (2006); Barbara Lounsberry (ed.), *The Tales We Tell: Perspectives on the Short Story* (1998); Carole Burns (ed.), *Off The Page: Writers Talk about Beginnings, Endings, and Everything in Between* (2008); Per Winther, Jakob Lothe, and Hans H. Skei (eds.), *The Art of Brevity: Excursions in Short Fiction Theory and Analysis* (2004); and Charles E. May (ed.), *The New Short Story Theories* (1994).

Works on specific genres are myriad. Some of the best on the novel are Jane Smiley, *Thirteen Ways of Looking at the Novel* (2005); David Lodge, *Consciousness and the Novel: Connected Essays* (2002); and Oakley M. Hall, *The Art & Craft of Novel Writing* (1989). Alexandra Johnson, *Leaving a Trace: On Keeping a Journal: The Art of Transforming a Life Into Stories* (2001), discusses journal writing. Mysteries are treated in Rosemary Herbert, *The Fatal Art of Entertainment: Interviews with Mystery Writers* (1994). Stephen Weissenburger, *Fables of Subversion: Satire and the American Novel, 1930–1980* (1995), examines satire in the 20th century; and Charles Kaplan and William Davis Anderson (eds.), *Criticism: Major Statements*, 4th ed. (2000), presents the fundamental arguments of criticism.

The science fiction genre has a host of resources. Paul K. Alkon, *Origins of Futuristic Fiction* (1987), examines 17th- through early 19th-century precursors of science fiction. Brian Aldiss and David Wingrove, *Trillion Year Spree: The History of Science Fiction* (1986, reprinted 2001), casts an objective yet interested eye on the SF world and its many unique customs and concepts. John Clute and Peter Nicholls (eds.), *The Encyclopedia of Science Fiction*, 2nd ed. (1999), is a work of remarkable scholastic rigour. John Clute and John Grant (eds.), *The Encyclopedia of Fantasy* (1997, reissued 1999), explores the murkier byways of the fantasy genre. Eric Leif Davin, *Pioneers of Wonder: Conversations with the Founders of Science Fiction* (1999), contains interviews with science fiction's veterans of the 1920s and '30s regarding the largely forgotten world of prewar pulp fiction. Frederik Pohl, *The Way the Future Was: A Memoir* (1978, reissued 1983), is one of the best and most deeply felt biographies of a hard-core SF professional. Darko Suvin, *Metamorphoses of Science Fiction: On the Poetics and History of a Literary Genre* (1979), presents an analysis and definition of the SF genre. David G. Hartwell, *Age of Wonders: Exploring the World of Science Fiction* (1984, reissued 1996), is an opinionated look at science fiction by a noted American SF critic and editor. Stanislaw Lem, *Microworlds: Writings on Science Fiction and Fantasy,* edited by Franz Rottensteiner (1984, reissued 1991), brings profound analytic brilliance to bear on the craft of science fiction. Damon Knight, *In Search of Wonder*, 3rd ed. enlarged and extended (1996), collects the scathingly funny criticism of science fiction by a gifted editor and expert short-story writer.